Arnold of Brescia

AMS PRESS

NEW YORK

Arnold of Brescia

by

GEORGE WILLIAM GREENAWAY

M.A.

Assistant Lecturer in History in the University College
of the South-West of England, Exeter;
late Scholar of Peterhouse

CAMBRIDGE

AT THE UNIVERSITY PRESS

1931

Library of Congress Cataloging in Publication Data

Greenaway, George William.
    Arnold of Brescia.

    Reprint of the 1931 ed. published by the University
Press, Cambridge, Eng.
    Bibliography: p.
    Includes index.
    1. Arnaldo da Brescia, d. 1155. 2. Christian
biography—Italy. 3. Church history—Middle Ages,
600-1500. 4. Popes—Temporal power. I. Title.
BX1256.G7   1978   282'.092'4 [B]   77-84710
ISBN 0-404-16116-2

Reprinted from the edition of 1931, Cambridge.
First AMS edition published in 1978.

Manufactured in the United States of America.

AMS PRESS, INC.
NEW YORK, N.Y.

To

the Reverend Claude Jenkins, D.D.
whose singular enthusiasm first inspired
in me a love of history
this book
is dedicated
in token of gratitude and affection
by
his friend and former pupil

Preface

The literature relating to Arnold of Brescia, though of considerable proportions, has not always been the fruit of impartial investigation and is therefore very unequal in value. One explanation for this is to be sought in the ease with which his story lends itself to party propaganda. The opportunity afforded by the dearth of contemporary evidence has been readily seized and from time to time historians and politicians, poets and dramatists have contributed their share towards the construction of what may be termed "the legend of Arnold". Some have seen in Arnold the pioneer democrat joined in mortal combat with the forces of political absolutism; others have hailed him as a premature apostle of free-thought and religious toleration, crushed by the mighty engine of ecclesiastical bigotry. It is only within the last fifty years that a series of foreign monographs on the subject has shown that by following the canons of historical scholarship it is possible to write of Arnold without either personal antipathy or religious or political prejudice.

The contribution of English historians to this happy process of the rehabilitation of Arnold is almost negligible. Save for Lord Bryce's few pages in *The Holy Roman Empire* there is still nothing of value except the older works of Gibbon and Milman. The absence of any biography of Arnold of Brescia in English is the *raison d'être* of this study, which is throughout based on original sources and was awarded the Prince Consort and Gladstone Prizes for 1930 in the University of Cambridge.

I must express my thanks to the Master and Fellows of Peterhouse for enabling me to embark on this piece of research by their generous grant of a post-graduate studentship; to the Syndics of the University Press for contributing towards the expenses of publication; to Prof. J. P. Whitney for many valuable suggestions and criticisms; to Dr C. W. Previté-Orton for help and advice on the early history of Brescia, and to my friends, Mr F. A. Ollett, M.A. and Mr W. E. Blackwood, M.A., for advice and assistance in the early stages of composition. Finally, I owe a deep debt of gratitude to the Trustees and Warden of St Deiniol's Library, Hawarden (where most of the following pages were written), for their unfailing kindness and consideration during my tenure of the Gladstone Studentship.

G. W. GREENAWAY

Exeter, September 1931

Contents

Appendices

Abbreviations

A.S.I.	Archivio Storico Italiano.
F.S.I.	Fonti per la Storia d' Italia.
M.G.H.	Monumenta Germaniae Historica.
M.H.P.	Monumenta Historiae Patriae.
M.P.L.	Migne, Patrologia Latina.
R.Q.H.	*Revue des Questions Historiques.*
R.S.	Rolls Series.
R.S.I.	*Rivista Storica Italiana.*
S.G.U.S.	Scriptores Rerum Germanicarum in Usum Scholarum.

Chapter I

INTRODUCTION. THE CHURCH IN THE TWELFTH CENTURY

IT is a common fallacy among students of the Church in the twelfth century that the Concordat of Worms (1122) marks the end of a distinct and sharply divided epoch in Church history, and ushers in a new and less heroic age.[1] Yet it may be fairly questioned whether this assumption is fundamentally sound. If viewed in a right perspective the Concordat of Worms would seem rather to denote the close of a single phase in the long struggle between *sacerdotium* and *regnum* for supremacy, a struggle destined to last till the end of the Middle Ages if not till the Peace of Westphalia in 1648.

The real importance of the Concordat of Worms is that by it Pope and Emperor were for the first time acknowledged co-equals in authority. Yet only one issue had been settled, namely the crucial problem of investitures. Other matters where a clash was imminent had not yet been clearly formulated.[2] Hence the Concordat was followed by a period in which the Church was engaged in taking stock of her new position. Slowly it dawned on men that the Hildebrandine triumph was little more than a Pyrrhic victory. In fact the need for reform was as urgent then as in the preceding century. The Church had won a measure of freedom from secular tyranny, but the more constructive part of Gregory VII's programme still remained to be carried out. Though lay investiture and secular interference

---

[1] For the ultimate effect on the Church of the Concordat see E. Bernheim, *Lothar III und das Wormser Konkordat* (1874); *Das Wormser Konkordat und seine Vorurkunden* (1906); D. Schäfer, "Zur Beurteilung des Wormser Konkordats", *Abhandlungen der Könige. Preussen Akad. der Wissenschaften*, I, Berlin (1905). Cf. Hauck, *Kirchengeschichte Deutschlands*, IV, pp. 116 seq.; Hefele-Leclercq, IV, p. 620, n. 2.

[2] Giesebrecht, *Geschichte der deutschen Kaiserzeit*, III, p. 958.

in ecclesiastical elections had been appreciably restricted by the provisions of the Concordat, the purely domestic problems of simony and clerical concubinage still remained unsettled, and since Gregory's day no concerted attempt had been made to eradicate the evils arising out of them.

The pages of the German prior, Gerhoh of Reichersberg, and of the cosmopolitan John of Salisbury, to take but two examples, abound in denunciations of simoniacal practices, scarcely less emphatic if more temperately expressed than those of St Peter Damiani and Cardinal Humbert three-quarters of a century earlier. The situation was such that even a "moderate" like Ivo of Chartres could speak of Simon Magus as reincarnate among men, and lament that none was found to correct him after the manner of St Peter aforetime.[1] Both simony and clerical marriage are the subject of frequent canons in twelfth-century Councils,[2] and to these practices, which some by dint of custom and tradition were wont to regard as natural and legitimate, were added in the course of the century corruptions arising out of the vast increase of appeals to Rome.

The finer spirits of the age were keenly alive to the worldliness and covetousness debasing the Church's life and the lethargy paralysing her limbs. It is no mere accident that a comparison of the Church with the physical organism makes a frequent appearance in the literature of the age.[3] "And whether one member suffereth, all the members suffer with it" is the burden alike of

---

[1] "Simonem magum nostris temporibus in Ecclesia suscitatum frustra extinguere verbis conaris, quia in hominibus qui corrigat non invenitur"—Ivo Carnot. Ep. 133. M.P.L. 162, col. 142.

[2] First Lateran, Canons 1, 7 and 21. Second Lateran, Canons 1, 6 and 7. Third Lateran, Canon 11. See Hefele-Leclercq, v; Lea, *Sacerdotal Celibacy*, I, pp. 385 seq.

[3] Gierke, *Political Theories of the Middle Age* (trans. F. W. Maitland, C.U.P. 1900), pp. 22 seq., 129 seq.

the *De Consideratione* of St Bernard and Adrian IV's curious confession to John of Salisbury narrated in the *Policraticus*.[1]

"Who will grant me", writes St Bernard in words that come ringing down the ages, "to see ere I die the Church of God as in the days of old when the Apostles let down their nets for a draught, not of gold or of silver, but of souls?"[2] In similar strain John of Salisbury stigmatises the whole Church as honeycombed with avarice and simony. "For in face of the Lord's interdiction His house of prayer has become a house of merchandise, and the temple built on His foundation is turned into a cave of robbers. The Church is given over to pillage....One trusting in the multitude of his riches has entered in with Simon Magus as his guide, finding none to bid him and his money depart to perdition. Another shuns approaching Peter openly with gifts, but creeps into the Church's lap secretly like Jupiter stealing in to Danae in a shower of gold."[3]

Unfortunately in respect of luxury and greed the Roman Church set a bad example to those of the provinces. The tendency towards display and magnificence manifest in the Curia and papal household may be traced back ultimately

---

[1] *Joannis Saresberiensis Policraticus* (ed. C. C. J. Webb, O.U.P. 1904), lib. VI, cap. xxiv.

[2] "Quis mihi det, antequam moriar, videre Ecclesiam Dei, sicut in diebus antiquis; quando apostoli laxabant retia in capturam, non in capturam argenti vel auri, sed in capturam animarum?"—Bern. M.P.L. 182, Ep. 238, col. 430. Cf. also his castigation of the worldliness of Papacy and Curia in the *De Consideratione*, lib. IV, col. 772 seq.

[3] "Domus namque orationis negotiationis, Domino prohibente, facta est domus; et templum fundatum in lapide adiutorii in latronum speluncam versum est. Siquidem Ecclesia data est in direptionem. ...Alius, sperans in multitudine divitiarum, Simone ducente ingreditur non inveniens ibi qui eum et pecuniam suam ire iubeat in perditionem. Alius in muneribus ad Petrum reformidat accedere; clanculo tamen per impluvium auri ac si per tegulas Iupiter illabatur in gremium Danae, sic in sinum Ecclesiae procus descendit incestus"—*Policrat.* lib. VII, cap. xvii, § 676.

to the time of Gregory VII, but it was during the papacy of Innocent II (1130–43) that it first received definite encouragement from the Pope. The struggle against the anti-Pope, Anacletus, in the early part of his reign had taught Innocent the supreme value of external splendour as a means of exalting the dignity of his office and of asserting the superiority of his claims.[1] The impulse once given the evil grew apace, and each successive Pope struggled in vain against the stranglehold of a Curia whose primary object was the accumulation of ecclesiastical dignities and material possessions.

Nor in reality was this state of affairs surprising. St Bernard in the *De Consideratione* might deliver a scathing indictment of the papal household for its unapostolic character,[2] but the worldly wise John of Salisbury showed a more sympathetic insight into the difficulties which the Pope had to face.

"The Pope's position at the present day", writes John in a passage of the utmost significance,[3] "is indeed wretched and unenviable. On the one hand he is for ever beset by the temptation to become the slave of avarice, and thus lose his spirituality; on the other hand, it is impossible to escape the hands and tongues of the Romans. He must secure freedom from three things, love of gifts, respect of persons, and a too ready disposition to give hearing to their requests. But hence arises a dilemma. If he is known to hate gifts, who will confer benefits on an unwilling person? And what shall he bestow who has himself received nothing? Or if he bestow not gifts, how will he appease the Romans? If he does not treat with them in person, how will he endure their proximity? For he is scarcely able to

---

[1] Cf. A. Hausrath, *Arnold von Brescia*, p. 28; F. Rocquain, *La Cour de Rome et l'esprit de réforme avant Luther*, I, pp. 185 seq., 194.

[2] *De Consid.* lib. IV passim.

[3] *Policrat.* lib. VIII, cap. xxiii, § 813 c.

ponder over a spiritual question [*causam sacerdotalem*] alone in his chamber, but is forced to admit them into his counsel. What of the presents and rewards he is compelled to condemn as simony? If he follow after these things does he not condemn himself out of his own mouth?" "For", the writer adds with thinly veiled irony, "in the present condition of the Church the Pope must needs act as *servus servorum.*" In conclusion John gives Adrian IV's account of the wretchedness of the Pope's position, and quotes his confession that he would never have left his native land but that he dared not rebel against the working of Divine Providence.

Elsewhere John abandons his sympathetic attitude for one of outspoken arraignment.[1] He represents himself as giving in Adrian's hearing the opinion of many men that the Roman Church, though she is the mother of all the churches, is acting the part of stepmother towards her children. "Scribes and Pharisees sit in her and bind heavy burdens on men's shoulders, refusing to touch them with their little finger."[2] He lays a special charge of luxury and extravagance against the Curia, and points out the grave harm wrought to the Church as a whole by the introduction of litigation into the provincial churches. In consequence a grievous blow is struck at ecclesiastical authority; confusion and open feuds between clergy and laity are the inevitable result. Justice is openly sold and everything has its price which changes with the morrow. The Pope himself has become grievous and insupportable. Whilst churches are tumbling into ruins and altars neglected, the Pope erects palaces and sits therein clothed not only in purple but also in gold. The palaces of priests shine in

[1] *Policrat.* lib. VI, cap. xxiv, § 623 c.

[2] "Sicut enim dicebatur a multis, Romana ecclesia, quae mater omnium ecclesiarum est, se non tam matrem exhibet aliis quam novercam. Sedent in ea Scribae et Pharisei ponentes onera importabilia in humeris hominum, quae digito non contingunt"—ibid.

splendour whilst the Church of Christ is defiled at their hands.

It has seemed worth while to give an extended account of these opinions, since they are not those of a professed writer of polemics, but of one who was both a dispassionate and acute critic of his times and also an able exponent of extreme hierarchical principles, a lineal descendant of the Hildebrandine school. Hence they are to be taken at their face value, since the author could have no ground for exaggerating the extent of the evil. Furthermore similar symptoms of disease were beginning to appear in the Transalpine Churches, and the enormous extension of the legatine system during the century served only to aggravate the malady.[1]

As far back as 1100 we find Ivo, Bishop of Chartres, writing to Pope Paschal II in complaint of the conduct of two of his legates.[2] "These men", he writes, "have aroused the suspicion that the Holy See seeks its own convenience and not the welfare of those placed in its care." Wherefore he and his fellow-bishops beg the Pope to send them another legate, who shall have both a closer acquaintance with their difficulties and power to effect a speedy settlement either in person or through report to the Holy See.

Some years later both John of Salisbury and St Bernard give graphic pictures of the misdeeds of Cardinal Giordano Orsini during his visitation of Germany (1151) and France (1152). "Everywhere", writes St Bernard, "he has left foul and horrid traces [*foeda et horrenda vestigia*] among us. From the foot of the Alps and the kingdom of the Germans, journeying about through all the churches of France and Normandy, as far as Rouen, this apostolic man has filled

---

[1] For a detailed study of the work of papal legates in Germany and the northern countries see J. Bachmann, " Die päpstlichen Legaten in Deutschland und Scandinavien (1125–59)", *Historische Studien*, No. 115 (ed. E. Ebering).

[2] Ivo Carnot. Ep. 109, col. 127.

them not with the Gospel but with sacrilege [*non Evangelio sed sacrilegio*]. Everywhere he is reported to have committed wickedness. Many bribed him not to come to them; but those whom he himself could not reach, he has oppressed and crippled through his emissaries. In the schools, the courts and the highways he has made his name a by-word [*fabulam*]. Seculars and religious alike speak ill of him. The poor, the monks and the clergy, all complain of him."[1]

Very similar is John of Salisbury's account of Giordano and of his colleague Cardinal Octavian, the future anti-Pope, Victor IV.[2] John roundly denounces them as wolves in sheep's clothing. He charges them with direct disobedience to the Pope's commands in respect of limitation of their retinue,[3] pecuniary exactions and respect of persons in their judgments. Not a jot nor a tittle of the papal instructions have they kept; on the contrary by sowing discord everywhere they have made the Roman Church a laughing-stock (*ludibrium*). They have "made innocence quake and purses shake", proving themselves to be torturers of men and extortioners of money.[4] The Pope (Eugenius III) wrote to them that they should mend their ways, but all to no purpose. Nevertheless, the matter could not be hushed up because folk returning from the city noised it abroad. In short, by their mission they have made the Roman Church hateful and contemptible in the eyes of the people.[5]

In the *Policraticus* John has no hesitation in comparing

[1] Bern. Ep. 290, col. 496.   [2] *Hist. pont.* cap. xxxviii, pp. 78–9.

[3] Cf. Gerhoh of Reichersberg's criticism of the immense equipages employed by legates. *De Invest. Antichristi*, cap. 1; *Lib. de lite*, III, p. 357.

[4] "Concutiebant innocentiam, loculos excutiebant, tortores hominum, pecunie extortores"—*Hist. pont.* loc. cit.

[5] *Hist. pont.* loc. cit. Cf. *Policrat.* VIII, cap. xvii, § 783 a. Gerhoh, however, writing in 1158 gives a favourable picture of Cardinal Octavian's activities in Germany based on personal knowledge. (Com. in Ps. lxiv, *Lib. de lite*, III, pp. 494 seq.; cf. Bachmann, op. cit. pp. 91–9.)

the ravages of papal legates with Satan's going forth from
the face of the Lord to scourge the Church.[1]

It would be wrong to infer from the instances quoted
above that most papal legates were of this type. The
majority were probably men of worldly experience, in
whom the flame of apostolic zeal had burned low by reason
of constant preoccupation with the administrative duties of
the Curia. Yet it should be noted that, when due allowance
is made for Bernard's rhetorical hyperbole, the concluding
words of his tribute to Cardinal Martin of San Stefano and
Cardinal Geoffrey of Chartres for their exemplary conduct
in Denmark and Aquitaine respectively would indicate that
even the ordinary standards of morality were seldom kept.[2]

In face of these revelations it must have been obvious to
the most casual observer that the Church stood in even
direr need of reform now than when Hildebrand had
launched his crusade against simony and lay investiture.
But the difficulty of securing a consensus of opinion among
reformers as to the direction which reform should take, and
the absence of a definite lead from the Papacy, prevented a
concerted programme from being framed. The old land-
marks of the investiture contest had been swept away by
its settlement and new problems of Church life and administration were presenting themselves for solution.
Gregory VII had secured for the Church an acknowledged

---

[1] "Sed nec legati sedis apostolicae manus suas excutiunt ab omni
munere, qui interdum in provinciis ita debaccantur ac si ad Ecclesiam
flagellandam egressus sit Sathan a facie Domini"—*Policrat.* lib. v,
cap. xvi, § 580 c. Cf. Gerhoh, *De Quarta vigilia noctis,* cap. xii, p. 513,
for instance of tyrannical conduct of Cardinal Gregory of St Angelo.

[2] "Quid dicis, mi Eugeni? Nonne alterius saeculi res est, redisse
legatum de terra auri sine auro? Transiisse per terram argenti, et
argentum nescisse? Donum insuper, quod poterat esse suspectum,
illico rejecisse?...O si talium daretur virorum copia, quales perstrinxi-
mus nunc! Quid te felicius, quid illo jucundius saeculo?"—*De
Consid.* IV, cap. v, col. 783. Cf. *Policrat.* lib. v, cap. xv, § 577 d;
Bachmann, p. 92.

position outside the feudal framework of society. Henceforth there was to be no question of the Church's subordination to the State. Unhappily Gregory's clearness of vision and lofty ideal were not imparted in the same degree to his immediate successors. What to him were merely symbols of spiritual freedom—investiture by ring and staff, the pallium, freedom of ecclesiastical elections—came to be regarded as in themselves the primary objects of the Church's zeal. The Hildebrandine ideal was obliterated by the mode of the Church's constitutional development.

There are several factors to account for this change. First may be set the increased importance of the College of Cardinals. Gregory was himself in part responsible for this, since it was at his inspiration that the Lateran synod of 1059 vested the right of papal elections in the hands of the Curia. In this way the cardinalate gained a means of control over future Popes and in course of time developed a policy of its own, sometimes diametrically opposed to that of the reigning Pope, as in the unhappy history of Paschal II's pontificate. During the successive schisms of Honorius II (anti-Pope Celestine) and Innocent II (anti-Pope Anacletus) the Curia rapidly gained political power at the papal expense.

Secondly, in 1115 died Gregory's powerful ally, the Countess Matilda of Tuscany, bequeathing most of her lands to the Papacy, and thereby presenting a conspicuous addition to the *damnosa hereditas* alleged to have been granted by the Emperor Constantine. The desire to secure this bequest was a potent factor in concentrating the attention of Pope and Curia on the temporal power of the Church.

Thirdly, a growing division between the German and Italian dominions of the Empire, markedly during the reigns of Lothaire and Conrad III, presented the Popes with a unique opportunity of extending their political claims. To some extent this was aided by the distinctive provisions for the two kingdoms in the matter of investitures contained in the Concordat of Worms.

Lastly, the growth of Canon Law, particularly the official sanction given to the Decretum of Gratian, indicated the Church's steady progress towards a centralised constitution.[1]

The period between the Concordat of Worms (1122) and the Third Lateran Council (1179) was for the Church unmistakably transitional. Neither the direction which reform should take nor the attitude of the hierarchy towards it was as yet clearly defined. And this largely because there was no common agreement as to the ultimate objective. Two schools of thought may be distinguished. The first was composed of the more enlightened churchmen, strong in the Gregorian principle of the Church's spiritual autonomy, and deeply perturbed by the increasing disproportion in wealth and status between the hierarchy, centred in the Roman Curia, and the body of the clergy. This seemed to them a flat contradiction of the sacerdotal principle so tenaciously held by Hildebrand, whereby every priest was equal in the sight of God in respect of his priestly functions. Accordingly these men looked for a remedy to a thorough overhaul of the Church's administrative machinery and not to any radical change in its constitution. This way of thinking was widely adopted in the Transalpine Churches, and was fundamentally in agreement with the views of St Bernard and John of Salisbury, though Germany was its peculiar stronghold.[2] Unfortunately it lacked a leader capable of welding its individual exponents into a distinct and united party.

The other school, sprung from the Patarin tradition of

[1] Gratian's work emphasised three points: (a) The unlimited character of papal sovereignty. (b) The Church's full independence in matters spiritual. (c) Subservience of the secular power to the ecclesiastical. Cf. Hauck, IV, pp. 165–6.

[2] See post, pp. 169–70.

northern Italy, was frankly iconoclastic in its aims, and represented a complete reaction from the Hildebrandine theory. According to this school no mere tinkering with the Church's constitution would meet the needs of the case. In fact the very idea of the Church as an institution sat lightly upon men of this persuasion. Their imagination was fired by the history and traditions of primitive Christianity; they desired a Church of a non-hierarchical, non-sacerdotal character basing its organisation on the practice and teaching of Christ and His Apostles. Nor was the movement utterly visionary in character; in some ways it was in full harmony with the spirit of the age. Its zeal was fed by the piety and devotion kindled by the Crusades[1] and indirectly stimulated by the new importance of the lay element in society prominent in the early decades of the twelfth century. In short, from one point of view it was the expression of the lay conscience of the age, a conscience deeply shocked at the spectacle of a Church steeped, as it seemed, in iniquity and wedded to secular pursuits.

But the strength which the movement drew from fervent zeal and disinterested ambition was largely neutralised by the fact that it was also committed to a political programme. This was almost inevitable since its ecclesiastical ideal involved a sharp distinction between spiritual and temporal functions (conceived not after the definition of Hildebrand but in accordance with the teaching of the Gospel) and ultimately the destruction of the feudal basis of society. Such ideas formed the core of Arnold of Brescia's teaching, and his career is the best illustration both of the strength and of the weakness of this position. For though Arnold himself can in no sense be termed the head of a party, there can be no doubt that his programme of ecclesiastical reform received the tacit approbation of all who shared the convictions outlined above.

[1] Hausrath, op. cit. p. 3.

Chapter II

BRESCIA AND THE PATARINI

NOT the least encouraging feature of the renaissance of mediaeval studies in the last half-century is the increasing interest shown in the economic and constitutional problems of the Italian city state. In this connection it was perhaps inevitable that in the first instance attention should have been focussed mainly on Milan, Florence and Venice to the neglect of smaller cities. For within broad limits Milan and Florence may be selected as representative respectively of the two different constitutional types evolved in Lombardy and Tuscany. The Venetian constitution, on the other hand, is unique among political systems and, so far as the Middle Ages are concerned, almost an anomaly. To this, and in a lesser degree to the character of the historical development engendered by her peculiar geographical position, Venice owes the meticulous study which historians have bestowed on her.

This concentration of attention on the larger cities has been the cause of a certain lack of proportion. Conspicuous among the states which have suffered is the city of Brescia. As yet no one has ventured to do for her what Villari and Davidsohn have accomplished for Florence[1] and Kretschmayr for Venice.[2] Indeed Brescia has hitherto attracted less notice than might have been reasonably expected considering the magnitude of her rôle in Lombard history, much less than has been given to some of her neighbouring rivals, for example Padua and Verona. In fact an adequate history of Brescia still remains to be

---

[1] P. Villari, *Two first centuries of Florentine History* (Eng. trans. L. Villari, London, 1901), first published in essay form in the *Nuova Antologia* (Florence, 1893–4). R. Davidsohn, *Geschichte von Florenz*, 4 vols. in 7 (Berlin, 1896–1927).

[2] H. Kretschmayr, *Geschichte von Venedig* (Gotha, 1905).

written. The only secondary work on a large scale is that of Odorici,[1] and both in scholarship and execution it is far inferior to the works on Florence and Venice mentioned above. In his own day Odorici performed a useful service by freeing us once for all from dependence upon the untrustworthy narrative of Biemmi,[2] but much remains to be done before the history of Brescia is stripped of legend and fantasy and established on a scientific basis of accredited fact.

Unfortunately such an enterprise is rendered more difficult of execution by the paucity of contemporary authorities before the fourteenth century. The local annals, though written in the thirteenth century, are, it is true, founded on older materials.[3] Yet the earliest entries are dated in the eleventh century, and the total number up to the middle of the twelfth comprises merely a couple of pages in the printed edition.[4] The local statutes[5] also afford little help and we are reduced to the chronicle of Malvezzi[6] and the *Codice diplomatico Bresciano*[7] for the

---

[1] F. Odorici, *Storie Bresciane dai primi tempi sino all' età nostra*, 10 vols. (Brescia, 1853–62).

[2] G. Biemmi, *Istoria di Brescia*, 2 vols. (Brescia, 1748). Biemmi's historical method in this and other works appears to have consisted in filling up gaps in knowledge by constructing a fictitious narrative and citing as authorities imaginary documents which he claimed to have in his possession. Cf. his account of Ardicio degli Aimoni, an eleventh-century personage of whose existence no trace is to be found in extant sources. Odorici, IV, pp. 143 seq. uncritically accepts this narrative in its entirety.

[3] R. L. Poole, Preface *Hist. pont.* p. lix. Giesebrecht, *Arnold von Brescia*, p. 9. K. Hampe, "Zur Geschichte Arnolds von Brescia", *Historische Zeitschrift*, cxxx, p. 63.

[4] *Annales Brixienses*, M.G.H. Script. xviii, pp. 812–13.

[5] *Leges Municipales*, ii, M.H.P. xvi.

[6] *Chronicon Brixiensis*, vol. xiv in Muratori. Though written in the fifteenth century it is fuller and more reliable for the twelfth than any other source.

[7] *Codice diplom.* (ed. Odorici, 6 Pts. in 2 vols. 1854–8). Also printed in form of appendices to volumes of Odorici's *Storie Bresciane*.

bulk of our information. Yet the early history of the city and the origins of the commune should be of no little interest in view of the prominent part taken by Brescia in Lombard politics during the twelfth and thirteenth centuries. It joined the Lombard League in 1167 soon after the League's inception and shared in the prosperity consequent upon the successful issue of the struggle against Frederick Barbarossa. It became next to Milan the largest cloth-manufacturing centre in Lombardy. Its city population was thus mainly composed of artisans, a fact responsible both for radical tendencies in politics and a highly developed civic patriotism. The dwellers in the *contado* were famed as good farmers and brave soldiers. From the thirteenth to the fifteenth century the city successfully withstood several sieges, the most notable being those of Frederick II in 1238 and Henry VII in 1311. Finally in 1512 came the great siege by the French under Gaston de Foix, which ended with the storming and sacking of the city. From this catastrophe she never recovered and henceforward declined in fame and prosperity. "Thus", writes Guicciardini, "fell in total ruin that city which was not inferior in nobility and dignity to any other in Lombardy, but in riches superior to all others save Milan."[1]

Brescia lies in the extreme north of the Lombard plain, fifty-two miles east of Milan and forty miles west of Verona. Its western flank is sheltered by the southernmost spur of the Alps dividing the valleys of the Chiesa and the Mella. On the north-east a strong castle commands the Lombard plain. The city was a place of great antiquity, even if we are compelled to reject the tradition which derived its name from the Celtic chieftain, Brennus.[2] Without doubt it was originally a Celtic township, being

[1] Guicciardini, *Istoria d'Italia*, v, p. 84 (Pisa, 1819).
[2] *Malvecii Chron.* p. 786. Johannis de Cermenate, *Historia*, F.S.I. cap. IV, p. 14.

taken by the Romans in 225 B.C. on the submission of the Cenomani. It was settled as a Roman colony in the reign of Augustus (27 B.C.), and its position on the great military road running from Como to Aquileia made it a place of strategic importance under the Empire. In 452 it was laid waste by Attila and suffered a momentary eclipse.[1] Under the Lombards it became once more an important centre, being made the capital of one of the Lombard duchies.[2] Hence Celtic, Gothic and Lombard strains were mingled with the Roman in its population. At the Frankish conquest its territory was absorbed in the Carolingian Empire.

The ninth century was a period of political disintegration throughout western Europe and symptoms of disorder were especially noticeable in Italy. The Lombard duchies fell apart into separate, self-contained units, each with its administration organised on feudal lines and virtually independent of the central authority, the Frankish Emperor. The one institution which emerged from the welter of the Dark Ages unimpaired in power and prestige was the episcopate. From time immemorial the bishop had been the leader and guardian of his flock, exercising a profound moral influence on the manifold vicissitudes of their lives. "The life of the Italian cities, and later of their communes", writes Dr Previté-Orton, "was almost inextricably intertwined with their church and its head, the bishop. Civic patriotism, religious emotion and the ordinary transactions of life, the market and the festival, all clustered round the city-saints and their fanes."[3]

[1] Odorici (*Storie Bresciane*, II, pp. 134 seq.) asserts that the city was rebuilt under Theodoric, but the evidence which he adduces for the statement is very slender and rests solely upon a doubtful interpretation of Theophanes (*Chronographia*, IV, p. 60), where Narses, the general of Justinian, is said "duas arces munitissimas Veronam et Brixiam a Gothis recepisse".

[2] Paulus diaconus, *Historia*, lib. v, cap. xxxvi, M.G.H. *Scriptores rerum Langobardarum*, p. 156.

[3] *Camb. Med. Hist.* v, p. 218.

By a spontaneous, if in part involuntary, process the bishops came to extend their jurisdiction into the temporal sphere. The development, by which they arrogated to themselves administrative functions formerly exercised by the Frankish counts, was rendered easier by the widening gulf between the Teutonic and Latin dominions of the Empire, partly a cause and partly a result of the breakdown of the centralised system of government set up by the Carolingians. The bishops, however, were not slow to realise the insecurity of their newly won powers in face of the legitimate claims of the Empire and the possible pretensions of the Papacy. They were driven to seek support from the citizens, and in return were willing to foster the growing spirit of municipal independence so long as it remained consistent with episcopal patronage.

This new spirit abroad in the Lombard cities was but one manifestation of a wider renaissance.[1] The tradition of the municipal liberties enjoyed under the Roman Empire had never quite died out in Lombardy, and assisted by favourable conditions was ripe for revival. Progress in industry and commerce accelerated the growth of the new movement. Old, disused trade routes were reopened and increased intercourse between town and town was fostered by the survival of the great Roman military roads traversing the Lombard plain. Each city gained in the process a consciousness of civic unity and a jealousy of its neighbours. In some cases the growth of the urban population necessitated a rebuilding of the city walls, the construction of new roads and the erection of new churches. A constant stream of immigrants from the *contado* swelled the numbers and increased the prosperity of the artisan class. Side by side with this economic revolution went a revival of culture and letters. Schools sprang up in every city,

[1] See C. W. Previté-Orton, *Outlines of Medieval History* (C.U.P. 1916), pp. 222 seq. for an admirable summary of its various facets.

learning became more secular in character and less strictly confined to the clergy, whilst a revival of Roman Law did something to educate the people in the basic principles of politics.[1] As a result what had at first been a vague aspiration towards political independence became in time a definite programme for the administration of local affairs on a self-governing, communal basis. Episcopal authority was threatened at the root, and before long the formation of political parties brought civil strife in nearly every city.

The situation was further complicated by disputes on ecclesiastical matters. The Lombard Churches of the eleventh century stood in dire need of reform. Nowhere were the grave evils corrupting the life of the Church more conspicuous. The hierarchy was tainted with simony, the inferior clergy were worldly and depraved. Many of them were openly married, a state of life acquiesced in or even approved by the mass of the people, but condemned by the zealots. The chief see and the seat of an archbishopric was Milan, whose clergy, writes a contemporary, were as numerous as the sand of the sea.[2] From the days of St Ambrose it had maintained a proud independence, acquiring peculiar traditions and privileges, of which the jealous preservation of the historic Ambrosian ritual provided a remarkable symbol. More than a score of the Lombard dioceses were included in its province, and in addition to his spiritual power the archbishop was a great feudal lord. Under the rule of the able Aribert (1018–45) the archiepiscopal power rose so high that Milan seemed well on the way towards the establishment of a strong theocratic government, its archbishop at the head uniting in his person both spiritual and temporal functions, and

---

[1] Previté-Orton, pp. 226–7.
[2] Bonitho Sutrien, "Liber ad amicum", lib. VI in Jaffé, *Mon. Gregoriana*, p. 639.

independent alike of Emperor and Pope. That such a
development fell short of completion was due mainly to
the outbreak of the agitation known as the Patarin
movement.

Many and varied were the elements composing the
latter.[1] Mere selfish, worldly motives, jealousy between
class and class, between clergy and laity, between the
hierarchy and the inferior clergy, were mixed with dreams
of political independence and outbursts of anti-sacerdotal
fanaticism. Envy of the superior status of the Lombard
hierarchy was linked with agitation against the existence of
manorial churches (*Eigenkirchen*) where the secular lord
was in effective control. It is easy to see how revolutionary
principles of this kind could be used by ambitious cities as
a weapon against their Imperial overlord, whose representative was often the bishop. This was especially the case
at Milan, where Aribert's successor was the Imperial
nominee, Guido of Velato. Aribert's success had been made
possible by the loyal support of the Milanese; Guido was
unfortunate in his antecedents,[2] and by no means skilful
enough to stem the rising tide of Patarin enthusiasm.
Hence the alliance between bishop and citizens was broken.
Gradually, as the movement for ecclesiastical reform
gathered strength under the guidance and inspiration of the
reformed Papacy, a new orientation of parties took place.
The cleavage came along religious rather than political
lines. For the moment the ideal of civic unity was eclipsed
by zeal for amendment of clerical morality. Yet political
grievances were not wholly left out of sight, for the attack
on simony and clerical marriage also involved a negation
of episcopal immunities. Rome was the indisputable head

[1] For a remarkable summary of Patarin ideals see G. Volpe, *Movimenti religiosi*, pp. 10 seq. Cf. E. Troeltsch, *Die Soziallehren der
Christlichen Kirchen und Gruppen*, pp. 384–5.

[2] "Vir illiteratus et concubinatus et absque ulla verecundia symoni-
acus"—Bonitho Sutrien, loc. cit.

of the movement. Not till the see of Ambrose had been brought to acknowledge the spiritual sovereignty of the see of Peter and the "vested interests" of the Milanese clergy destroyed, could the inveterate abuses in the churches of Lombardy be eradicated. Hence the laity, drawn both from the artisan and the merchant classes, joined with the lower clergy in enforcing the papal programme of reform on an unwilling hierarchy, while the nobles of the *contado* rallied to the bishop in defence of episcopal privilege.

From a particular district of the city, the quarter of the rag-pickers, where their numbers were strong, the re-formers became known as the Patarini. It is impossible to enter here into the confusing history of these years of strife (1056–75) or to sketch the motives of the popular leaders, Ariald and Erlembald.[1] But two significant factors emerge from the chaos of warring parties; first, a dis-interested desire for a readjustment of the social relation-ship between clergy and laity, and secondly, a passionate attachment to the idea of apostolic poverty as the ruling principle in the life of the priesthood. The former took practical shape by the establishment of communal govern-ment, the latter, if it were ever to be realised, would

---

[1] Good narrative accounts are given in *Camb. Med. Hist.* v, chap. i, pp. 39 seq.; H. C. Lea, *Sacerdotal Celibacy* (3rd ed.), I, pp. 243–63; and F. Tocco, *L'eresia nel medio evo*, pp. 207–31. Monographs by H. Paech (1893) and A. Krüger (1903). Also C. Pellegrini, *I santi Arialdo ed Erlembaldo* (1897). On the derivation of the term "Patarin" see *Camb. Med. Hist.* v, p. 219; Lea, I, p. 249, n. 2; C. Mirbt in *Herzog's Realencyklopädie*, art. Pataria, pp. 761 seq. Originally it was a term of opprobrium cast at the reformers by their opponents, who in turn were branded as Nicolaitans, though there can have been little in common between the principles and practice of the married clergy of Milan and those of the sect of that name mentioned in the Apocalypse. In the twelfth century Patarini came to be synonymous with Cathari and derived from "pati" (to suffer) implying those who suffered for their opinions. See Mirbt, p. 764; Döllinger, *Beiträge zur Sektengeschichte des Mittelalters*, I, pp. 128 seq.; Volpe, op. cit. p. 24.

necessitate the destruction of the temporal power of the bishop. Though these objects were only partially achieved, something was gained by the abolition of episcopal immunities and the subjection of the see to the spiritual authority of the Pope. The power of the Milanese hierarchy, however, was still by no means negligible. On the death in 1075 of Erlembald, the most statesmanlike of the popular leaders, the hierarchical party took advantage of the ensuing confusion in the Patarin ranks and regained a substantial share in the city government.

Two separate systems of administration existed side by side within the city; the feudal, monarchical jurisdiction of the archbishop and the democratic organisation of the commune led by its consuls. In practice this was no such anomaly as it seems in theory. It is difficult at all times to square the constitutional practice of the Italian city republics with the academic theories of sovereignty propounded in modern text-books. This dyarchical arrangement was by no means peculiar to Milan; nearly all the Lombard cities went through a similar transitional stage at some period in their history. In every case the commune achieved full autonomy only after a long contest with ecclesiastical authority for temporal sovereignty. Normally several decades elapsed before the goal was reached. In the interim a clash of jurisdictions was inevitable.

The twenty years' strife at Milan was no isolated phenomenon but the greatest local manifestation of the radical change wrought by Patarin principles. These were rapidly pervading Lombardy, and in every city were to be found men of courage and conviction eager to emulate the saintly patriots Ariald and Erlembald. Very early in the movement Brescia had become one of its chief strongholds.[1] Geographical proximity to Milan, the strength and prosperity of its artisans and the corrupt character of its clergy

[1] Bonitho Sutrien, op. cit. Jaffé, p. 644.

were factors eminently calculated to promote the spread of Patarin doctrines.

Ecclesiastical grievances were especially conspicuous. Despite frequent canons of reform passed in local synods the evil of simony continued unabated. Churches and livings were sold to the highest bidder and the sole object of the clergy appeared to be the amassing of material wealth. The bishop was a great feudal lord who owned more than one-fifth of the province.[1] Hence arose continual friction between bishop and citizens on questions of land ownership. As the eleventh century progressed, social and economic disputes merged into political, producing a class hostility similar to that found in Milan though less prone to break out into open war. Already in 1029 under Bishop Landulph II the commune had begun to entrench on episcopal jurisdiction by securing a statute regulating the disposal of feudal contracts in the case of a debtor dying without an heir.[2] This proved to be, to use a convenient if somewhat hackneyed phrase, the thin end of the wedge. The municipality had in effect wrung from the bishop a recognition of its claim to be consulted where its economic interests were concerned. It was soon in a position to extend this claim to other spheres. In 1037 under Bishop Odoric I a convention was made between people and episcopate whereby the bishop was forced to admit serious limits to his feudal jurisdiction.[3]

The accession of Hildebrand to the papal throne ushered in troublous times for Brescia as for other Lombard cities.

---

[1] Vacandard, "Arnauld de Brescia", *R.Q.H.* xxxv, p. 59 and n.2. Odorici (*Storie Bresciane*, IV, p. 258) relying on the fictitious chronicle of "Ardicio degli Aimoni", says that *three-fifths* of the land was held in fee from the bishop.

[2] *Codice diplom. Bresciano*, Pt. III, No. xl, pp. 48–9. Cf. Odorici, *Storie Bresciane*, III, p. 328, IV, p. 123.

[3] *Codice diplom.* Pt. III, No. xlvi, p. 52. Cf. Odorici, III, p. 325, IV, p. 124.

The new Pope's first attempt to put down simony and concubinage precipitated a conflict on ecclesiastical grounds. In 1074 all the Lombard prelates were summoned to attend the Lenten synod in Rome, there to discuss questions of clerical morals and lay investiture.

Neither Tedaldus, the Imperialist Archbishop of Milan, nor any of his suffragans put in an appearance, and all incurred the penalty of excommunication. Among them was Odoric II, Bishop of Brescia.[1] The Lombard bishops in fact were fast bound both by feudal contract and political interest to their Imperial overlord. Of Odoric's immediate successors Conon (1080–5), a native of Saxony and a distant relative of the Emperor Henry IV, John (1085–96) and Obertus (1096–8) had all received investiture from the secular power.[2]

As each succeeding bishop was a minion of the Emperor the citizens of Brescia leaned more and more on the arm of the Papacy. The untimely death of Gregory VII in 1085 increased the confusion of parties and debased their principles. The contest over investitures had divided every city into factions, papalist and imperialist, Guelf and Ghibelline. Thus far the two sides had been so evenly matched that few cities showed a united front in support either of the one cause or of the other. Now, however, the papalists began to secure a numerical superiority. The forceful personality of the Countess Matilda of Tuscany, Gregory VII's loyal ally of earlier days, succeeded in detaching Milan from the Imperial alliance and effecting a *rapprochement* with the Pope. Other cities followed the lead and the rise in papal prestige caused by Urban II's enthusiastic preaching of the First Crusade helped to complete the process.

Changes in the larger arena of politics invariably pro-

---

[1] Odorici, IV, p. 127. See rescript in Jaffé, pp. 61 seq.
[2] Odorici, p. 128.

duced like changes in local affairs. In a synod of the Lombard clergy held at Milan in 1098 the Imperialist bishops were condemned as simonists and deposed, among them being Obertus (*invasor Brixiensis*). Arimannus, a native of Brescia and a cardinal, already distinguished for his part in winning over Milan to the papal camp, was appointed in his stead.[1] He was welcomed by the citizens as a fellow-countryman and as a liberator from the yoke of alien and Imperialist prelates. In Lombardy he acquired a unique position, wielding an influence greater than his metropolitan at Milan, and actually succeeded in imposing his own nominee on the archiepiscopal throne.[2] Able, unscrupulous and gifted with a fair measure of political prescience, Arimannus steered the city through a difficult period with considerable skill. Yet his autocratic bearing and overweening ambition alienated the democratic sentiments of the people. The death of the Countess Matilda in 1115 removed his staunchest supporter, and in the same year occurred a revolt of the citizens culminating in the schismatic election to the see of the archpresbyter Villanus. At the Lateran Council of 1116 Pope Paschal II confirmed the popular choice. Arimannus was declared deposed and the usurper Villanus consecrated in his stead.[3]

During the latter's tenure of office occurred two events, which taken together were not without influence in shaping the destinies of the Lombard communes. In 1122 the settlement of the investiture dispute by the Concordat of Worms removed one potential source of civic strife. Unhappily another equally fertile was provided by the papal schism of 1130, which divided the ecclesiastical allegiance of western Europe for nearly eight years. In Brescia the conflict between the two parties was long and bitter. In

---

[1] Mansi, *Concilia*, xx, col. 957. [2] Odorici, p. 134.
[3] Landulph, *Hist. Mediolanensis*, cap. xxx. Muratori, v, col. 499 seq. Odorici, p. 226.

common with his metropolitan at Milan and most of the
Lombard bishops, Villanus was a warm supporter of the
anti-Pope Anacletus. This of itself was sufficient to enlist
the sympathies of the citizens on behalf of Innocent II.

Moreover St Bernard's heroic labours in Innocent's
cause during his missionary tour through Lombardy
appeared to give the highest sanction to the choice made
by the citizens of Brescia. The history of the struggle is
obscure, but Villanus with the aid of the nobles of the
contado contrived to retain possession of his see till 1132.
Then Innocent II declared him deposed and set up a
certain Manfred in his place.[1]

Such is the bare outline of the political history of
Brescia from about 1030 to 1130. The pattern is blurred,
but the medley of colours need not blind us to the unity of
the design. Beneath the vicissitudes of party politics, the
clash of principles and interests, the bewildering sequence
of movement and counter-movement, of revolt and counter-
revolt, went on the steady, ordered growth of civic institutions and the gradual diffusion of civic ideals. Land-
marks in constitutional history are generally few in number,
and the case of Brescia is no exception to the rule. The
subject is fringed with doubts and discrepancies; we have,
however, sufficient data to mark the salient changes in the
governmental system during this period. These are almost
wholly connected with the distribution of powers between
the bishop on the one side and the officials of the municipality on the other. At the beginning of the period the
bishop virtually exercised an undisputed control over all
departments of government, executive, administrative and
judicial. By the time of Villanus a very different state of

---

[1] "Anno 1132. Innocentius papa Brixiam venit et eiecit Villanum
de episcopatu"—*Annal. Brix.* p. 812. Cf. Malvecius (*Chron.* VII, cap.
xxx, p. 876) who speaks of a popular rising while the Pope was in the
city. He also wrongly gives the year 1135 as the date of Villanus'
deposition.

affairs meets our gaze; the constitution now approximates to the dyarchical model, which we have mentioned as existing at Milan fifty years earlier.[1] The chief cause of this change is undoubtedly the emergence of the consulate, the chief magistracy of the commune.[2] The date of the earliest appearance of consuls in Brescia is still undetermined. It would, however, seem safe to assume that the office was firmly established by the beginning of the twelfth century, since by then nearly all the Lombard cities show evidence of its existence.[3] Our earliest documentary evidence is given in a treaty dated 1127, signed by bishop and consuls jointly and effecting a compromise in a dispute over the control of administration.[4]

Thus by 1130 the commune of Brescia may be said to have attained its political majority and to have emerged from the semi-autonomy of the preceding century. Its organisation, based on the ideal of a self-governing democracy, with political principles the complete negation of the feudal traditions of the episcopate, was now established. Through the consuls, its elected representatives, it had obtained an equal share with the bishop in the control of civic administration. But the process of encroachment on episcopal privilege was not yet finished. We have seen how the cleavage both of principle and policy widened under stress of the larger politics of the period, how in every dispute bishop and commune were found in opposite camps. With the growth of a new generation this antagonism became instinctive and permanent. The city's debt to the episcopate in distant days was forgotten, nor did the lives and characters of the twelfth-century bishops inspire either affection for their persons or respect for their

---

[1] See ante, p. 20.

[2] On the origin and development of the consulate see *Camb. Med. Hist.* v, pp. 220 seq.

[3] *Camb. Med. Hist.* loc. cit.

[4] *Codice diplom.* Pt. III, No. xxxviii, pp. 94–5.

office. Neither Manfred nor Villanus was comparable with Arimannus in talent or personality. They were puppets dependent on the benevolent support of external powers, Pope or Emperor, and neither efficient administrators nor worthy pastors.

The lists were set for the final clash, a veritable combat *à outrance*. It was no longer to be a struggle between two competing jurisdictions, but a battle for the existence of the bishop's temporal power. The issue would decide whether or no the bishop was to share the fate of Emperor and count before him. There was a further aspect of the situation equally fraught with significance for the future.

Though aspirations towards the ideal of a reformed and purified Church had been temporarily diverted by the immediate practical issues raised by the investiture contest, the ideal itself still exercised a dynamic attraction. True, the Patarin movement had in Milan largely failed of its object and its organisation had been suffered to decay. Yet in Brescia, at any rate, its principles survived and needed only a leader to put them to practical use. In Arnold of Brescia such a one was at hand. His entry into the movement revived its drooping energies and infused into it a new and purer spirit. In him all ignoble or petty strains were purged away, all pursuit of personal or class ambitions was relinquished, and the cause for which he fought raised to a higher plane by the disinterestedness of his motives and the earnestness of his convictions. Henceforward Brescia was destined to lead the van in a renewed battle against the secularisation of the Lombard Church.

Chapter III

ARNOLD'S EARLY LIFE. THE DISCIPLE
OF ABAILARD

THE circumstances of Arnold's birth are lost in obscurity. All accounts agree in giving Brescia as his native city, but no mention is made of him in the local annals.[1] The exact year of his birth is unknown. It cannot be placed earlier than 1090 or later than 1110 (if the story of his student days in Paris be accepted) and historians are fairly evenly divided in opinion as to which side of the century mark is more probable. Giesebrecht and Gregorovius would fix it within the first decade of the twelfth century[2]; the Abbé Vacandard argues for the last decade of the eleventh, basing his conclusion on Otto of Freising's statement that Arnold had already taken minor orders before his departure to France (c. 1115).[3] Most of the later biographers have followed this, the more probable of the two alternatives. Further it is by no means certain that he was born within the city walls; Otto of Freising's phrase, *ex Italia civitate Brixia*,[4] may refer to the whole of the territory bound by the feudal jurisdiction of the bishop.[5] Nor have we any knowledge of Arnold's parents and their station in life. The statement of Walter Map that he came of a noble family[6] is not in itself improbable. He would seem to have received his early education in the

---

[1] *Annal. Brix.* M.G.H. XVIII, pp. 812 seq. Mention is made of one, Arnold, who suffered a similar fate in 1153, and Dr K. Hampe, pp. 61 seq. thinks that Arnold of Brescia is here indicated despite the discrepancy of date.

[2] Giesebrecht, *Arnold von Brescia*, p. 7; Gregorovius, *Rome*, IV, p. 480.

[3] Otto of Freising, *Gesta Fred.* lib. II, cap. xxviii (S.G.U.S. p. 133). Vacandard, op. cit. p. 56, n. 1.

[4] Otto of Freising, loc. cit.   [5] See ante, chap. ii, p. 21.

[6] Map, *De Nugis Curialium* (ed. M. R. James, O.U.P. 1919), p. 39.

episcopal school, one of the many set up by Eugenius II,[1] which owed its continuing existence to the reforming zeal of Hildebrand.

The young scholar grew to manhood amid the civil and religious discords which accompanied the successive stages of the investiture contest. How far the sorry spectacle influenced Arnold's mental development it is difficult to gauge. It is easy and tempting to ·stress too heavily the effect of environment upon character. In Arnold's case it probably produced a series of impressions, some of which were effaced by the hand of time, whilst others remained to provide a background of experience on which the ripening intellect could draw in later days.

Somewhere about the year 1115, driven by a thirst for knowledge Arnold crossed the Alps and became a pupil of Abailard, then at the height of his fame as a teacher at Paris. This piece of information we owe to Otto of Freising; all our other authorities are silent on the point. At first sight the story seems improbable, and, as Dr Poole suggests, there is always to be considered the possibility of a confusion with Arnold's later association with Abailard at the Council of Sens.[2] Further St Bernard's silence on the point is undoubtedly remarkable. Every scrap of information concerning Arnold's past history is imported into the fervid letters wherein the orthodox champion summons the episcopal legions to arms against the philosophic heretic. In the letter written to Innocent II at the time of the Council of Sens, in which so damaging an account is given of Abailard's teaching, Bernard takes special pains to indicate the closeness of the links binding the two men.[3] Here, if anywhere, the student would search

---

[1] Jaffé-Loewenfeld, *Regesta*, p. 321; Mansi, *Concilia*, xiv, col. 1008.
[2] R. L. Poole, *Illustrations of Mediaeval Thought and Learning*, p. 141, n. 29.
[3] Bern. Ep. 189, col. 355.

expectantly for some intelligence as to the beginnings of the connection. But not a hint is dropped of any earlier intercourse than that under discussion in the letter. Yet even if infallible the Abbot of Clairvaux was not omniscient, and his omission of the fact may be satisfactorily explained by his ignorance of it. A quarter of a century divides the two events. In 1115 Bernard was on the point of setting out to found the new monastery at Clairvaux,[1] and the cares of its administration were sufficient to tax his energy during the years immediately following. He had then no opportunity, and possibly little inclination, to assume the rôle of Defender of the Faith which was responsible for his unhappy conflict with Abailard.

Of graver import is the silence of our most dependable authority, the *Historia Pontificalis*. John of Salisbury, himself a pupil of Abailard,[2] might have been expected to give the episode at least a passing mention. Yet even this omission is far from being conclusive evidence, for Arnold and John were associated with the Paris master at two distinct periods of the latter's teaching. Arnold's sojourn in France cannot with certainty be extended beyond the year 1120, the date of Abailard's entry into the monastic order at St Denis, whilst John's discipleship did not begin till 1136,[3] when Abailard returned to the Mont Ste Geneviève. We have therefore a gap of at least fifteen years. John could have no first-hand knowledge of the event but would be dependent on the recollections of Arnold's fellow-students and any local traditions of him that happened to survive. There is, however, no reason to suppose that Arnold was likely to attract the curiosity of his fellows. In short the fact can neither be definitely proved nor disproved. No

[1] Bern. *Vita Prima*, lib. 1, cap. vii, M.P.L. 184, col. 245.
[2] *Joannis Saresberiensis Metalogicon*, lib. 11, cap. x (ed. C. C. J. Webb, O.U.P. 1929), § 867 b.
[3] R. L. Poole, *Dict. Nat. Biography*, art. John of Salisbury.

evidence exists to give the lie to Otto's statement, and in a case of this kind the *argumentum ex silentio* is of doubtful value. Further it is worth stressing that Otto is by no means an ill-informed writer for the earlier part of Arnold's life. To reject his very explicit statement[1] in the absence of any other evidence to the contrary merely because no corroboration is available from other sources would scarcely be in accord with the canons of scholarship.[2]

It was the age of the wandering scholar, and for every youth of studious ambition Paris was the first objective. Years before Abailard himself and Otto of Freising had journeyed thither from afar, and in the near future John of Salisbury and other English scholars were to cross the channel to add one more tongue to the Babel of the Latin Quarter. There is therefore nothing strange in the fact that Arnold should cross the Alps and make his way thither. He was merely following a trail well blazed since the distant days when the great Lombard lawyer made his perilous journey across France to find rest and shelter in the monastic house of Bec. At the time of Arnold's arrival Abailard was incomparably the ablest and most successful teacher in Paris. The manner, no less than the substance, of his lectures transcended the barren discourses of more orthodox teachers, and the originality of his thought coupled with the lucidity of his expression struck a note of

---

[1] The exact words used by Otto deserve close attention: "Petrum Abailardum olim praeceptorem habuerat", he writes (p. 133). There is here none of the caution implied for example in Otto's words giving Arnold's opinions on the Sacraments. See p. 198, n. 2. It is difficult to escape the deliberation of such a phrase.

[2] Cf. Neander, *Gen. Church History*, VII, p. 199, n. 2. Neither Gregorovius nor Giesebrecht shows any disposition to impugn the validity of Otto's statement. Similarly Vacandard, Breyer and Hausrath are all inclined to admit it. The first writer openly to deny it is Michele de Palo, "Due Novatori del XII secolo" in *Archivio Storico Italiano*, XIV, pp. 79–114. He is followed by E. Comba, *I nostri Protestanti*, pp. 173 seq.

novelty which his hearers were quick to appreciate. Such were the characteristics of the man whom Arnold now took for master, and whose vagaries of genius were at once the pride and the terror of the scholastic world.

Peter Abailard[1] was born in Brittany at the village of Pallet or Palais near Nantes in or about the year 1079. The eldest son of a noble house, at an early age he abandoned his ancestral rights to his brothers and, forsaking the path of military glory marked out for him by the custom of the period and the traditions of his lineage, dedicated himself to a life of study or, to use his own expression, he forsook the court of Mars for the lap of Minerva.[2] He first attached himself to Roscelin,[3] the eminent Nominalist, whose daring speculations on the Trinity had drawn down upon himself a charge of tritheism and ecclesiastical censure by the Council of Soissons (1092). So outraged were the master and his more faithful followers at the keenness of the pupil's criticism, so runs the story, that Abailard judged it prudent

---

[1] The standard biography is Charles de Rémusat (Paris, 1845). Where later study has thrown fresh light on various aspects of his career S. M. Deutsch (Leipzig, 1883) and A. Hausrath (Leipzig, 1893) are useful. Dr R. L. Poole gives a brilliant study in his *Illustrations of Mediaeval Thought and Learning*, 2nd ed. Joseph McCabe, *Peter Abélard*, is vivid and written with insight but should be read with caution. For Abailard's philosophy see Reuter, *Geschichte der religiösen Aufklärung*, 2 vols. (1875-7), and Rashdall, *Med. Universities*, I, chap. ii. For his conflict with St Bernard, Neander, *Der Heilige Bernhard*, and Vacandard, *Vie de St Bernard*, chaps. xxii, xxiii. The chief original authority for his life is his own *Hist. Calam.* M.P.L. 178.

[2] *Hist. Calam.* cap. i, M.P.L. 178, col. 115.

[3] Abailard makes no mention of this in the *Hist. Calam.* and we owe the information to Otto of Freising (*Gesta Fred.* lib. I, cap. xlix, S.G.U.S. p. 69). Grave doubts were formerly held as to the accuracy of this statement, but the fact is now definitely established by Cousin's publication of Roscelin's letter to Abailard, *Opera*, II, pp. 794 seq. See also Cousin, *Ouvrages inédits d'Abélard*, introd. pp. xl seq.; *Dialectica*, Pt. v, p. 471: "Fuit autem, memini, magister nostri Ros(cellini) ...." Cf. Rashdall, I, p. 48, n. 2. R. L. Poole, *Illustrations*, App. VIII, p. 315.

to change his place of study. After the fashion of the age he wandered from school to school[1] till about 1100 we find him settled at Paris in the cathedral school over which presided William of Champeaux, the greatest dialectician of the day.[2]

The abrupt change from Roscelin, the Nominalist champion, to William, the chief exponent of the dominant Realism of the day, bears eloquent testimony to the voracious character of Abailard's intellectual appetite. From Roscelin he had equipped himself with the kind of argument most potent to destroy the insecure foundations of the Realist teaching. With his customary impetuosity he made full use of the opportunity afforded and began openly to assail William's position, hitherto regarded as impregnable. Criticism from the one side provoked jealousy and persecution from the other, till at length Abailard resolved to set up as a teacher of philosophy on his own account. He deemed it imprudent to make this bold venture in Paris but removed to Melun where under the shadow of the royal fortress he opened a school with a few of William's discontented pupils as a nucleus.[3] Here so immediate a success attended his first pedagogic efforts that he was encouraged to move his quarters to Corbeil a little further up the Seine. A true instinct was drawing him steadily back to Paris, later the centre of the great Scholastic Renaissance, of which he was himself to become the harbinger. In 1102 we find him teaching on the Mont Ste Geneviève.[4] Here students of every nation flocked to his lectures, attracted in the main by the novel methods of his exposition. William of Champeaux endeavoured to renew

---

[1] "Proinde diversas disputando perambulans provincias, ubicumque hujus artis (Dialecticae) vigere studium audieram, Peripateticorum aemulator factus sum"—*Hist. Calam.* cap. i.

[2] *Hist. Calam.* cap. ii.   [3] Ibid.

[4] Ibid. col. 120.

the unequal contest but soon suffered a final discomfiture. According to Abailard's own account the master was completely vanquished in argument and driven to make modifications which ultimately involved a total abnegation of the extreme Realist position.[1] In all probability the motive power behind Abailard's criticism was not so much the dialectical arguments acquired from Roscelin as his own innate repugnance to accept any teaching on the mere warrant of authority. His mind was essentially of an open and enquiring nature, and to his keen critical faculty he added the rarer ability of viewing all philosophical problems from more than one angle. William's credit was wholly destroyed by the retreat that Abailard had forced upon him. His school was fast emptying, and for the sake of the little reputation that remained to him he found it expedient to discover a sudden desire for a more religious calling. Quitting the academic battleground he retired to the comfortable seclusion of the vacant bishopric of Châlons in 1113.[2]

But the intellectual avidity of the Breton scholar—he was now a little over thirty—was still unsated. Hitherto he had confined his energies both as student and as teacher to the subjects of dialectics and grammar. He now aspired to glory in the more attractive lists of the theological tournament, and to this end in 1113 he left Paris and entered the school of Anselm of Laon. The latter had been a pupil of St Anselm of Canterbury, and possibly owing to this connection some of the elder teacher's renown had been reflected on him. At any rate he enjoyed a marked reputation as a lecturer in Divinity, and being now advanced in years was content to rest upon his laurels. Undoubtedly Abailard's account of Anselm's methods is

---

[1] *Hist. Calam.* col. 119. Cf. Rashdall, I, p. 50.
[2] *Hist. Calam.* col. 122.

grossly prejudiced.[1] Even so it would appear that his fame as a theologian far exceeded his merits. Stripped of the eloquent language in which they were delivered his lectures contained little more than a bundle of texts collected from the writings of the Latin Fathers, and dispensed as the authoritative teaching of the Church on sacred subjects. It can easily be conjectured that Abailard was not the man to be impressed by teaching of this kind. The method of free enquiry characteristic of his dialectical studies is brought to bear also on this field of knowledge. His impudent assertion that a master was not indispensable for the learning of theology aroused against him the rancour of Anselm and his more fervent admirers. The challenge Abailard rashly issued was accepted, yet the lectures he had undertaken to give as a wager were so remarkable that his experience at Paris was repeated here in Laon. Subjected to continual persecution at the hands of Anselm's chosen pupils[2] the philosopher knight-errant was compelled to retrace his steps to Paris, where in 1116 he once more set up his standard on the Mont Ste Geneviève, on this occasion as a teacher of theology.[3] Here he remained till 1119, when the tragic sequel to his love for Heloise drove him as a monk disillusioned and broken to the Abbey of St Denis.[4]

At the beginning of Arnold's discipleship, however, the great philosopher, conscious of an increasing grasp of intellectual problems, stood forth with a confidence based on past experience and an ambition unchecked by any external force. It is of the highest importance for Arnold's later

---

[1] "Mirabilis quidem erat in oculis auscultantium, sed nullus in conspectu quaestionantium. Verborum usum habebat mirabilem, sed sensu contemptibilem, et ratione vacuum. Cum ignem accenderet, domum suam fumo implebat, non luce illustrabat"—*Hist. Calam.* cap. iii, col. 123.

[2] *Hist. Calam.* cap. iv, col. 125.

[3] Ibid. cap. v, col. 126.

[4] Ibid. cap. viii, col. 135.

career that we should investigate any reaction to be traced directly to Abailard's teaching. Superficially the two men present to a later observer a striking contrast both in temperament and power of intellect. Abailard with a genius for dialectics mainly confined his attention to the philosophical problems engaging the academic world around him. He was never at ease save in the realm of theoretical speculation. His lot was cast amid the intellectual ferment of the Paris schools. His churchmanship he habitually placed in a secondary relationship to his philosophy, and the goal of his studies was determined by the intellectual curiosity that was perhaps the most potent factor in his character. The famous sentence in the *Sic et Non* became the touchstone of his speculation and the fundamental principle of his teaching. "By doubting", he writes, "we are led to enquire, by enquiring we arrive at truth."[1] Believing with his whole heart that the *Civitas Dei* could be reached by more roads than one, he conceived it his mission to explore every channel of thinking whereby the human mind might achieve a closer apprehension of the Divine. But not in every case did he show either the desire or the capacity to press his discoveries to their logical conclusion. Further in the pursuit of so exalted an ideal there existed a danger lest his intellectual brilliance and fearless investigation should lead him into positions where he might find himself deprived of a stable foundation for the structure of his thinking. And this impulse of mental instability was augmented rather than checked by peculiarities of temperament and character. The vacillation, that more than once marked his conduct in the crises of his life, was the physical counterpart of those ingenious subtleties and mental reservations which puzzled his friends and angered his foes. Amid all the vicissitudes of his career he remained

---

[1] "Dubitando enim ad inquisitionem venimus; inquirendo veritatem percipimus"—M.P.L. 178, col. 1349.

at heart a pilgrim with the melancholy upon him of one
who is a prey to restless unquiet searchings.

Arnold was a man of an entirely different type. To quote
the apt expression of Reuter: "Er ist ein Mann aus einem
Stück".[1] But to be all of one piece may involve limitations
not always salutary. Arnold's dominant interest was ethical
rather than intellectual. Zeal for righteousness, personal
and social, was united to a vivid consciousness of the goal
of his endeavour and a grim tenacity of purpose resolved to
let nothing block the path of his reforming programme.
He could never be satisfied with half measures. The spirit
which reaches out towards compromise was foreign to his
nature; he possessed in full measure the Italian's love of
change and disregard of tradition. Above all he was endowed with an inflexible will and untiring energy, which
impelled him to attempt in face of incalculable odds a
thorough reform of the mediaeval system, both in its
ecclesiastical and political administration. Hence unlike
those of a reforming turn of mind among his contemporaries he was in no way deterred by sentiments of fear or
reverence from acting in open defiance of ecclesiastical
authority, whenever in his judgment such a course was
necessary for the prosecution of his plans.

It is difficult at first to trace the hidden springs of
attachment between two such men, differing so remarkably
in character, talents and interests, or to understand what
Arnold found in Abailard or Abailard in the younger man
to surmount these obstacles. Yet the influence of each
upon the other is undeniable; over and above the community of interest later forced on them by circumstance
there existed from the first a real spiritual kinship. Each
felt the other's labours to be in a sense complementary to
his own. Abailard's task was to invigorate the Church with
the new truths brought to light by philosophical disputa-

---

[1] H. Reuter, *Geschichte Alexanders des Dritten*, I, p. 82 (Berlin, 1845).

tion, and thus to make easier a reconciliation between the Christian Fathers and the Greek philosophers in order to achieve ultimately a complete system of ethics. Arnold's function was of a humbler kind and more immediate in its application, namely, the cleansing of the Christian Church in all its members so that the ancient vessels of its doctrine might be purified for the new wine of Abailard's teaching.

Perhaps as a final judgment it is safest to say that Abailard's influence on Arnold is most strongly marked in awakening qualities of heart and mind hitherto dormant, and by indirect suggestion of practical ways in which they might be employed. Thus the independence shown by Abailard in the realm of the intellect is transferred by Arnold to the field of action; the fearlessness which Abailard displayed in philosophical speculation is shown by Arnold in scathing indictment of Pope and hierarchy; the ruthlessness with which Abailard pursued his adversaries in disputation is employed by Arnold in furtherance of a political programme.[1]

Our examination of the character and genius of the two men has carried us beyond the chronological limits of our previous narrative. Arnold would seem to have remained in Paris till 1119. Abailard, as we have seen, had by then retired in despair to St Denis, where his castigation of the monks' evil life subjected him to continual persecution.[2] So bitter was the strife occasioned by his presence that the

[1] Cf. Bernhardi, *Konrad III*, p. 733; Vacandard, *R.Q.H.* xxxv, pp. 57–8; S. M. Deutsch, *Herzog's Realencyklopädie für protestantische Theologie und Kirche*, art. on Arnold of Brescia, p. 118. Odorici in his life of Arnold, while accepting Otto of Freising's narrative, minimises Abailard's share in shaping Arnold's opinions, and draws a comparison entirely unfavourable to Abailard. This, however, is plainly done with the intention of glorifying his hero: "Spogliato quindi Abelardo da quell' aureola che mal regge di fronte alla nuda realtà della storia, come poi contrapporvi la stupenda e colossale figura del nostro Arnaldo?" —p. 55. Cf. p. 52.
[2] *Hist. Calam.* cap. viii, col. 136.

abbot removed him from the monastery and sent him to the dependent house of Maisoncelle in Champagne.[1] Here, freed in a measure from the restraint of authority, he began once more to teach. So great a throng of students came to attend his lectures that the neighbouring cathedral school of Rheims was almost denuded of pupils.[2] But the "second Origen" was not for long to enjoy peace and prosperity. The masters of the school at Rheims, Alberic and Lotulph, were those same pupils of Anselm of Laon who had been the principal agents of Abailard's expulsion. To these antagonists was added Abailard's old enemy, Roscelin, now ending his stormy career as a canon of Tours. Together they concocted a charge of tritheism based on an extract from Abailard's treatise on the nature of the Trinity.[3] The sequel was Abailard's summons before the Council of Soissons (1121), his condemnation and the burning of his book. We cannot here delve into the details of the sorry story.[4] Suffice it to say that the trial was a mere travesty. Abailard was allowed no chance to defend himself by public disputation; such a course would have been too dangerous for the prosecution. A half-hearted attempt to prove the truth of the charge was soon relinquished, and the great philosopher was formally condemned on the technical ground of presuming to teach theology in public without either the authorised degree or the sanction of the Pope. With a bitter cry upon his lips[5] Abailard submitted to the Council's decision. After a brief

[1] *Hist. Calam.* col. 137.   [2] Ibid. col. 138.
[3] *Tractatus de unitate et trinitate divina* (ed. R. Stoelzle, Freiburg, 1891).
[4] *Hist. Calam.* col. 150 seq. Cf. Bern. Ep. 189. For full account see R. L. Poole, op. cit. pp. 149 seq.; Rémusat, I, pp. 80 seq.; Hefele-Leclercq, v, pp. 593–602.
[5] "Deus qui judicas aequitatem quanto tunc animi felle, quanta amaritudine teipsum infamis arguebam, te furibundus accusabam, saepius repetans illam beati Antonii conquestionem: 'Jesu bone, ubi eras?'"—*Hist. Calam.* col. 151.

stay at the monastery of St Médard he was allowed to return to St Denis.[1] But henceforth there was to be little peace for the returned prodigal. Ere long his researches into the history of the patron saint and reputed founder of the monastery brought down upon his head the renewed wrath of Abbot Adam and his monks. From the pages of Bede he drew the discovery that Dionysius the Areopagite was Bishop of Corinth not of Athens as was then generally believed.[2] The outraged community threatened to bring the matter before the king. Abailard was constrained to flee again to Champagne, but shortly afterwards the death of Abbot Adam and the appointment of the famous Suger to the vacancy smoothed the path for a settlement of the difficulties. Abailard was permitted once more to retire as a hermit in the neighbourhood of Troyes on condition of living in accordance with the rules of the abbey.[3]

Here at last the tired exile found rest. With but a single companion he built a rude hut of reeds and straw, and dedicated it as an oratory to the Holy Trinity. Physical necessity compelled him to seek a livelihood, and he fell back on his old profession of teaching. At the first rumour of his activity his old pupils returned to him and once more the desert began to blossom as the rose. So great was the press of students that soon the surrounding country was filled with small huts and cabins built by the hands of devoted disciples. When the original oratory could no longer contain the numbers of those who thronged it, Abailard rebuilt it and dedicated it afresh to the Comforter, the Paraclete, an act on which his enemies speedily seized as a pretext for resuming their attacks.[4] It is not

---

[1] *Hist. Calam.* col. 153.

[2] Ibid. col. 154 seq. Abailard afterwards modified his opinion and rejected both Bede's account and that held by the monks. Actually the saint of the abbey was neither the Areopagite nor the Bishop of Corinth. Cf. Poole, *Illustrations*, p. 132, n.21.

[3] *Hist. Calam.* col. 159.   [4] Ibid. col. 162.

easy to estimate the extent of his danger at the Paraclete. He himself speaks of renewed persecutions to which he was subjected,[1] but there is at this time nothing but his own fears to account for them. St Bernard and St Norbert, the two "reformers" whom he has in mind, had not yet begun to trouble themselves with his activities; their interests lay elsewhere.[2] Nevertheless, when suddenly summoned to the post of abbot in the monastery of St Gildas on the grim, rocky coast of his native Brittany, Abailard gladly seized the opportunity of escape from real or imaginary perils.[3] Never was radiant hope doomed to more bitter disappointment. Abailard found the life of the monastery corrupt in the extreme. The monastic vows were continually and shamelessly broken and the monks themselves were savages and rebels. His first attempt to introduce some sort of order into the community led to threats of violence against his person, and before long attempts were even made upon his life. He remained at St Gildas, however, for either six or eight years,[4] the misery of his existence relieved only by periodical visits to the Paraclete where in 1129 he had installed Heloise and the nuns of her community.[5] At last unable longer to endure the life there he fled, and appears to have remained in hiding for at least two years. It was then that he wrote to an anonymous friend the letter now known as the *Historia Calamitatum*, from which most of our knowledge of his earlier life is derived. In 1136 he suddenly reappeared as a teacher on the Mont Ste Geneviève, and once more became the storm centre of the scholastic world.[6]

[1] *Hist. Calam*. col. 163.
[2] Vacandard, *Vie de Saint Bernard*, II, p. 119.
[3] *Hist. Calam*. col. 164 seq.
[4] See Poole, *Illustrations*, p. 135, n. 26, for a discussion of the chronology.
[5] *Hist. Calam*. col. 168 seq.
[6] *Joannis Saresberiensis Metalogicon*, loc. cit. ante.

The question now presents itself; how far was Arnold associated with Abailard's fortunes during these years? It would scarcely need much attention were it not that the earlier biographers were responsible for a number of erroneous statements on the subject. Thus Guadagnini suggests that Arnold was numbered among the pupils who gathered round the master at Maisoncelle (1120).[1] This is pure conjecture; there is not a shred of evidence in its support. Moreover for this part of the reformer's life our authorities are very sparse in information. Otto of Freising and his versifier, the author of the *Ligurinus*, pass straight from the mention of his attendance at Abailard's lectures to a discussion of his character and doctrine, only resuming the narrative with the disturbances at Brescia (1135–7).[2] The *Historia Pontificalis* has nothing to tell save the fact of his ordination presumably after his return to Brescia.[3] Arnold would seem in fact to have left Paris either in 1119 or 1120. He may possibly have been a witness of Abailard's condemnation at Soissons,[4] but it is more probable that he had already recrossed the Alps by the time Abailard entered St Denis. But the thirst for romance is difficult to assuage, and Francke early seized an occasion of indulging it. We have noted that when Abailard retired to the Paraclete in 1122 he was accompanied by a single follower willing to share with him a life of privation and of solitude.[5] Without hesitation Francke identifies this faithful companion with Arnold of Brescia and proceeds to make the most of the opportunity thus picturesquely afforded.[6] Both de Castro and Guerzoni repeat the statement. Clavel is

---

[1] Guadagnini, *Vita di Arnaldo*, p. 7.
[2] Otto of Freising, *Gesta Fred.* p. 133. Gunther, *Lig.* M.P.L. 212, col. 570.   [3] *Hist. pont.* cap. xxxi, p. 63.
[4] Vacandard, *Arnauld de Brescia*, p. 57.
[5] *Hist. Calam.* loc. cit. ante.
[6] H. Francke, *Arnold von Brescia und seine Zeit* (Zurich, 1825), pp. 31 and 65.

more cautious though he also admits its probability.[1]
Gregorovius, Giesebrecht and the better informed of the
later writers either give a firm denial or pass over the
suggestion in silence. Hence it is disconcerting to find that
the most recent writer on Arnold repeats the familiar
story as a plain fact and makes no attempt to indicate that
it is at best an open question.[2]

Here for a while we leave Abailard re-installed on the
Paris rostrum and turn to follow Arnold's fortunes on his
return to Lombardy. John of Salisbury tells us that he was
now ordained priest, became a canon regular of an Augustinian house at Brescia and ultimately attained the dignity
of abbot.[3] True, John is our only authority for this, and it
is worthy of note that neither St Bernard nor Otto, themselves monks, makes mention of the fact or charges him with
apostasy from his vows. John's testimony, however, is
not lightly to be disregarded, and the monastic cast of
Arnold's later teaching on religious reform certainly lends
colour to the suggestion that his ideas were shaped by
personal experience of the life within the cloister.[4]

We have now come to Arnold's active intervention in
the political and ecclesiastical problems of the period. It
was at Brescia that he first appeared openly as a reformer,
and certain aspects of the local situation will shortly engage
our attention. It will be well first to attempt a delineation
of his character now that he may be said to have reached
the age of maturity. In the comparison with Abailard

---

[1] G. de Castro, *Arnaldo da Brescia e la Rivoluzione Romana* (Leghorn,
1875), pp. 169, 200 seq. G. Guerzoni, *Arnaldo da Brescia* (Milan,
1882), p. 25. V. Clavel, *Arnauld de Brescia et les Romains du XII
Siècle* (Paris, 1868). De Castro, p. 160, produces an ingenious argument
to account for the fact that neither on this occasion nor on any other
is Arnold's name mentioned in Abailard's correspondence.

[2] E. Scott Davison, *Forerunners of St Francis*, pp. 112 and 114.

[3] "Erat hic dignitate sacerdos, habitu canonicus regularis....
Fuerat abbas apud Brixiam"—*Hist. pont.* cap. xxxi, p. 63.

[4] Giesebrecht, p. 8. De Castro, p. 238.

drawn a few pages earlier we have noted some aspects of Arnold's mentality; we turn now to consider other traits responsible to some degree for the direction of his energies. We have unfortunately no information as to his personal appearance; we would give much to have had from Otto of Freising's pen a detailed portrait similar to that given of his own hero, Frederick Barbarossa. Yet it would hardly be presumptuous to infer that some part of the magnetism which drew men to Arnold was due to his personality. Whatever the true source of his appeal it cannot be wholly explained by the enthusiasm evoked by his ascetic practices. Much is told us of these by our authorities, and it must be accounted a remarkable tribute that, in an age when personal abuse was regarded as a legitimate weapon of controversy, none of his adversaries has cast the slightest reproach on his moral character. Even Otto of Freising, who in general adopts a tone of scornful superiority towards him, and in particular describes him as a wolf in sheep's clothing, proves by his use of this biblical metaphor that Arnold at least wore the garb of humility.[1] A yet more striking example is to be found in the letters wherein his bitterest enemy, St Bernard, slanders his character with pen dipped in gall. More than once in the middle of a series of diatribes the Abbot of Clairvaux is driven to admit the innocency of Arnold's morals. "Would that the purity of his teaching", he writes, "matched the strictness of his life", and goes on to depict him as "a man who came neither eating nor drinking save", he adds maliciously, "with the devil hungering and thirsting after the blood of souls."[2]

[1] "Sub ovina pelle lupum gerens"—Otto of Freising, p. 133.
[2] "Utinam tam sanae esset doctrinae quam destrictae est vitae. Et si vultis scire, homo est neque manducans neque bibens, solo cum diabolo esuriens et sitiens sanguinem animarum"—Bern. Ep. 195, col. 362. Cf. Ep. 189, col. 355. "Vir nimis austerus dureque per omnia vite, in victu modicus"—Gesta di Federico (ed. E. Monaci, F.S.I. Rome, 1887), line 762.

Thus in works of practical piety Arnold more than attained to the high standard set and demanded by the Cistercian Order and its chief apostle. But Arnold was no mere ascetic occupied with bodily austerities as a means towards the salvation of his soul.[1] He was a man of culture, probably above the standard of his age, well versed in literary topics, so the author of the *Gesta di Federico* tells us.[2] John of Salisbury, while corroborating the testimony of the Bergamasque poet, speaks also of his acute intellect employed in diligent study of the Scriptures.[3] All our witnesses tell likewise of the power of his eloquence directed principally to the castigation of worldly indulgence.[4] Bishops, secular priests and monks, all felt the lash of his invective, and if, as Otto states, he showed more favour to the laity,[5] this was partly because he found in them more of the essence of true Christianity, that spirit of evangelical poverty of which his own life was a faithful pattern. A full century before the sons of St Francis he chose the practice of the Gospel precepts for the high road of salvation and strove "as naked to follow the naked

[1] "He seems to have been sane, manly, and clear; whether it is that he really was so, or that history has withheld many circumstances of his life"—Gregorovius, IV, p. 548.

[2] *Gesta di Fed.* lines 765 and 850. Cf. Walter Map, *De Nugis Curialium*, loc. cit. ante.

[3] "Ingenio perspicax pervicax in studio scripturarum"—*Hist. pont.* p. 63.

[4] "Facundus eloquio, et contemptus mundi vehemens predicator"—*Hist. pont.* loc. cit. "Cujus maledictione et amaritudine os plenum est....Cujus dentes arma et sagittae, et lingua ejus gladius acutus. Molliti sunt sermones ejus super oleum, et ipsi sunt jacula"—Bern. Ep. 195. "Sed verbi prodigus, et qui ultra oportunum saperet"—*Gesta di Fed.* lines 763–4. Otto of Freising regards him as a mere wind-bag: "Plus tamen verborum profluvio quam sententiarum pondere copiosus"—p. 133.

[5] "Clericorum ac episcoporum derogator, monachorum persccutor, laicis tantum adulans"—Otto of Freising, loc. cit. "Clerumque procaci insectans odio, monachorum acerrimus hostis. Plebis adulator, gaudens popularibus auris"—Gunther, *Lig.* col. 369.

Christ". But with him it was no mere maxim of individual conduct, least of all did it involve any renunciation of intercourse with one's fellow men, as with the hermits of the Egyptian or Palestinian deserts six centuries before. On the contrary it was to be the hall-mark of a true Christian society.

In a manner therefore Arnold was a prophet of what, anticipating modern terminology, we may call a "social Christianity", inspired by the teaching of the Gospel and fortified by the example of the infant Church. But if Arnold was thus a prophet he also appeared to his contemporaries as a man of action,[1] as truly such as his victorious enemy, Barbarossa. Both his merits and defects well fitted him for the part. Bold at a venture he was too often prone to adopt heroic measures without waiting to consider whether the end in view could be attained by a more cautious method of procedure, to assume that every knot was a Gordian knot to be loosed only by the sword. A restless passion for change and the firm conviction that nothing could be worse than present conditions engendered a regrettable turbulence of disposition.[2] Most of the difficulties which beset his later career were due as much to lack of patience as to unfavourable circumstances. This impetuosity of temper he never learned to curb. So intent was he on reaching the goal of his endeavour, so acutely conscious of the purity of his ideal and the disinterestedness of his intention, so pathetically confident in the invincibility of his own example that he never paused to debate the consequences of a line of action or to count the cost either to himself or to his followers. Yet he was no mere idealist heedless of the practical difficulties attending the

[1] A. de Stefano, *Arnaldo da Brescia e i suoi tempi* (Rome, 1921), p. 3.
[2] "Facundus et audax, confidensque sui"—*Gesta di Fed.* loc. cit. "Singularitatis amator, novitatis cupidus"—Otto of Freising, loc. cit. ante. "Ut aiunt sediciosus erat"—*Hist. pont.* loc. cit. ante. Cf. Bern. Ep. 195: "Tanquam leo rugiens circuiens quem devoret".

execution of his plans; on the contrary he showed himself fully alive to their existence. His failure to surmount them was due partly to a grave depreciation of the strength of his opponents and a corresponding exaggeration of the value of popular support, and partly to a fatal illusion as to the compelling logic of his cause.

Undoubtedly Arnold possessed in great measure the instinct of the demagogue, and the cause of truth is not advanced by shirking the fact. We may even hazard a suspicion that he occasionally courted popularity for its own sake. Certainly he knew how to flatter the people's vanity by holding out to it the prospect of a larger liberty, and to arouse enthusiasm for his principles by his oratory.[1] Nevertheless, to impugn the reformer's honesty on this account would ignore an additional strain in his character, which, though of no great prominence in his activities at Brescia, formed an integral part of his convictions and loomed more largely in his later days at Rome. This was a spirit of reverence for antiquity common to the enlightened citizenship of his age and one of the motives inspiring the communal movements throughout Italy. We shall have occasion later to examine more closely the sources of this unexpected renaissance. For our immediate purpose the important fact is the peculiar fashion in which this vague belief in the half-mythical civic piety of antiquity was blended in Arnold's mind with aspirations for a return to the apostolic piety of the early Christian Church. The two strands of thought, religious and political, were closely interwoven and came to appear complementary

---

[1]   "Et fateor, pulchram fallendi noverat artem,
        Veris falsa probans; quia tantum falsa loquendo
        Fallere nemo potest; veri sub imagine falsum
        Influit, et furtim deceptas occupat aures"—
Gunther, *Lig*. col. 370. Cf. ibid. line 294: "Impia mellifluis admiscens toxica verbis". *Gesta di Fed*. line 774: "Veraque miscuit falsis multisque placebat". Cf. also line 810.

aspects of the same ideal. And from this point of view, in the desire to restore a golden past, which had in reality never existed, Arnold is a perfect type of the reaction against the dominant political theory and practice of the Middle Ages, even though his personal fame was acquired in a monk's cowl.[1]

Such were the principal characteristics of the man who resolved henceforward to consecrate his powers to the cause of ecclesiastical reform. In the situation at Brescia under Bishop Manfred he found the opportunity he sought, and embarked on a struggle with the recognised and legitimate rulers of the Church which ended only with his death.

[1] Cf. Hausrath, p. 5: "Bei ihm durchdringt sich das Mönchsideal des Mittelalters mit antiken Errinnerungen und juristischen Doctrinen. Aus Motiven der christlichen Askese, der antiken Freiheit und des aufstrebenden Bürgersinnes entspringt sein reformatorisches Auftreten".

Chapter IV

THE COMMUNE AT BRESCIA

BY the appointment of Manfred to the see of Brescia Innocent II had hoped to bring peace to that distracted Church. The choice did not prove a happy one. The new bishop was by no means the right man for the emergency. Of weak will and timid disposition the best that can be said for him is that his actions were inspired by honourable motives. From the first his hold on power was insecure. The city factions created by the papal schism still survived, and the deposed Villanus possessed formidable allies in the nobles of the *contado*. Manfred's own position was distinctly invidious. He had been "coadjutor" to Villanus and some share in the responsibility for the latter's misgovernment was rightly or wrongly attributed to him by the people. Again, the circumstances of his elevation by Innocent II implied on Manfred's part a moral obligation to introduce the reforms indicated by the Pope in the synod of 1132. Nothing short of a thorough purge of the Church's corrupt administration would meet the needs of the case. This Manfred fully recognised, and there is no reason to doubt the sincerity of his professions. But the path to reform was beset by thorny difficulties. On the one side Villanus and the malcontent nobles were threatening a *coup d'état*, on the other the clergy, entrenched in the traditional license which they miscalled privilege, set their faces like flint against their new pastor at the first hint of reform.

The bishop was thus thrown back on the support of the laity, among whom the Patarin ideal still retained something of its pristine vigour. That Manfred failed to enlist their sympathies for his cause was due in part to a natural suspicion of the sincerity of his motives. So complete a break with the traditional episcopal policy did his proposals involve that the popular party saw in them some deep-laid plot to crush its civic liberties. The dual capacity of the bishop, at once a spiritual pastor and a feudal landowner, must always be remembered in connection with the situation. Further the laity could scarcely avoid entertaining grave doubts as to Manfred's personal character; they recalled his past activities as agent and adviser to Villanus and drew the obvious inference from the discrepancy of policy that marked the two phases of his career.

But Manfred's failure was due in still greater measure to the involved character of the political situation and the conflicting ideals of the several parties within the city. The mass of the laity gave indeed a qualified approval to the bishop's reforming programme, but in their eyes it was merely the prelude to more sweeping changes in the system of government. Their ultimate ideal of an independent, self-governing commune, completely severed from the purely spiritual administration of the bishop, could never be realised whilst the clergy retained the feudal right to temporal possessions. A reformed Church meant a Church that should "live of its own", a clergy dependent on tithes and almsgiving, on revenue derived from purely ecclesiastical sources. To the popular party therefore ecclesiastical reform was no mere pawn on the political chess board but the sole remedy for a grave social evil.

Behind all loomed the shadow of the Papacy. No longer as in the days of the Patarin agitation at Milan did Pope and Curia recognise in the laity of the Lombard cities fellow-workers in the same noble cause, inspired by the same lofty ideal of a purified Church. The politics of Innocent II were of baser metal than those of Alexander II or of Hildebrand. In his struggle to maintain his claim to the title Innocent had fought a long and desperate campaign with the anti-Pope Pierleone. Now that the end was in sight his mind was set more on tranquil enjoyment of the fruits of victory than on a voyage in the turbulent waters of Lombard politics. The vicissitudes of his pontificate prompted him to look for aid mainly to the monarchs and the aristocracy of Christendom. By temperament also he was averse to democratic sentiments. His elevation of Manfred to the see at Brescia was directed by the same desire for peace. But the laity's interpretation of the transaction was not so simple. In their eyes Manfred was a papal satellite, the means whereby the traditional independence of the Lombard bishoprics was to be destroyed. On the ruins of clerical privilege and through the unwitting agency of the bishop the temporal supremacy of the Pope was to be erected.

Such would appear to have been the popular party's diagnosis of the situation. Hence the mass of the people stood aloof; they would bear no part in so insidious a design. On the contrary, should the bishop succeed in carrying into effect the first part of his programme, they were determined to oppose him to the utmost of their power.

There was little prospect of so dangerous a situation arising. Manfred had neither the energy nor the courage to go forward on so bold a venture. Active support he had almost none, and his first attempt to put down simony and clerical marriage was the signal for the outbreak of hostilities. An alarming recrudescence of these twin evils had taken place during the chaotic days of the papal schism. When milder measures failed Manfred confiscated the benefices of the refractory priests. This bold but injudicious stroke united the whole body of the clergy against him and soon the city was in uproar. The actual sequence of events is obscure; the chronology of the local annals seems to have gone astray at this point.[1] The situation was

[1] See p. 56, n. 4.

complicated by an unsuccessful attempt on the part of Villanus to regain possession of his see. It is difficult to fix the date of this event. The disturbances certainly began in 1135, yet it would appear that this, the climax of the struggle, was not reached till two years later. Certainly Manfred lingered in the city amid the relics of his fallen state, for not till 1138 is he found journeying to Rome to seek papal aid.[1]

How far Arnold was associated with the movement at its inception is a question that must now be faced. John of Salisbury implies that it was not till Manfred's departure for Rome that Arnold actively intervened.[2] There is much inherent probability in this statement, though unfortunately the other authorities are so vague that we are forced to conjecture the correct chronology of events. Yet even if Arnold took no part in the first revolt,[3] his general attitude towards it can be surmised from the events of 1138 and their sequel. He probably viewed the situation with mixed feelings. Confusion of principles in the various parties made it impossible for him to take sides immediately. With the stubborn selfishness of the recalcitrant clergy he could have no sympathy. Nor probably was he directly interested in the constitutional schemes of the popular party. Yet in so far as the latter aimed at destroying the bishop's temporal authority it was working towards the same end as Arnold's own later teachings here and in Rome. On the other hand, Manfred's attempt to inaugurate a

---

[1] Poole, Preface, p. lx.   [2] *Hist. pont.* p. 63.

[3] Most of the earlier Italian biographers assume Arnold to have been the acknowledged leader of the movement. Cf. Odorici, *Arnaldo da Brescia*, p. 61: "Che levasse Arnaldo fra quei civili contendimenti la voce, proverò più innanzi non doversene dubitare, come parrebbe che il popolo bresciano, seguendo il novatore, mutasse i consoli, altri eleggendone fra quel tumulto, di *arnaldici pensieri*, avvivatori della spenta disciplina e della cadente libertà del commune". De Castro (pp. 239 seq.) admits that there is no proof of these statements. Vacandard (p. 60) gives a decisive negative to the suggestion.

series of reforms in the lives of the clergy equally commanded his respect, since it constituted the preliminary
stage in his own programme. This dilemma explains his
hesitation at the beginning of the crisis; his actions were
not usually marked by indecision. When Manfred by his
appeal to Rome reintroduced the papal factor into the
situation, Arnold was obliged by his principles to cast in
his lot with the popular party.

His advent at this critical juncture fanned the smouldering embers of discontent into flame.[1] By the power of his
eloquence he persuaded the people to secure their newly
won liberties. Manfred gained but small success from his
mission; the Pope was too fully occupied with the settlement of the schism to grant material aid. On his return
Manfred found the city in revolt and its gates shut against
him.[2] He was compelled to retrace his steps to Rome, there
to await remedial measures from the meeting of the
Lateran Council summoned for the following year. The
popular party was now master of the city, and Arnold was
the organising genius behind it. His first incursion into
public life had been successful beyond expectation. The
bishop's authority was momentarily suspended and a
popular government established in its place. Yet success
was more apparent than real. The hierarchical party was
subdued but not crushed. If material weapons failed, there
remained the Church's spiritual armoury at its disposal.
It looked to Rome to supply the necessary equipment, and
Rome was not slow to furnish it.

The second Council of the Lateran[3] was convened early

---

[1] "Ipsam, in qua natus est valde atrociter commovit terram, et con-
turbavit eam"—Bern. Ep. 195. The author of the *Gesta di Fed.* says
that he also created disturbances at Milan; lines 807 seq. This is by
no means improbable. Cf. Gunther, *Lig.* col. 370, line 295: "Alias
plures adeo commoverat urbes". [2] *Hist. pont.* loc. cit. ante.
[3] For a detailed account see Hefele-Leclercq, *Histoire des Conciles*,
V, pp. 721–38. A useful summary is given in E. H. Landon, *A Manual
of Councils of the Catholic Church* (2nd ed. 1909), I, pp. 325 seq.

in 1139 and formally opened by Innocent II on April 4 of that year. It was a large and imposing gathering, more than a thousand prelates being present.[1] The principal objects of the Council were three: the final extinction of the papal schism, the condemnation of various heretical sects and the initiation of a number of reforms in the administration of the Church. The anti-Pope, Anacletus, together with his chief adherents,[2] was condemned by name, and certain bishops consecrated by him were deposed and degraded. Roger of Sicily, who alone among Christian kings still maintained allegiance to Anacletus, incurred a solemn excommunication which he chose to disregard and did so with impunity.

The relics of the schism thus summarily dealt with, the Council turned its attention to reform. Thirty canons were passed,[3] mainly of a disciplinary nature and designed to correct abuses in the life and administration of the clergy. The twenty-third alone demands notice here. It pronounced heretical all who denied the Real Presence in the Eucharist, the efficacy of infant baptism, Church orders and the priesthood, and the legitimacy of marriage: such were declared severed from the Church and handed over to the secular arm.[4] This canon was patently directed at the Petrobrusians of Provence with whose Manichaean

---

[1] Five English bishops and four abbots were present. Hefele-Leclercq, p. 738; Landon, p. 325. For their identity see R. L. Poole in *Eng. Hist. Review*, XXXVIII (1923), pp. 61 seq.

[2] Gerard, Bishop of Angoulême, and Giles, Bishop of Tusculum. Hefele-Leclercq, p. 723.

[3] The full text is given in Mansi, *Concilia*, XXI, col. 523 seq. and Hefele-Leclercq, pp. 725 seq.

[4] "Eos autem, qui religiositatis speciem simulantes Dominici corporis et sanguinis sacramentum, Baptisma puerorum, sacerdotium et caeteros ecclesiasticos ordines et legitimarum damnant foedera nuptiarum, tamquam Haereticos ab Ecclesia Dei pellimus et damnamus, et per potestates exteras coerceri praecipimus: defensores quoque ipsorum ejusdem damnationis vinculis innodamus"—Mansi, col. 532. Hefele-Leclercq, p. 732.

tenets the list of errors enumerated closely corresponds.[1]
It is worthy of note that the text is a literal transcription of
the third canon of the Council of Toulouse (1119), a city
in which this particular sect had many adherents.[2] Thus
there is not the slightest ground for accepting Francke's
conclusion that Arnold was included in this anathema.[3]
He was not at this time under suspicion of heresy; the
charge preferred against him was one of schism, of interference with the Church's administration, not of denying
its doctrines.

Here, as elsewhere in dealing with Arnold, it is of the
utmost importance to keep a true historical perspective.
Too often historians have allowed their interpretation of
this event to be warped by consideration of Arnold's later
activities. Remembering the magnitude of his part in the
Roman commune ten years later, they have tacitly assumed
that in 1139 the question was of equal gravity for Innocent
II and the Council. Yet this may justly be doubted. In the

---

[1] Peter of Bruys, the founder of the sect, was a priest of Narbonne,
born in the last quarter of the eleventh century. Expelled from his
living on account of his anti-sacerdotal opinions, he became a wandering preacher in Provence, inciting men to rebel against the bishops,
and polluting the morals of the faithful by his own excesses and sacrilegious example. He was burned as a heretic at St Gilles, c. 1126.
The chief authority for his doctrines is the treatise written against him
by Peter the Venerable, Abbot of Cluny (M.P.L. 189, col. 719 seq.).
Cf. also Abailard, Introductio ad Theologiam, lib. II, cap. iv (M.P.L.
178, col. 1056). Among secondary works the best account is in Döllinger,
Beiträge zur Sektengeschichte des Mittelalters, I, pp. 75 seq. Cf. also
Herzog's Realencyklopädie, art. Petrus von Bruys; H. C. Lea, Inquisition of the Middle Ages, I, pp. 66 seq.
[2] Mansi, Concilia, XXI, col. 226–7. Vacandard, p. 65, n.2.
[3] Francke, op. cit. p. 86. The supposition is based on Otto of
Freising's vague allegation of Arnold's erroneous opinions on the
Eucharist and infant baptism: "De sacramento altaris et baptismo
parvulorum non sane dicitur sensisse", p. 133. For a full discussion of
the vexed question see pp. 198–200 of this essay. Francke's opinion is
rejected by Clavel, pp. 84–7, De Castro, pp. 262 seq. and Vacandard,
p. 65. Cf. Hefele-Leclercq, pp. 732, n.1, 735.

eyes of ecclesiastical authority the dispute at Brescia was a local disturbance similar in character to the faction fights which frequently troubled the peace of the Lombard Churches, and hardly of sufficient importance to warrant the attention of the Council. It is unlikely that any man then foresaw the tempest which this cloud speck on the horizon was to bring. To contemporaries the matter appeared of much less moment than the ravages of the heretic wolves, Peter of Bruys and Henry of Lausanne, among the sheepfolds of Provence.[1]

Nor does the argument that his case was not covered by any of the Council's canons conflict with the statements of our authorities. According to Otto of Freising, though Manfred's accusation was brought before the Council, it was the Pope who actually imposed silence on the upstart demagogue and decreed his banishment.[2] Gunther in the *Ligurinus* does indeed mention a specific condemnation by the Council,[3] but he is not a first-hand witness and depends largely on Otto's account. John of Salisbury and the poet of Bergamo make no mention of the Council but ascribe the conviction to the Pope.[4] Finally St Bernard says de-

---

[1] Cf. Bern. Ep. 241, where a graphic description is given of the woeful state of the Church in those parts. "Basilicae sine plebibus, plebes sine sacerdotibus, sacerdotes sine debita reverentia sunt, et sine Christo denique Christiani, Ecclesiae synagogae reputantur; sanctuarium Dei sanctum esse negatur: Sacramenta non sacra censetur: dies festivis frustrantur solemniis."

[2] "In magno concilio Romae sub Innocentio habito ab episcopo civitatis illius virisque religiosis accusatur. Romanus ergo pontifex, ne perniciosum dogma ad plures serperet, imponendum viro silentium decernit; sicque factum est"—Otto of Freising, p. 133.

[3] Gunther, *Lig*. col. 370: "Mox in concilio Romae damnatus".

[4] "A domino Innocentio papa depositus et extrusus ab Italia"— *Hist. pont.* p. 63.

> "Papa, dolens populum vitiari dogmate falso
> Et cupiens aliqua morbo ratione mederi
> De gremio matris, reputans anathemate dignum,
> Expulit ecclesia doctorem scisma docentem."
> *Gesta di Fed.* lines 818 seq.

fiuitely that Arnold was accused of schism before the Pope and on that account sent into exile.[1] It is therefore a tenable proposition that Arnold's case was not examined by the whole body of the Council but reserved to the judgment of the Pope. The absence of any rescript or brief makes it impossible to settle the matter with any confidence.

One further point remains to be discussed before resuming the narrative. In the letter already cited St Bernard says that the Pope imposed on Arnold an oath binding him not to return to his native city without the Apostolic permission.[2] Giesebrecht has suggested that this implies Arnold's presence in Rome at the time of the Council.[3] It is certainly difficult to see how such a promise could have been extracted unless this were the case. Yet it must be noted that neither John nor Otto expressly mentions it. On the other hand, such a visit is not impossible and would be perfectly consonant with the general intrepidity of Arnold's character.

Considerations of place and manner apart the fact of Arnold's condemnation is, as we have seen, well attested. Its effect on the situation in Brescia was electric. Manfred, returning in haste fortified by the papal decision, found the revolution already tottering to its fall. His entry into the city was the signal for its final collapse. The Republic was overthrown, the consuls, Rebaldus and Persicus, set up by the popular party in 1135 were compelled to flee,[4] and

[1] "Accusatus apud dominum Papam schismate pessimo natali solo pulsus est: etiam et abjurare compulsus reversionem, nisi ad ipsius Apostolici permissionem"—Bern. Ep. 195.   [2] Ibid.

[3] Giesebrecht, p. 11. Mansi, XXI, col. 536 seq. See Hausrath, p. 160, n.49, for a skilful marshalling of the evidence.

[4] *Annal. Brix*. M.G.H. XVIII, p. 812: "Consules pravi a Brixiensibus expulsi sunt". The two recensions of the annals respectively give 1135 and 1139 as the date of the eviction. Cf. *Malvecii Chron*. Muratori, XIV, p. 877: "Duo consules haeretici a consulatu Brixiae depositi....Rebaldus et Persicus viri hipocriti et heretici qui eo anno regebant a Brixiana civitate cum suis sequacibus expulsi sunt".

before long the episcopal authority was restored to its former status. Arnold's movements during these calamitous events are uncertain. For a while he appears to have wandered about the cities of Lombardy till in 1140, moved by the rumour of Abailard's approaching disputation with St Bernard at Sens, he recrossed the Alps to resume the thread of his acquaintance with the Paris master.[1]

The failure of his early effort at reform had in no wise damped the ardour of his spirit or shaken his convictions. His schemes had been shipwrecked on the rock of papal politics; but it was impossible for him to put his principles in action without sooner or later encountering papal antagonism. It was worse than useless to attack the secular authority of bishops whilst the temporal power of the Popes remained unlimited. To adopt such a course was to court disaster. There was but one way open, one plan offering a reasonable chance of success in the future. A mere frontier warfare was doomed to failure: the fight must be carried into the heart of the enemy's territory. The decisive blow must be struck at the most vulnerable point of the hierarchical system; the papal patrimony itself must be destroyed.

Whether Arnold, learning wisdom from his experiences at Brescia, now realised this it is difficult to guess. Certainly he made no attempt to renew the struggle in another field, but it must be admitted that he was afforded little opportunity. Henceforward he was a marked man, and his subsequent actions were not calculated to remove suspicion from his name. On the contrary by his courageous support of Abailard's cause at Sens he incurred the undying enmity of the man whose counsels stood highest in the Church, the Abbot of Clairvaux.

[1] *Hist. pont.* p. 64. It is not impossible that Arnold may already have been leading a nomadic life in Lombardy at the time of his condemnation.

Chapter V

ABAILARD AND THE COUNCIL OF SENS

THE contest between Abailard and St Bernard which reached its climax in the Council of Sens was not wholly due to personal antipathy. Doubtless this was a potent factor preventing either of the two men from achieving a just appreciation of the other's standpoint. But beneath the clash of personality lay vital principles, each subversive of the other, each held with passionate conviction and defended with stubborn tenacity. To understand both the principles and the situation which they created, a brief study of the intellectual movements of the twenty years separating the Council of Soissons from the Council of Sens is essential.

The years immediately preceding Abailard's return to Ste Geneviève (1136) were years of great intellectual productivity. He not only revised many of his earlier treatises including the *Sic et Non* and that on the Trinity condemned at Soissons, but it was now that the *Theologia Christiana* and the *Introductio ad Theologiam* finally assumed the shape in which they are known to-day. One completely new work on ethics, the *Scito te ipsum*, also first saw the light.[1]

The same acute reasoning and challenging conclusions mark both the earlier and the later works, and once more the exponents of orthodoxy awoke to a sense of the danger threatening the traditional dogmas of the Church. In particular Abailard's juxtaposition of contradictory texts from the Fathers in the *Sic et Non* was regarded as an insidious attempt to undermine the very basis of Christian dogma.

Slowly the opposition gathered strength. Important changes were taking place in the scholastic world. The centre of controversy had appreciably shifted. New

---

[1] Poole, *Illustrations*, p. 137. Vacandard, *St Bernard*, II, p. 121.

problems were stirring men's curiosity, new methods of approach were employed and new solutions, theological rather than philosophical, were adopted. In place of the barren disputes between Nominalist and Realist a new and deeper cleavage had opened between the exponents of a mystical and supernatural theology and the followers of the rationalist principles developed by Abailard. The arguments of Roscelin, William of Champeaux and Anselm of Laon were discredited, and their authors either dead or retired from active controversy. The acute perception and dialectical skill, which had served Abailard so well against them, proved entirely ineffective against the leaders of the new movement. In the earlier contest the dispute concerned the inferences drawn from premises on which there was common agreement, and something like an established code of rules regulated the conduct of the disputants. But the controversy in which Abailard now came to be involved could provide no *modus intelligendi*, no common philosophic basis. It was rather a contest between two fundamental and mutually destructive principles than an academic debate, and an intelligent appreciation of the strength of the opposing case was lacking to either side.[1]

The new movement was chiefly associated with the Abbey of St Victor. The origin and development of the school is an interesting commentary on the intellectual currents of the age. When in 1108 William of Champeaux suffered his first defeat at the hands of Abailard[2] he retired to the ancient chapel of St Victor on the bank of the Seine a few miles below Paris. Here, aided by a few staunch supporters, he founded a community of Augustinian canons, and opening a school resumed his lectures on dialectics. Though he remained but four years the community grew

[1] Cf. J. G. Sikes, "Conflict of Abailard and St Bernard", *Journ. Theol. Studies* (1926), pp. 398 seq.

[2] See ante, p. 32.

in numbers and speedily achieved a considerable repute for learning. Much of its prestige was due to an interesting personality. The life of Hugh of St Victor was almost entirely spent in the daily round of monastic duties and has therefore little of outward interest.[1]

A Saxon of noble birth, like Abailard he early renounced his inheritance and entered the cloister of Halberstadt. About 1115 he removed to the Abbey of St Victor, became a teacher in the monastic school and in 1133 succeeded to the office of prior, which he retained till his death in 1144. There can be no doubt that he was a capable scholar, for his fame as a teacher of theology continued undiminished throughout the later Middle Ages. Hitherto the school of St Victor had been noted mainly for its studies in dialectics, a legacy of William of Champeaux. It was due to Hugh more than to any other that henceforward it became the acknowledged centre of the forces opposed to the rationalism of the school of Abailard. "The spirit which he infused", writes Dr Poole, "was more theological and religious, less instinctively literary, far less secular."[2] For Hugh was by nature a mystic, inspired more with the spirit of Plato than that of Aristotle, though in common with his contemporaries he knew only the *Timaeus*. Yet he also contrived to extract something of the real Plato from the study of Augustine, Plotinus and the Neo-Platonists. The governing factor of Hugh's system is the inability of unaided reason to explain the nature of God or to guide men to salvation. Not that he despised or under-

[1] See A. Mignon, *Les origines de la Scolastique et Hugues de Saint Victor* (Paris, 1895), chap. i, pp. 7–25. For his writings: Hauréau, *Les Œuvres de Hugues de Saint Victor, Essai critique* (Paris, 1886); G. Santini, *Ugo da San Vittore: Studio Filosofico* (Alatri, 1898). For his general position in twelfth-century scholasticism: H. O. Taylor, *Mediaeval Mind*, II, pp. 385 seq.; J. de Ghellinck, *Le mouvement théologique du XII siècle* (Paris, 1914).

[2] *Illustrations*, p. 96.

valued the intellectual faculties, though he is frankly suspicious of logic. Rather for him intellect and emotion are complementary faculties: each has its proper function in promoting the soul's ascent to the heavenly mount. Thus the three stages of man's spiritual progress are defined as *cogitatio*, *meditatio* and *contemplatio*. The first is exclusively an intellectual process; in the second, meditation, emotion and intellect are equally blended, in the final stage of contemplation the intellect is quiescent whilst emotion soars sublime and the soul becomes fully conscious of the ineffable beauty and unfathomable mystery of God.[1]

The link between St Bernard and the school of St Victor was particularly close. Not only was St Bernard on several occasions brought into personal relationship with Hugh, but in the spirit and method of their theological studies they were akin.[2]

Hence Abailard's proclamation of the supremacy of reason in the realm of theology ranged against him not only that ever-growing body of men trained according to the principles of the Victorines but also the Abbot of Clairvaux and his numerous personal following.

Ultimately the issue lay between authority and reason. On which of these two grounds ought the Church to base her claim to obedience? The one depended on a system of dogma, fashioned by the accumulated wisdom and experience of generations of saints and scholars, and stamped with the Church's official approval. The other proclaimed the inalienable right of the individual to investigate for himself the mysteries of his faith and in so doing to subject all traditional teaching to the test of private judgment. Had the former a greater sanction than the latter? Was

---

[1] *Homilia Prima in Ecclesiasten*, M.P.L. 175, col. 115 seq. Cf. Bern. *De Consid.* lib. 11, cap. ii, col. 745.

[2] A comparison of Hugh's short treatise, the *De Amore Sponsi ad Sponsam* (M.P.L. 176, col. 987 seq.), with Bernard's sermons on the Song of Songs (M.P.L. 183, col. 786 seq.) will show this.

there a legitimate place in the scheme for the exercise of the critical faculty? Did there remain any aspect of the Christian ethic undiscovered or but partially revealed, or had the Faith in all its fullness been delivered once for all to the saints? Such were the problems underlying the crisis we are about to review, and the solution reached was of the greatest moment for the future of theological and philosophical studies.

We have said that in essence the problem was one of authority against reason. Enough has been indicated of Abailard's intellectual outlook and mental processes to show to which side he gave his allegiance. Yet it would be untrue to assert that he was contemptuous of authority or allowed no place for it in his system.[1] On the contrary it was an essential part of his intellectual creed that authority and reason were two paths to ultimate truth, which must necessarily converge the nearer the mind of man attained to its goal. Such was the framework of his theory, yet so far as concerned its practical application he was adamant. In the first instance man's progress must depend on the questionings of his own mind, and the test of his advance must be the appeal to reason.[2] If doubts and apparent contradictions ensue they but serve to remind the enquirer that truth is many-sided and only partially to be apprehended by the mind of man. Only in the omniscient and infallible intelligence of the Divine are they capable of reconciliation.

To St Bernard much of this was anathema. An example of the gulf between the intellectual systems of the two men is afforded by their divergent views on faith. To Abailard

[1] The exaggerated language occasionally used by Abailard in dealing with the subject should not blind us to this fact. It must be remembered that every exponent of a new philosophical method tends to over-emphasise what is novel therein, and correspondingly to depreciate the elements of truth in the older system. Cf. Poole, *Illustrations*, p. 140.

[2] Ibid. p. 116.

faith was private opinion tentatively held and subjected to the searching test of reason, capable of change both in substance and mode of expression, essentially subjective, the product of the individual's own thinking. To St Bernard faith went deeper than this. It was no mere intellectual affirmation, no tentative hypothesis serving as a basis for conduct, but a certitude, an act of will enshrining the soul's trust in its Maker and Redeemer, an instinct implanted by God's grace, nourished by the teaching and sacraments of the Church, and finding concrete expression in works of charity and devotional exercises. Such an interpretation, avowedly mystic rather than philosophic, is poles asunder from the rationalistic definition of Abailard.[1]

Yet it was not so much Abailard's distinctive teachings which aroused Bernard's indignation: it was rather the spirit which launched him on his speculative ventures and the methods he employed. And in this he was a worthy representative of the new spirit abroad in the twelfth century. Everywhere the breath of free enquiry was stirring the stagnant waters of the intellect, quickening interest in the mind of man and the problems of existence. In scholar and theologian the speculative faculty long dormant sought fresh channels for its employ, and the weapon of ruthless criticism which Abailard had forged became the standard arm for all who warred with the Church's claim to supremacy over man's intellect. And just here in Bernard's eyes lay the point of danger. Already the movement threatened to over-reach the academic bounds of its origin. From the desk of the schools and the monastic cell the new doctrines were penetrating to the market place. Italy and southern France teemed with

---

[1] Abailard would have regarded it as worse than useless as a definition, a mere empty form of words leaving the problem exactly where he found it. Cf. J. Cotter Morison, *Life and Times of St Bernard* (1894), pp. 317–19; Sikes, op. cit. pp. 399 seq.

heresy. The very foundations of the Faith were being undermined by the combined onslaught of sceptical philosopher and wandering heresiarch. The faith of the common people was being sapped at the roots. The movement begun by the harmless criticism of the schools ended by promoting the flagrant antinomianism of fanatical and ignorant sectaries.

Such was Bernard's gloomy diagnosis of the situation, and without hesitation he ascribed the major portion of the blame to Abailard. Abailard's repeated professions of personal orthodoxy and ingenious explanations of his most daring subtleties entirely failed to meet the case. So long as he remained at liberty to sow the fatal seed of philosophic doubt among his fellows, so long the Church's prestige and authority must suffer irreparable damage in the world at large.[1] Whether or no Abailard was conscious of the drift of his teaching[2] there can be little doubt that Bernard's view was substantially correct. In any case it is scarcely surprising that Abailard's motives were unjustly suspected by the more conservative churchmen of his day. His opponents were not bigoted obscurantists; for the most part they were men of respectable character but limited intellect, fearful of the consequences to the Church's sacred heritage if this noxious teaching were left unchecked. The times were out of joint; the Church stood in dire need of a

---

[1] "Irridetur simplicium fides, eviscerantur arcana Dei, quaestiones de altissimis rebus temerarie ventilantur, insultatur patribus, quod eas magis sopiendas, quam solvendas censuerint....Ita omnia usurpat sibi humanum ingenium, fidei nihil reservans. Tentat altiora se, fortiora scrutatur, irruit in divina, sancta temerat magis quam reserat, clausa et signata non aperit sed deripit, et quidquid sibi non invenit pervium id putat nihilum, credere dedignatur"—Bern. Ep. 188, col. 353.

[2] Cf. G. G. Coulton, *Five Centuries of Religion*, I, p. 297, n.1: "Abailard must have known at the bottom of his heart that his methods and arguments were essentially solvent of a great deal in the established religion of his time".

champion to defend her citadel against the increasing assaults of rationalism. With one accord men turned to the Abbot of Clairvaux. No other could successfully accomplish so difficult a task, no other had the like prestige among the laity or the same ascendancy over the hierarchy. Not without reluctance was he persuaded to accept the challenge; yet when the moment for intervention came, he threw himself into the struggle with all his wonted energy.

When in 1139 the storm broke on Abailard it came from an unexpected quarter.[1] Two of his works, the *Introductio ad Theologiam* and the *Theologia Christiana*, fell by chance into the hands of William of St Thierry, a friend and correspondent of St Bernard, and at this time a monk of Signy in the diocese of Rheims.[2] William was a man of small learning and simple faith. So startled was he at the daring innovations contained in the two works, whose purport he can scarcely have understood, that he was moved to record a passionate protest in the form of a letter addressed jointly to St Bernard and the papal legate, Bishop Geoffrey of Chartres.[3] "Peter Abailard", he writes, "is again teaching new doctrines and putting them into writing; his books both cross the seas and leap over the Alps, his new propositions and teachings concerning the Faith are borne through province and kingdom, openly preached and freely defended. They are even said to have influence in the Roman Curia." There follows a vehement indictment of Abailard's methods. He treats Holy Scripture as if it were an exercise in dialectics, is the burden of

---

[1] Good accounts of the events leading up to the Council of Sens are to be found in: Deutsch, *Die Synode von Sens, 1141;* Hefele-Leclercq, v, pp. 747–60; Rémusat, *Abélard,* I, pp. 183–205; Vacandard, *St Bernard,* pp. 121–4, 141 seq.; J. Cotter Morison, *St Bernard,* pp. 253–7 301 seq.

[2] Good accounts of William and his earlier relations with St Bernard are found in Cotter Morison, pp. 55 seq. and Deutsch, p. 8.

[3] The letter is given among those of St Bernard, M.P.L. 182, Ep. 326. Deutsch (pp. 9 and 10) thinks it is Bernard's own composition.

William's complaint. "He is a censor of the Faith and not a disciple, an innovator rather than a follower."[1] The writer then enumerates thirteen errors drawn from the two works in question, and calls the attention of the recipients to two other works, the *Sic et Non* and the *Scito te ipsum*, which he himself has not seen but whose titles suggest the probability of equally questionable opinions. Wherefore he begs them to take immediate steps to procure official condemnation of such pernicious heresies; if they preserve silence it will be at peril to themselves and to the Church, for the evil will spread and infect the whole body of the faithful.[2]

Bernard's reply was cautious and non-committal. He praises William's zeal for the Faith and assures him that he will acquaint himself further with the subject when time permits. He would welcome later an opportunity of discussing the position with him.[3]

The projected "council of war" took place. Bernard undertook to visit Abailard and remonstrate with him on the evil effects of his doctrines. According to Geoffrey of Auxerre, Bernard's biographer, Abailard won over by the saint's earnest entreaties agreed to amend his writings at Bernard's discretion. But there is good reason to doubt the accuracy of this version,[4] and the issue proved unsatisfactory. Abailard had not the slightest intention of

[1] "Censor fidei, non discipulus; emendator non imitator"—Bern. loc. cit. col. 532.

[2] Bern. loc. cit. col. 531.

[3] Bern. Ep. 327. Geoffrey of Chartres, the other recipient of William's letter, appears to have made no response. He had been one of Abailard's supporters at the Council of Soissons.

[4] "Cum quo etiam tam modeste, tamque rationabiliter egit (Bernardus), ut ille (Abailardus) quoque compunctus ad ipsius arbitrium correcturum se promitteret universa"—Bern. *Vita Prima*, lib. III, cap. v, M.P.L. 185, col. 311. In the letter sent by the French bishops to Innocent II announcing their decision at Sens (M.P.L. 182, Ep. 337) no mention is made of any such retractation on Abailard's part. Cf. Rémusat, I, pp. 191-2, n. 1; Poole, p. 142.

submitting to Bernard's dictation in intellectual matters. If he ever made such a momentary retractation, it was probably designed to gain time for the preparation of his defence.

His position was not devoid of strength. At Soissons he had stood alone, a free-lance theologian braving the Church's claim to an exclusive interpretation of her doctrine. Now he was the leader of a definite school, a small band of devoted disciples, who drew inspiration and confidence from his creative genius, and were imbued with a sense of loyalty to the methods he employed. Men like Gilbert de la Porrée and Berengar of Poitiers were no mean upholders of his cause. Of yet greater importance his teachings had secured recognition and approval in the Roman Curia.[1] Hyacinth, subdeacon and later cardinal, was the leader of a party jealous of Bernard's interference in ecclesiastical administration and therefore favourable to Abailard on political grounds.[2] Conscious of his improved prospects and desirous of conducting the struggle on his own chosen ground, Abailard determined to forestall his adversaries by challenging St Bernard to a disputation. A convenient opportunity presented itself. A solemn exhibition of relics had been arranged for the Whitsun festival in Sens Cathedral. To the Archbishop Abailard wrote asking him to hold at the same time a public synod, where in the presence of his accusers he, Abailard, might clear himself of the charge of heresy. By this means he hoped to gain a spectacular victory over the Abbot of Clairvaux and his friends. It was a challenge which could not be ignored. Abailard had taken the initiative and placed the responsibility for the counter-

---

[1] Ep. 330, 331, 333 passim.
[2] Hyacinth together with John of Salisbury was a pupil of Abailard in 1136; he was created cardinal in 1144 by Celestine II. Poole, Preface to *Hist. pont.* p. lxi. Watterich, *Pont. Rom.* II, pp. 301, 708–9.

stroke on the shoulders of his adversaries. Henry "the
Boar", a prelate with a wild and dissolute past, was
nothing loth at the prospect of an "intellectual tourney".
He entered forthwith into the spirit of Abailard's challenge
and invited Bernard to the contest.

The latter was placed in an unenviable position. He
knew himself unable to vanquish Abailard in debate. Even
had he done so, it would not have advanced his purpose
one step. He desired to appear as Abailard's accuser before
a properly constituted and lawful Council of the Church
and not as a party to a disputation reminiscent of the
schools. No need for words, he maintained, the man's
writings were sufficient warrant for the charge of heresy.[1]
Further, it was no part of his, Bernard's, duty to judge
matters of doctrine; that function belonged to the bishops.[2]

At first, therefore, he refused the invitation, excusing
himself on the ground of his inexperience and lack of skill
in dialectical pursuits. "When all fly before his face", he
writes in a letter to Pope Innocent after the Council, "he
selects me, the least of all, for single combat. I refused",
he continues, "because I was but a lad, and he a man of
war from his youth."[3] Abailard's disciples were elated at
the rumour of Bernard's refusal. They indulged in premature prophecies of a crowning triumph for their master.
But the vocal entreaties of Bernard's friends caused him to
change his mind. He fully recognised that persistence in

[1] "An non justius os loquens talia fustibus tunderetur, quam
rationibus refelleretur?"—*Tractatus de Erroribus Abailardi*, cap. v, 11,
M.P.L. 182, col. 1063.

[2] "Dicebam sufficere scripta ejus ad accusandum eum; nec mea
referre, sed episcoporum, quorum esset ministerii de dogmatibus
judicare"—Ep. 189, col. 355.

[3] "Cum omnes fugiant a facie ejus, me omnium minimum expetit
ad singulare certamen....Abnui quia puer sum, et ille vir bellator ab
adolescentia"—Ep. 189, loc. cit. It is curious that Bernard forgets the
context of his quotation and that by using such language he is declining
the part of David against Goliath. See post, p. 76.

refusal would mean Abailard's victory by default. With extreme reluctance he finally consented to appear at the Council, and set out without preparation or forethought save that he pondered on the words of Scripture, "Be not anxious how or what ye shall speak for it shall be given you in that hour what ye shall speak".[1]

This is Bernard's account of events, but without casting doubts on his honesty it must be admitted that the aptness of the scriptural parallel is not sustained by an examination of the facts. His mind once bent to the task he used all the weapons at his command to further the success of his cause. A letter to the French bishops summoned to the Council, exhorting them to act courageously in defence of the Faith,[2] was followed by another to Pope Innocent in which his horror of Abailard's teachings receives eloquent expression. "A new faith", he writes, "has been forged in France, a faith which does not treat morally of virtue and vice, nor faithfully of the Sacraments, nor simply and soberly of the mystery of the Holy Trinity, but goes beyond what we have received. We escaped the roar of Peter the Lion (the anti-Pope Pierleone) when he sat in Simon Peter's seat, only to encounter Peter the Dragon assailing Simon Peter's faith. The one persecuted the Church of God openly like a ravening lion, the other like a dragon sits concealed in ambush that he may slay the innocent. Finally, to put much in a few words, our theologian puts steps and ladders in the Trinity like Arius; sets free-will above grace like Pelagius; and dividing the Christ separates

---

[1] "Cedens tamen (licet vix, ita ut flerem) consilio amicorum, qui videntes, quomodo se quasi ad spectaculum omnes pararent, timebant ne de nostra absentia et scandalum populo, et cornua crescerent adversario, et quia error magis confirmaretur, cum non esset qui responderet aut contradiceret, occurri ad locum et diem, imparatus quidem et immunitus, nisi quod illud mente volvebam, *Nolite praemeditari*. . ., etc."—Ep. 189, loc. cit.

[2] Ep. 187.

the assumed humanity from the fellowship of the Trinity like Nestorius. But in all these things he boasts that he has opened the fountains of knowledge to the cardinals and clerks of the Curia, that he has implanted his works in the hands and his opinions in the hearts of the Romans, so that he takes those who ought to be his judges for guardians and patrons of his errors." He concludes with a passionate plea for the Pope's co-operation in silencing so obnoxious a heretic.[1]

We now approach the climax of the drama. The first Sunday after Whitsun in the year 1140[2] the Council of Sens was formally opened with pomp and ceremony. King Louis of France, Theobald, Count of Champagne, and a host of lay barons were present. The higher clergy of the northern provinces of France attended in large numbers, the most notable being the Archbishop of the diocese, Geoffrey, Bishop of Chartres, Hugh of Auxerre, and the Archbishop of Rheims. Widespread curiosity had

---

[1] "Nova fides in Francia cuditur, de virtutibus et vitiis non moraliter, de sacramentis non fideliter, de mysterio sanctae Trinitatis non simpliciter ac sobrie sed praeter ut accepimus, disputatur.... Evasimus rugitum Petri Leonis, sedem Simonis Petri occupantem: sed Petrum Draconis incurrimus, fidem Simonis Petri impugnantem. Ille persecutus est Ecclesiam Dei manifeste, sicut leo rapiens: iste vero, tanquam draco, sedet in insidiis in occultis, ut interficiat innocentem.... Denique, ut pauca de multis dicam, theologus noster cum Ario gradus et scalas in Trinitate disponit, cum Pelagio liberum arbitrium gratiae praeponit; cum Nestorio Christum dividens hominem assumptum a consortio Trinitate excludit. Sed in his omnibus gloriatur, quod cardinalibus et clericis curiae, scientiae fontes aperuerit; quod manibus et sinibus Romanorum libros et sententias incluserit, et in tutelam erroris sui assumit eos a quibus judicari debet et damnari"—Ep. 330, col. 535 seq. Cf. also Ep. 331, 332, 336 and 189.

[2] The year of the Council, whether 1140 or 1141, has been a matter of dispute since the time of Baronius. Deutsch (*Die Synode von Sens*, pp. 50–4) advanced substantial but inconclusive arguments in favour of 1141. The Abbé Vacandard has contested this view (*R.Q.H.* L (1891), pp. 235–43). In the absence of further evidence the earlier date may be taken as the more probable.

been aroused by the prospect of a dialectical tournament between the two leading figures in the French Church, and the occasion was marked by many as worthy of comparison with the great crusading Council of Clermont in 1095. Abailard came attended by a chosen band of disciples, Bernard supported by a small company of monks from Clairvaux. Popular feeling was hot for the saint and Abailard soon found himself in the midst of enemies. When he appeared in the streets his life was in danger. If he had hoped for a more impartial tribunal than that which had condemned him at Soissons he was soon un-deceived. His adherents were outnumbered by about ten to one. Too late he realised that, in the existing state of opinion, what he had designed to be a public debate might easily become a trial in which his orthodoxy would be impeached.

The first session was mainly occupied with the exposi-tion and adoration of the sacred relics. On the morrow the Council met in the Church of St Stephen and turned to deal with the question of Abailard's doctrines. Abai-lard entered with his disciples, among whom Arnold of Brescia and Gilbert de la Porrée were prominent. Bernard mounted the pulpit and read aloud seventeen pro-positions abstracted from Abailard's works, which he de-clared suspect of heresy. He called upon Abailard either to deny them or to vindicate his orthodoxy. To the conster-nation of the assembled company Abailard refused to plead or to answer any questions but lodged an appeal to the Pope and straightway left the church.[1]

The motive behind this dramatic action has provoked much discussion and is still partially unexplained. Otto of Freising ascribes it to a fear of violence to his person,[2]

---

[1] Bern. Ep. 189, col. 356; 191, col. 357 seq.; 337, col. 542. *Vita prima*, lib. III, cap. v, M.P.L. 185, col. 311.

[2] Otto of Freising, *Gesta Fred.* lib. I, cap. xlix, p. 70.

Geoffrey of Auxerre, Bernard's apologist, to a miracle.
Abailard, he says, later confessed that at this moment he
was smitten with a sudden malady which obscured his
mental faculties and deprived him of his wonted eloquence.[1]
More probably it was due to natural causes. The vague
forebodings of ill which had long troubled him now gave
place to a definite suspicion that his fate was already determined in the minds of his judges. In the Council his
cause was lost before he could plead his defence. Ignominy
and defeat stared him in the face. We have seen what
bitterness of soul he suffered through his earlier condemnation at Soissons.[2] It can well be imagined that he would
seize any loophole which offered deliverance from a repetition of such anguish. At Rome, he was persuaded, matters
would be different. There he had able and loyal allies
working for him, the psychological influence of Bernard's
personality would be removed, and he might count on an
impartial hearing of his cause. Above all a delay would
afford him ample time to extend his interests in the Roman
Curia. Some such thoughts in all probability were responsible for his action.[3]

There is, however, a further point to be considered.
The version of the Council's proceedings given above is
derived from the letters of St Bernard, his biography by
Geoffrey of Auxerre and the official account contained in

[1] "Nam et confessus est postea suis, ut aiunt, quod ea hora, maxima
quidem ex parte memoria ejus turbata fuerit, ratio caligaverit, et
interior fugerit sensus"—Bern. *Vita prima*, loc. cit.

[2] See ante, p. 38.

[3] Dr Poole thinks that Abailard acted merely on impulse: "At the
close of his life as at every juncture in its progress, Abailard's fortunes
turned upon the alternations of his inner mood. He believed his
actions to be under the mechanical control of his mind; yet he was
really the creature of impulse. At the critical moment, that lofty self-
confidence of which he boasted would suddenly desert him and change
by a swift transition into the extreme of despondency, of incapacity
for action"—*Illustrations*, p. 144.

a synodal letter despatched to the Pope above the signa-
tures of the bishops of the province. All these documents
omit an important piece of evidence which may also have
affected Abailard's conduct. For this we are indebted
mainly, though not solely, to a pamphlet from the pen of
Berengar of Poitiers called an Apology for Peter Abailard.[1]
Written after the synod it is in fact a venomous and libel-
lous attack on the Abbot of Clairvaux. As a specimen of
satirical writing it is unrivalled in contemporary literature.[2]
The bitterness of the invective matches anything to be
found in Bernard's own works, and the author is a master
of irony. He begins the tractate in a strain of mock
flattery. Bernard's fame has gone out into all lands, bearing
his writings on its wings. This in itself is a great marvel
seeing that he is a man ignorant of letters and the arts;
such fecundity of eloquence must be the Lord's doing.
Almost imperceptibly the tone changes from delicate irony
to blatant sarcasm. Happy indeed is the world with such
a meteor to light it; on the words of his mouth seemed to
hang the laws of nature and the fruits of the earth. Yea,
even the very demons obeyed his commands. But now the
sting of the serpent is revealed to all men.[3] Berengar taunts
him with intellectual pride and spiritual vainglory, which
he endeavours to conceal by a pretended zeal for the
Church's faith. His repute for sanctity and his claim to
work miracles the audacious author tears to shreds, and
we are left with the portrait of a hypocrite and a charlatan.
Now this impostor has attacked Peter Abailard, a true

---

[1] Printed at the end of Abailard's works. M.P.L. 178, col. 1857 seq.

[2] The Abbé Vacandard gives an entirely contrary judgment on the
work: "C'est un amas de calomnies, relevé parfois par des traits de
satire assez heureux, mais le plus souvent assaisonné de citations
puériles, d'ignobles plaisanteries, qui bravent même l'honnêteté de la
langue latine"—St Bernard, II, p. 169. Rémusat exaggerates in the
opposite sense. Cf. I, p. 234: "C'est une Provinciale du XII siècle".

[3] Berengarii Apologia, loc. cit. col. 1857.

follower of Christ; he has accused him of heresy before the Synod. In public he has besought the faithful to offer prayers for him; in private he has taken care to secure his ostracism by the whole Christian world.[1]

Berengar then proceeds to draw a lively picture of the Council. He tells of a private conference held by the bishops on the evening of the first day. Abailard's suspected propositions were read aloud and discussed. But the recital was tedious and the full-fed prelates heavy with wine lay sprawling in a drunken stupor. When, after each proposition has been dealt with, the reader asks, "Do you condemn it?" the sleepy response comes back, "Damnamus". Some, roused by the chorus of condemnation, merely echo "Namus" (We swim).[2]

That Bernard presided over a drunken orgy is a monstrous charge which cannot be substantiated, and in point of fact Berengar under pressure from authority afterwards disavowed his statements. Yet that some kind of private conference did take place is confirmed by a passage in the official report of the Council sent to the Pope.[3] Whatever be the truth of the matter it can be taken as certain that

---

[1] "Concionabaris ad populum, ut orationem funderet ad Deum pro eo; interius autem disponebas eum proscribendum ab orbe Christiano"—Berengar, *Apologia*, col. 1858.

[2] "Cum itaque lector in Petri satis aliquod reperiret spinetum, surdis exclamabat auribus pontificum 'Damnatis'? Tunc quidam vix ad extremam syllabam expergefacti, somnolenta voce, capite pendulo: 'Damnamus' aiebant. Alii vero damnantium tumultu excitati, decapitata prima syllaba,...'namus' inquiunt"—Berengar, *Apologia*, col. 1859.

[3] Where an examination of Abailard's works "pridie ante factam ad vos appellationem" is mentioned. Ep. 337, col. 542. Cf. Vacandard, *St Bernard*, II, p. 147, n.1; Deutsch, pp. 39–40. Cf. also John of Salisbury (*Hist. pont.* cap. ix, pp. 20–1) where in an account of the trial of Gilbert de la Porrée at the Council of Rheims (1148) he tells how the cardinals present condemned Bernard's procedure, "dicentes quod abbas arte simili magistrum Petrum aggressus erat". Poole, Preface, pp. xliii and xliv; Deutsch, pp. 30 seq.

Abailard's condemnation had already been resolved before the public hearing of his case began.[1] Had he gleaned tidings thereof, and, if so, did it contribute at all to his decision to appeal to Rome? An affirmative answer to each of these questions should probably be given.

Abailard's appeal placed the Council in an awkward situation. Unquestionably it was a perfectly legitimate move, and would be welcomed at Rome where every opportunity of promoting the centralisation of ecclesiastical jurisdiction was turned to account. Hence arose a difficult problem for St Bernard and the bishops. Was the malignant heretic to escape their clutches notwithstanding their careful preparations? For a while his person was secure from molestation. The fact of his appeal, however, had not deterred the bishops from venturing a formal condemnation of his doctrines. Fourteen propositions were declared heretical, contrary to the teaching of Augustine and other Fathers of the Church. The Council's decision was communicated to the Pope in three epistles, all of which were probably composed by Bernard. The first was the official "minutes" of the Council signed by the Archbishop of Sens and his suffragans.[2] The second was despatched in the names of the Archbishop of Rheims and the Bishops of Soissons, Châlons and Arras[3]; the third in Bernard's own name.

In the last we get the first mention of Arnold of Brescia's part in the controversy. Bernard couples his name with

---

[1] The Abbé Vacandard (loc. cit.) argues that this preliminary meeting was entirely legitimate. Deutsch (p. 23) holds that Abailard should have been allowed to appear. The fact that he was not and the incompleteness of the gathering seem to tell against the Abbé's view.

[2] Bern. Ep. 337. Deutsch (p. 29) argues against Bernard's authorship of this letter. His objection is based on the difference between the style of composition and the vigorous, terse sentences characteristic of the saint's epistles.

[3] Bern. Ep. 191.

Abailard and draws a graphic picture of "the new Goliath, tall of stature and clad in war apparel, preceded by his armour-bearer (i.e. Arnold). Scale is so closely joined to scale that not a breathing space is left between them. The bee of France has hissed to the Italian bee[1] and together they have advanced against the Lord and against His Christ. In life and habit they wear the mask of piety, but they deny its virtue and deceive many by disguising themselves as angels of light while in reality they are angels of Satan. Together they stand between the lines and Goliath shouts against the hosts of Israel, reproaching the ranks of the saints with greater boldness in that he knows no David is there to thwart him ".[2] The motive underlying this caricature is difficult to determine. Two explanations may be offered. First that St Bernard saw in Arnold the most devoted and most dangerous of Abailard's disciples; the man of action placing his practical ability and greater knowledge of the world at the service of the ingenuous philosopher.[3] Such an interpretation is perfectly in keeping with Bernard's mentality, but receives little support from the actual course of events and is inconsistent with the Goliath *motif*. There is no evidence that Arnold took any active part in the proceedings any more than did the armour-bearer. He can hardly have been in Abailard's full confidence, for he

[1] An allusion to Isaiah vii, 18.

[2] "Procedit Golias procero corpore, nobili illo suo bellico apparatu circummunitus antecedente quoque ipsum ejus armigero Arnaldo de Brixia. Squama squamae conjungitur, et nec spiraculum incedit per eas. Siquidem sibilavit apis quae erat in Francia, api de Italia: et venerunt in unum adversus Dominum et adversus Christum ejus.... In victu autem et habitu habentes formam pietatis, sed virtutem ejus abnegantes, eo decipiunt plures, quo transfigurant se in angelos lucis, cum sint Satanae. Stans ergo Golias una cum armigero suo inter utrasque acies, clamat adversus phalangas Israel, exprobratque agminibus sanctorum, eo nimirum audacius, quo sentit David non adesse"—Ep. 189, col. 355.

[3] "Adhesit Petro Abaielardo, partesque eius...adversus abbatem Clarevallensem studiosus fovit"—*Hist. pont.* loc. cit. ante.

would certainly never have countenanced the appeal to Rome. A more specious explanation is that Bernard was seeking to discredit Abailard in the eyes of the Pope by depicting him as the inseparable companion of Arnold, the turbulent demagogue. If successful it would counteract the intrigues of Hyacinth's party in the Curia. From this point of view the letter is a skilful document. Innocent would readily recollect Arnold's part in the schism at Brescia and the condemnation it incurred. Bernard's assertion that Abailard and Arnold were united in principle implied that Abailard's opinions not only menaced the Church's doctrines but also the whole hierarchical system, a conviction which Bernard himself held in all sincerity.[1]

The closing scenes of the drama were now being enacted. Both parties made feverish preparations for the impending struggle in Rome. The day following his appeal Abailard drew up a confession of faith wherein he endeavoured to interpret his beliefs in an orthodox sense. At the same time he made a violent attack on the Abbot of Clairvaux, accusing him of gross ignorance in theology, malicious distortion of facts and insensate fury.[2] Such a polemic was little calculated to improve his prospects at Rome. But it proved to be the last flicker of his old fighting spirit. In a subsequent *apologia* addressed to Heloise all bitterness has vanished and the deepest convictions of his soul find utterance in an exposition of his faith entirely sincere and almost sublime. "I would not be a philosopher", he writes, "if that implies disobedience to Paul. I would not

---

[1] Bern. Ep. 195, col. 363: "Adhaeserat Petro Abaelardo cuius omnes errores, ab Ecclesia tam deprehensos atque damnatos, cum illo etiam et prae illo defendere acriter et pertinaciter conabatur". Cf. Vacandard, *St Bernard*, ii, p. 155.

[2] This treatise is not fully extant. Otto of Freising (*Gesta Fred.* lib. i, cap. xlix) gives only the beginning of it. Its contents can be gauged from the reply of an anonymous monk known as the "Disputatio anonymi abbatis". M.P.L. 180, col. 283 seq.

be an Aristotle and separated from Christ. For there is
none other name under heaven wherein I must be saved."
There follows a formal profession of his orthodoxy and
a condemnation of the various heresies charged to his
name. "Such is the faith in which I stand", he concludes,
"and from which I draw the strength of hope. Firmly
planted in this, I fear not the barking of Scylla, I laugh at
the whirlpool of Charybdis, I shudder not at the fatal songs
of the sirens. If the storm breaks I am not shaken, if the
winds blow I am not moved, for I am founded on the rock
which shall never be removed."[1]

Having unburdened his soul with this courageous *con-
fessio fidei*, Abailard set out on the long road to Rome in
order that by attendance in person before the Curia he
might be better able to advance his suit. But age and
failing health constrained him to break his journey at
Cluny where he was kindly received by Abbot Peter the
Venerable.

Meanwhile Bernard and his partisans were moving
heaven and earth to secure a speedy condemnation from
Rome. In addition to his lengthy treatise refuting Abailard's
doctrines and dedicated to the Pope,[2] a flood of letters from
Bernard's pen inundated the Curia.[3] On friend and foe
promiscuously he lets loose the torrent of his eloquence,

---

[1] "Nolo sic esse philosophus, ut recalcitrem Paulo. Non sic esse
Aristoteles, ut secludat a Christo. 'Non enim aliud nomen est sub
caelo, in quo oporteat me salvum fieri.'...Haec itaque est fides in qua
sedeo, ex qua spei contraho firmitatem. In hac locatus salubriter,
latratus Scyllae non timeo, vertiginem Charybdis rideo, mortiferos
sirenarum modulos non horresco. Si irruat turbo, non quatior; si
venti perflent, non moveor. Fundatus enim sum supra firmam pe-
tram"—Abailard, Ep. 17, M.P.L. 178, col. 375 seq.

[2] *Tractatus de erroribus Petri Abaelardi*, M.P.L. 182, col. 1053 seq.

[3] Fifteen letters on the subject are printed in M.P.L. 182 under
Bernard's name. Of these all save Ep. 187 and 330 were probably
written after the Council. Deutsch, p. 41. Vacandard, *St Bernard*, II,
p. 158, n. 1. Poole, *Illustrations*, p. 145, n. 35. Rémusat differs in placing
some of them earlier. Ep. 330 appears to be an earlier draft of Ep. 189.

now entreating, now threatening, according to the known disposition of each recipient. His dexterous fingers sweep the whole range of human emotions, appealing now to pride, now to fear, and sometimes to the ignoble passions of hatred and envy. In every letter the old weapons of argument are furbished and the old calumnies reiterated. That addressed to the Pope closes with some harsh words against Hyacinth, and the fact that these are repeated in a letter to Haimeric, the papal chancellor, indicates that it was from this quarter that Bernard anticipated most opposition.[1] His fears on that score proved in the event to be groundless. The astute monk had completely out-manœuvred the skilled dialectician, and the latter was condemned by the Pope without a hearing. Two rescripts, both dated July 1140, upheld the decision reached by the Council of Sens. The first, addressed to the Archbishops of Sens and Rheims together with "our very dear son in Christ", the Abbot of Clairvaux, declared the propositions forwarded by the Council to be pernicious and altogether contrary to Catholic teaching, and condemned their author to perpetual silence.[2] The second, with a similar super-scription, ordered both Abailard and Arnold of Brescia to

---

[1] "Jacinctus multa mala ostendit nobis; non fecit tamen non quia non voluit, sed quia non potuit"—Ep. 338, col. 543. Cf. Ep. 189, col. 357. Hyacinth had called in question the legality of the Council's action in condemning Abailard's works pending the hearing of the appeal in Rome. Cf. Ep. 337, col. 542 where the bishops in their synodal letter appear unduly anxious to affirm that appeals are of doubtful validity—"licet appellatio ista minus canonica videretur".

[2] "Dolemus autem, quoniam sicut litterarum vestrarum inspectione et missis a fraternitate vestra nobis errorum capitulis cognovimus, in novissimis diebus, quando instant periculosa tempora, magistri Petri Abaelardi perniciosa doctrina, et praedictorum hereses, et alia perversa dogmata catholicae fidei obviantia, pullulare coeperunt. Nos itaque...destinata nobis a vestra discretione capitula, et universa ipsius Petri dogmata, sanctorum canonum auctoritate, cum suo auctore damnavimus, eique tamquam heretico perpetuum silentium imposuimus"—Mansi, XXI, col. 564.

be interned in separate monasteries and the books containing their errors to be confiscated and burned.[1] In respect of this last provision the Pope himself set an example to the faithful by consigning to the flames such works of Abailard as were accessible in Rome.[2]

Bernard's triumph appeared complete and permanent. Goliath and his armour-bearer lay rolling in the dust, the one stricken to death, the other bound with the chain of ecclesiastical censure, and the new David, improving on the example of his prototype, retired in befitting modesty to the shelter of the monastic sheepfold.

Abailard was still at Cluny when the terrible blow fell. He made no attempt to prolong the struggle but meekly accepted the papal decision as the Church's irrevocable judgment on his life and work. The proud spirit and the headstrong will crumpled before the shafts of fate. Henceforward he desired nothing better than to renounce the fleeting and uncertain triumphs of the schools and to end his days in the shelter of the abbey, cherished and consoled by the overflowing charity of its saintly abbot. The latter gladly complied with his request and wrote to the Pope entreating his consent. Further by arrangement with the Abbot of Citeaux, Abailard and St Bernard were once more brought face to face. A personal reconciliation was effected, and they parted on friendly terms.[3] Abailard drew up yet another profession of his faith, making therein a full submission to the Pope, retracting his errors and promising to correct them in his books.[4] At Cluny he dwelt many months, edifying his brother monks by the sanctity of his life and the charm of his conversation. With astonishment somewhat akin to awe men beheld "the

[1] Mansi, xxi, col. 565.
[2] Gaufridi *Ep. ad Albinum cardinalem*, M.P.L. 185, col. 595–6. Cf. Bern. *Vita prima*, lib. iii, cap. v, col. 311 seq.
[3] Petrus Venerabilis, lib. iv, Ep. 4. M.P.L. 189, col. 305 seq.
[4] Apologia, in *Petri Abaelardi Opera*, ed. Cousin, ii, pp. 719–23.

lawless, rule-less monk" of other days[1] living in love and concord with his fellows, distinguished above them all in piety, humility and obedience. His character, marred in earlier days by an overweening conceit in his own intellect and a scornful contempt for those of his fellows, seems to have been purged and purified in the fire of his tribulations, leaving a candour and gentleness, a humility and devotion, which in the Abbot of Cluny's eyes fitted him to stand as a perfect example of "the servant and true philosopher of Christ".[2] For in quitting the schools Abailard had not wholly renounced the pursuits of the intellect. In the intervals of the Divine offices he read widely in theology and philosophy, with long and frequent meditations on spiritual things. His malady increasing Abbot Peter removed him to a daughter house in the sunny district of Châlons. But the shadow of death had fallen upon him and in the spring of 1142 the weary, tortured spirit shed its earthly garment. "With what holiness, with what devotion, in how Catholic a spirit he made confession of his sins, with what heart's desire he received the sustenance for his journey, the pledge of eternal life, verily the Body of the Lord Redeemer, how faithfully he commended his body and soul to Him both here and in eternity, the brethren and the whole congregation are witnesses. Thus Master Peter finished his days, and he who for his singular mastery of learning was famed throughout the world became meek and lowly in the service of Him Who said, 'Learn of me for I am meek and lowly of heart', and, so we may believe, passed into His presence."[3] So wrote Peter the Venerable to Heloise after his death. No more fitting tribute to Abailard's memory can be conceived than this from the pen of the man whose affection had assuaged the sorrows of his declining days to the woman whose love had sweetened the victories of his prime.

[1] Bern. Ep. 332, col. 537.   [2] Pet. Ven. Ep. 21, col. 350.
[3] Ibid. col. 352.

Chapter VI

ARNOLD IN EXILE

THE stir raised by the Council of Sens quickly subsided in the days following Abailard's retreat to Cluny. The Pope's ratification of the sentence passed on him effectually silenced the few who maintained that the Council had acted *ultra vires*. Nevertheless opinion veered round unexpectedly in favour of the stricken teacher. On deeper reflection men felt that he had been harshly treated. The popular horror of heresy, which Bernard so skilfully exploited at the Council, was effaced by genuine awe at the report of Abailard's death in the odour of sanctity and in full communion with the Church. The challenge to the Church provoked by his career was obliterated from the mind of subsequent generations, and he was remembered only as an illustrious teacher and the pious founder of the Paraclete.

This revolution in popular feeling also affected the fortunes of Arnold of Brescia. So harsh was the judgment which had associated him with Abailard's condemnation, so palpably the fruit of Bernard's representations to the Pope, that no French bishop was found willing or able to carry out the papal decree. Arnold was made of sterner stuff than the sensitive and volatile Abailard. He was young and active, and the series of misfortunes which had attended his evangelical crusade only succeeded in whetting his appetite for further adventure. The Council ended he returned to Paris, established himself on the Mont Ste Geneviève, the site of his master's triumphs, and opened a school of theology.[1] For a year he dwelt there unmolested. Vehement indictments of the avarice and immorality of bishops and the worldliness of the clergy were inter-

[1] *Hist. pont.* p. 64.

spersed among his academic discourses. "He taught",
remarks John of Salisbury dryly, "things most consonant
to the law of Christians but as remote as possible from
actual life."[1] Such tirades, reminiscent of the popular
preacher, were entirely out of harmony with the atmosphere of the schools, and naturally failed to attract the
intellectual youth of Paris. Then as now the practice of
evangelical poverty seldom consorted well with a love of
letters. Arnold, it appears, had few for audience save poor
scholars accustomed to win their daily bread as public
mendicants.[2] Further his prestige was lowered by the
bitter polemics he launched against St Bernard. The
latter he denounced as a seeker after vainglory, jealous of
all who, not being of his school, won distinction in letters
or theology.[3] The shrewd thrust appears to have struck
home. At any rate the sneer rankled in Bernard's mind.
Henceforward he reckoned Arnold chief among his personal enemies and pursued him ruthlessly like a common
criminal.[4] As the French bishops were still unwilling to
execute the papal ban[5] Bernard appealed to the secular
arm. King Louis VII at length responded to his im-

[1] "Dicebat que Christianorum legi concordant plurimum et a vita
quam plurimum dissonant. Episcopis non parcebat ob avariciam et
turpem questum, et plerumque propter maculam vite, et quia ecclesiam
Dei in sanguinibus aedificare nituntur"—*Hist. pont.* p. 64.
[2] "Sed auditores non habuit nisi pauperes et qui ostiatim eleemo-
sinas publice mendicabant, unde cum magistro vitam transigerent"—
ibid.
[3] Ibid.
[4] How far Bernard was capable of allowing his sense of proportion
to be warped by personal animosity is shown by the extraordinary
terms in which he denounces his secretary, Nicholas, after the latter had
betrayed him. Writing to Eugenius III to warn him against the traitor
he concludes: "Mementote Arnaldi de Brixia, quia *ecce plus quam
Arnaldus hic*. Nullus perpetua dignior inclusione, nihil ei perpetuo
silentio justius"—Ep. 298, col. 501. This letter was written in 1151
in the heyday of Arnold's fortunes in Rome.
[5] Bern. Ep. 195, col. 363.

portunate clamour, and Arnold was driven from the kingdom, a wanderer and a fugitive (*vagus et profugus super terram*), ultimately finding a precarious shelter at Zürich in Switzerland.[1]

On the Mount, as in Brescia, the core of his teaching was the incompatibility of spiritual ministration with enjoyment of material possessions. At Brescia, Otto of Freising tells us, he had taught that bishops who retained the *regalia* and monks who held property could in no wise hope for salvation. These belonged of right to the secular power, whom it behoved to use them to the best advantage of the laity.[2] The rights of the clergy were restricted to tithes and first-fruits, and in addition free-will offerings prompted by the devotion of their flocks.[3]

Zürich, whither Arnold had fled, though outside the limit of the Duchy of Swabia, formed part of the territory bestowed as a fief on Berthold, Duke of Zähringen, by Frederick of Hohenstaufen in 1098.[4] But the Dukes of Zähringen were at all times little more than titular rulers, after 1139 the real power being lodged in the hands of the

---

[1] "Optinuit ergo abbas, ut eum Christianissimus rex eiceret de regno Francorum"—*Hist. pont.* op. cit. Cf. Bern. Ep. 195, col. 362 seq. Otto of Freising, *Gesta Fred.* p. 133.

[2] "Dicebat enim nec clericos proprietatem nec episcopos regalia nec monachos possessiones habentes aliqua ratione salvari posse. Cuncta haec principis esse, ab eisque beneficentia in usum tantum laicorum cedere oportere"—Otto of Freising, p. 133.

> "Nil proprium cleri, fundos et praedia nulla
> Iure sequi monachos nulli fiscalia iura
> Pontificum, nulli curae popularis honorem
> Abbatum sacras referens concedere leges
> Omnia principibus terrenis subdita, tantum
> Committenda viris popularibus, atque regenda."
>
> Gunther, *Lig.* col. 370.

[3] Gunther, *Lig.* loc. cit.

[4] Otto of Freising, *Gesta Fred.* p. 24. Hausrath, pp. 65, 165, n.4. E. Heyck, *Geschichte der Herzoge von Zähringen* (Freiburg, 1891), pp. 185 seq.

Imperial Prefect (Reichsvogt), the Count of Lenzburg, who exercised supreme executive and judicial authority over the city.[1] Over against the temporal jurisdiction of the Prefect was set the ecclesiastical dominion of the Bishop of Constance, within whose diocese the city lay. Gradually as the twelfth century progressed a new power arose, destined to dispute with both the claim to supremacy. This was composed of the city burghers, aspiring to municipal self-government and growing ever stronger in consciousness of civic unity. At the period with which we are concerned this movement was in its infancy. Scarcely had the municipality attained a semi-autonomy in the social and economic spheres. Certainly it could not compare in political status with the Lombard communes. Not till the succeeding century do consuls, the invariable sign of civic autonomy, make their appearance.[2] Unhappily we have little knowledge of the strength and number of the various crafts and gilds out of which municipal organisation normally developed. The fact that the city lay in a remote corner of the Empire, though not entirely severed from the commercial highways of Lombardy and the Rhineland,[3] accounts for the comparative slowness of its institutional development. Yet from the account given us by Otto of Freising it would appear that from a very early date some intercourse existed between Zürich and the Lombard cities. "Zürich", he writes, "the noblest town of Swabia, ...is situated in the passes of the mountains towards Italy above the lake whence flows the river 'Leman'.[4] It was formerly a colony of the Emperors or kings and, according to the tradition of our ancestors, of such importance that the Milanese, when summoned over the Alps to judgment

[1] Hausrath, pp. 65 and 69. Heyck, op. cit. p. 295.
[2] Hausrath, p. 69.
[3] It lay on the Roman road from Chur to Basle, and so was linked with Como and Milan.
[4] I.e. River Limmat.

by the Emperor, had to go there to have their cases dealt with."[1]

Such was the political structure of Zürich as Arnold found it. We have next to determine the length of his stay and the nature of his activities. Each is a task fraught with considerable difficulties. From the time of his flight from Paris to his reception at Viterbo by Pope Eugenius III the materials for Arnold's history are of the most meagre character. Neither the *Historia Pontificalis* nor the *Gesta di Federico* affords a clue to the problem. Otto of Freising merely records the fact of his sojourn at Zürich, together with the ambiguous statement that he "assumed the office of doctor, sowing the seeds of his pernicious doctrine there many days".[2] Some words of Gunther in the *Ligurinus* gave rise among the earlier biographers[3] to the extraordinary opinion that Arnold adopted a disguise, teaching under the assumed name of "Doctor Lemannus". This is palpably an error due to an imperfect understanding of the Latin construction in the poem.[4] Our most

---

[1] "Turegum, nobilissimum Sueviae oppidum...in faucibus montium versus Italiam super lacum, unde Lemannus fluvius fluit, situm imperatorum seu regum olim colonia fuit tantaeque iuxta maiorum nostrorum traditionem auctoritatis, ut Mediolanenses, si quando ab imperatore ad Transalpina vocarentur iudicia, ibi discuti vel iudicari de iure deberent"—Otto of Freising, *Gesta Fred.* op. cit.

[2] "Ita homo ille de Italia fugiens ad Transalpina se contulit ibique in oppido Alemanniae Turego officium doctoris assumens pernitiosum dogma aliquot diebus seminavit"—Otto of Freising, p. 133.

[3] Francke, p. 133. Odorici, p. 77. De Castro, p. 337.

[4]   "Fugit ab urbe sua, transalpinisque receptus,
                  Qua sibi vicinas Alemannia suspicit Alpes,
                  Nomen ab Alpino ducens, ut fama, Lemanno,
                  Nobile Turregum, doctoris nomine falso,
                  Insedit."   Gunther, *Lig*. col. 370.

All the poet says here is that "Alemannia" derives its name from "Lemannus". Cf. Otto of Freising, p. 25: "A praedicto etiam Lemanno fluvio...tota illa provincia Alemannia vocatur". The phrase "doctoris nomine falso" can only mean that Arnold assumed the title of doctor under false pretences, i.e. since he was not qualified for the

fruitful source of information is a letter sent by St Bernard to the Bishop of Constance,[1] though even here very little of concrete fact is given us. The Abbot of Clairvaux would appear to be relying mainly on reports gathered from monks of local Cistercian houses, who invariably adopted the rôle of secret service agents with skill and equanimity.[2] Even so Bernard shows no definite knowledge of the shape and scope of Arnold's activities.

Herman of Arbon, the recipient of the letter, was a prelate whose path of destiny more than once crossed that of Arnold of Brescia. His elevation to the see of Constance in 1138 was disturbed by schism, and it was only after a prolonged suit at Rome, which put him to vast expense, that his election was ratified by Innocent II in the Lateran Council of 1139, about the time Arnold was condemned for schism. A friend and correspondent of Wibald of Corvey, Herman became also a trusted servant of Conrad III and Frederick Barbarossa, being frequently employed by them on diplomatic missions beyond the Alps. He accompanied Frederick on the latter's first expedition to Italy, and in all probability was present in the Imperial camp when the man whom he had once sheltered in his diocese was handed over to the Roman Prefect for execution.[3] Essentially politically minded, tolerant of opinions and lax in the administration of his diocese, there is no reason to suppose that Herman in any degree shared Arnold's opinions on the Church.[4] He was not of the stuff

degree. Cf. Hausrath, p. 165, n. 1; R. Breyer, "Arnold von Brescia", *Maurenbrecher's Historisches Taschenbuch* (1884), p. 142, n.3.

[1] Bern. Ep. 195, col. 361 seq.

[2] There were two important monasteries at Zürich, the Augustinian canons of the Grossmünster and a nunnery whose abbess owned much property in the town. These may not be unconnected with Arnold's stay. See Escher and Schweizer, *Urkundenbuch der Stadt und Landschaft Zürich*, I, p. xi.

[3] Hausrath, pp. 68–9, 167, n.6.   [4] Cf. Hausrath, op. cit.

of which reformers are made. His inactivity in the
matter of Arnold's presence in Zürich was probably due
to preoccupation with affairs of state. Once his eyes
were opened to the danger of heresy at his very threshold
he would be prompt to act. And there was that in
Bernard's letter calculated to stir the most sluggish will
to action.

From beginning to end the letter is a cascade of vitupera-
tion directed against the exiled reformer and couched in
the author's inimitable phraseology. Arnold indeed had
shaken the dust of France from off his feet, but the im-
placable saint was hot on his trail. Opening with an invidious comparison between the bishop and the man in the
Gospel parable who failed to keep watch at night against
the coming of the thief, Bernard passes to the evil deeds
and machinations of Arnold. Wherever the latter has
dwelt he has left footprints so foul and terrible behind
him that he never dares to return thither.[1] A recapitulation
of Arnold's escapades in France and Italy follows. To
describe his wickedness in anything like appropriate terms
the saint is driven instinctively to borrow the language of
the psalter mingled with St Paul. Like a roaring lion he
goes about seeking whom he may devour, eating up the
people as it were bread. His mouth is full of cursing and
bitterness, and his feet swift to bloodshed; destruction and
unhappiness are in his ways, and the way of peace has he
not known. He is an enemy of the cross of Christ, a sower
of discord and a maker of schisms, a disturber of peace and
a sunderer of unity; whose teeth are spears and arrows
and his tongue a sharp sword; his words are smoother than
oil and yet they are very darts. Thence it is that he is wont
by flattering speeches and the pretence of virtue to bind

[1] "Ubicumque conversatus est, tam foeda post se, et tam saeva
reliquit vestigia, ut ubi semel fixeret pedem, illuc ultra redire omnino
non audeat"—Bern. op. cit. col. 362.

unto himself the rich and powerful.[1] The letter closes with an earnest appeal for the bishop's co-operation in enforcing the papal ban against the proscribed teacher.

Whether Arnold succumbed to this scriptural indictment and left Zürich of his own accord, or whether he was forcibly ejected from the diocese, cannot be determined with certainty. It is safe, however, to affirm that his stay was not prolonged beyond the year 1142, for about that time we find him living at Passau under the protection of Cardinal Guido, who in August 1142 had been sent on a legatine mission to Moravia and Bohemia.[2] The evidence for this is a letter of Bernard's to the legate which, since Innocent II is mentioned as still alive, must be dated prior to September 1143.[3] The tone of the epistle is similar to that sent to the Bishop of Constance. "Arnold of Brescia", Bernard writes, "whose conversation is honey and whose doctrine is poison; whose head is a dove's but his tail a scorpion's; whom Brescia cast forth, Rome abhorred; whom France has rejected, Germany curses and

---

[1] "Tanquam leo rugiens, circuiens et quaerens quem devoret... et devorat plebem vestram sicut escam panis. Cujus maledictione et amaritudine os plenum est, veloces pedes ejus ad effundendum sanguinem: contritio et infelicitas in viis ejus, et viam pacis non cognovit. Inimicus crucis Christi, seminator discordiae, fabricator schismatum, turbator pacis, unitatis divisor: cujus dentes arma et sagittae et lingua ejus gladius acutus. Molliti sunt sermones ejus super oleum, et ipsi sunt jacula. Unde et solet sibi allicere blandis sermonibus et simulatione virtutum *divites et potentes*." (A reference to the abbess of the Fraumünster?) Bern. op. cit. col. 363.

[2] Jaffé-Loewenfeld, *Regesta*, 8238. *Innocentii Ep.* M.P.L. 179, col. 597. It was formerly held that the legate was Guido of Castello, Abailard's friend and pupil, who afterwards became Pope Celestine II. Giesebrecht (pp. 16–17) has proved that this identification is an error on the part of Baronius, and that the legate was a cardinal-deacon of the same name. Cf. Bernhardi, *Konrad III*, p. 740, n.21; Vacandard, p. 70, n.1; Poole, Preface, p. lxii; De Stefano (p. 11) repeats the old error.

[3] Giesebrecht, p. 16. Innocent II died at Rome on the 24th September 1143. Jaffé-Loewenfeld, I, p. 911.

Italy will not receive, is said to be with you. Take care, I beseech you, lest he do greater harm under cover of your authority. For, since he has both the art and the will to do injury, if he gain your favour, he will, I fear, like a triple cord, which is with difficulty broken, be harmful beyond measure." He assumes that either the legate is ignorant of Arnold's past or that he has succeeded in discovering in him signs of repentance. The saint adds a pious aspiration that this expectation may not prove vain. "Who could grant that from this stone should be raised up a child unto Abraham? How pleasing a gift would it be to our Mother Church to receive from your hands as a vessel for honour him whom she has so long suffered as a vessel of dishonour!" It is lawful to make the attempt but a wise man will give heed to the limit laid down in the Apostle's counsel: "A man that is an heretic after the first and second admonition reject; knowing that he that is such is subverted and sinneth, being condemned of himself." (Titus iii, 10 and 11.)[1]

But on this occasion the Abbot of Clairvaux's remonstrance proved unavailing. Despite the lurid language in

[1] "Arnaldus de Brixia, cujus conversatio mel, et doctrina venenum: cui caput columbae, cauda scorpionis est; quem Brixia evomuit, Roma exhorruit, Francia repulit, Germania abominatur, Italia non vult recipere, fertur esse vobiscum. Videte, quaeso, ne vestra auctoritate plus noceat. Nam cum et artem habeat, et voluntatem nocendi, si accesserit favor vester, erit funiculus triplex, qui difficile rumpitur, supra modum, ut vereor, nociturus. Et unum existimo de duobus, si tamen verum est quod vobiscum hominem habeatis: aut minus scilicet notum vobis esse illum; aut vos, quod est credibilius, de ejus correctione confidere. Et utinam id non frustra. Quis det de lapide hoc suscitare filium Abrahae? Quam gratum munus susciperet mater Ecclesia de manibus vestris vas in honorem, quod tamdiu passa est in contumeliam? Licet tentare; sed vir prudens cautus erit non transgredi praefinitum numerum ab Apostolo, qui ait: 'Hereticum hominem post unam et secundam correptionem devita; sciens quia subversus est qui ejusmodi est, et delinquit proprio judicio condemnatus'"—Bern. Ep. 196, col. 363 seq.

which the refugee's crimes were painted the appeal for his expulsion fell on deaf ears. Arnold had at last secured a friend. It is probable also that the legate was not without support from Rome. The accession to the papal chair of Guido of Castello (Celestine II) in September 1143[1] had vastly increased the influence of that enlightened minority in the Curia which had countenanced the teachings of Abailard. Furthermore, to the casual observer Bernard's unflagging zeal for the purity of the Church's doctrine came to look suspiciously like the prosecution of a personal vendetta. Judging from Bernard's letter Guido would seem to have treated the exile more as an honoured guest than as a prisoner on parole. "To be on intimate terms with him", writes Bernard, "and to admit him frequently to private converse, to say nothing of inviting him to feast with you, is suspiciously like showing him favour, and a strong weapon in the hand of an enemy. A member of the household and a boon companion of a legate of the Holy See will preach with impunity and easily persuade what he will."[2]

Bernard's letter is a single beam of light illuminating an obscure phase of Arnold's career. From 1143 to 1145 the reformer vanishes from the page of history. In the latter year he reappears in Italy,[3] about the time that the legate Guido returned from his mission.[4] In the absence of definite proof it is fair to conclude from this coincidence that Arnold remained in the cardinal's household during

---

[1] Jaffé-Loewenfeld, II, p. 1.

[2] "Alioquin familiarem habere, frequenter admittere ad collo-quendum, ne dicam ad convivandum, suspicio favoris est, et inimici hominis fortis armatura. Secure annuntiabit et facile persuadebit quae volet domesticus et contubernalis legati apostolicae Sedis"—Bern. op. cit.

[3] Otto of Freising, *Gesta Fred.* p. 134. *Hist. pont.* p. 64. Boso, "Vita Adriani IV" in Watterich, *Pont. Roman.* II, p. 324.

[4] Jaffé-Loewenfeld, 8930, 8931. *Eugenii Ep.* M.P.L. 180, col. 1142–3.

these years.[1] In 1145, or possibly 1146, the much-
travelled exile made his peace with Pope Eugenius III at
Viterbo.[2] Doubtless this reconciliation was brought about
through the good offices of the legate, upon whom the
charm of Arnold's personality seems to have made a deep
impression during the two years of their companionship.[3]

Such is the bare outline of Arnold's exile reconstructed
from the scattered notices of contemporary authorities.
As a catalogue of his activities during these years it is
manifestly incomplete. Furthermore, there are not lacking
stray hints in other sources that his teachings met with a
ready welcome at Zürich and left tangible results. But for
the most part the way is left regrettably open to conjecture
and hypothesis, and the earlier and partisan biographers
have made full use of the opportunity. Thus Francke in
dealing with this period of Arnold's history gives full play
to his fantastic imagination. National pride and sectarian
prejudice combine to depict Arnold as a mediaeval pre-
cursor of Zwingli, awakening in the sturdy Swiss a livelier
appreciation of pure religion and winning for them a larger
measure of civic freedom.[4] His chronology is hopelessly
inexact; he prolongs Arnold's stay from 1139 till 1146.[5]

---

[1] Giesebrecht, p. 17. Poole, Preface, *Hist. pont.* p. lxiii.

[2] *Hist. pont.* loc. cit. John of Salisbury was probably an eye-witness
of this reconciliation. See post, p. 208. Cf. Poole, Preface, p. lxxiii.
For chronology ibid. pp. lxiv, lxv.

[3] It would appear safe to make this inference without going the
length of the Abbé Vacandard (*Arnauld de Brescia*, p. 71; *St Bernard*,
II, p. 253) who postulates a formal submission by Arnold to the legate
himself.

[4] Francke, pp. 132 seq. The extent of the harm wrought by ro-
mancing of this nature may be gauged from the fact that so sane
and scholarly a critic as Milman without hesitation accepts Francke's
narrative. "It is singular to observe", he writes, "this more than
Protestant, sowing as it were the seeds of that total abrogation of the
whole hierarchical order, completed in Zürich by Zwingli." Milman,
Latin Christianity, IV, p. 380.

[5] Francke, p. 140. Cf. Giesebrecht, p. 15, n.27.

He also speaks of the reformer being offered a public chair in the city,[1] and, to complete the toll of errors, gives a graphic picture of Arnold descending into Italy at the head of an army of Swiss mountaineers and marching on Rome in aid of the revolution.[2] Equally doubtful assertions are found in the works of Guadagnini and Odorici. These are not so much errors of fact as anachronisms due to a deficient historical sense. Thus Guadagnini transplants the political ideas current in the Lombard cities to the totally different environment at Zürich. Arnold is depicted as the leader of a communal revolt, freeing the citizens from the irksome bonds of feudal custom, resisting the claim of bishop and hierarchy to secular power, much as he had done in Brescia four years earlier, and in general laying the foundations of civic freedom and civic autonomy.[3] All this is sheer surmise. No extant document confirms the existence of such a movement, let alone the supposition that Arnold had any share in promoting it. In similar strain Odorici acclaims him as the real author of Swiss independence, the historical prototype of that hero of legend, William Tell.[4] A justification for these intemperate judgments has been sought in a phrase used by St Bernard in his letter to the Bishop of Constance.[5] The saint writes of Arnold as one employing armed force (*fretum tyrannide militari*) to provoke rebellion against the bishops and run amok amongst (*desaevire*) the whole ecclesiastical order. Yet this is no

---

[1] Francke, p. 133. A statement apparently based on the assertion of Otto of Freising and Gunther (loc. cit. ante) that Arnold assumed the title of "doctor". See p. 86 ante.

[2] Francke, pp. 178 seq. Milman, op. cit. p. 388. The source of this remarkable story is a passage in the *Fasti Corbeienses*: "Arnoldus Alpinorum turbam ad se traxit et Romam cum multitudine venit". Unfortunately this is an interpolation by a later hand and has been omitted in Pertz (ed. in *Mon. Germaniae* series, III).

[3] Guadagnini, *Vita di Arnaldo*, p. 38.

[4] Odorici, pp. 87 and 79.

[5] De Castro, p. 341.

adequate proof. Taken in its context the passage does not imply that this had actually happened; the sentence is cast in the future tense and merely indicates Bernard's acute anxiety for the outcome, should the bishop persist in allowing the reformer full liberty of speech and action.[1] No doubt the saint had in mind Arnold's proceedings at Brescia.

In brief it is more than doubtful whether Arnold's activities at Zürich were of a political character. No evidence of this is forthcoming, and it is hard to believe that Guido, a cardinal and papal legate, would have taken under his wing a man whose fame had twice been tarnished by participation in a political revolution.

There remains only one solution of the problem which will provide an ostensible ground for Bernard's persistent hostility and also square with Otto of Freising's brief notice. Arnold's days at Zürich were spent in preaching his gospel of ecclesiastical reform, and we have reason to believe that he achieved a measure of success. Possibly the way had been prepared for him by the wandering heretic, Henry of Lausanne,[2] and his doctrine of evangelical poverty fell on fruitful soil. Certainly from this time forward his peculiar tenets were accepted as the basic elements of Christian teaching by the pious and primitive communities of the Swiss uplands, though there is no evidence of a definite sect tracing its origin back to him.[3] In the city of Zürich itself we have naught but spasmodic outbreaks of anti-sacerdotal fanaticism which may or may not have been inspired by the memory of his teaching.[4]

[1] "Demum cum fuerit de illorum captata benevolentia et familiaritate securus, *videbitis hominem aperte insurgere in clerum fretum tyrannide militari, insurgere in ipsos episcopos, et in omnem passim ecclesiasticum ordinem desaevire*"—Bern. Ep. 195, op. cit.

[2] Vacandard, p. 69.

[3] Giesebrecht, p. 34. E. Scott Davison, *Forerunners of St Francis*, p. 163.

[4] A revolt of Augustinian canons against Bishop Herman in 1153 is thought by Hausrath (p. 79) to be an echo of Arnold's preaching.

Yet that Arnold secured a personal following is proved by evidence derived from an unexpected source. In the letter sent by Wetzel, one of Arnold's republican allies in Rome,[1] to Frederick Barbarossa in 1152, mention is made of three men of eminent status in the diocese of Constance, who had in varying degrees shown themselves sympathetic towards the reformer's teaching.[2] Of the three the best known to us is the second name, Ulrich of Lenzburg, Imperial Prefect at Zürich. The mere fact that a man occupying this supreme office could be designated one of Arnold's adherents is a weighty argument against the view that the reformer took part in the politics of the city. Ulrich was a trusted counsellor of Conrad III, being on several occasions employed as his envoy in affairs of State.[3] It would be going too far to claim him as a wholehearted believer in Arnold's doctrines; his support was probably based on political expediency. Frequent conflicts with episcopal authority over the question of jurisdiction would dispose him to look with favour on Arnold's teaching concerning the relations between "Church" and "State". Also he had no love for the monastic orders and was at this time engaged in litigation with the house of Einsiedeln over the abbey's lands, an additional motive for according protection to the sworn enemy of that archpatron of monks, the Abbot of Clairvaux.[4] In any case it was probably due to Ulrich more than any other that Arnold remained so long free from molestation.[5]

Nothing is known of a definite connection between Arnold and the other two men mentioned in the letter. Hausrath

---

[1] For question of his identity see pp. 137–8.
[2] They are described as "Comitem Rodulfum de Ramisberch (Ravensburg?) et comitem Oudelricum de Lenzenburch et alios idoneos, scilicet Eberhardum de Bodemen". Jaffé, *Mon. Corbei. Wibaldi* Ep. 405, p. 541. Giesebrecht, p. 14, n.24.
[3] Bernhardi, *Konrad III*, I, passim.
[4] Hausrath, pp. 70, 168, n.10.   [5] Ibid. p. 71.

indeed has suggested that Count Rudolf of Ravensburg was not a direct associate but an acquaintance of Wetzel if, as seems probable, the latter came of Teutonic stock.[1] Eberhard of Bodmen was probably one of the great land-owners of the neighbourhood. Besides these representatives of the aristocratic, landowning class Arnold would appear to have won the sympathies of the prosperous burghers of the city; so much, at least, is indicated by Bernard's mention of the *divites* whom the reformer gained for patrons.[2] This of itself provides some sort of justification for the Abbot's gloomy prophecies and shows that his fulminating rhetoric was not wholly pointless.

Wetzel's letter completes the evidence at present available. It would be folly to attempt to build an imposing structure on so slender a foundation, to postulate, for example, the existence of a distinct Arnoldist sect here in Zürich. All we dare venture as a final judgment is that Arnold's visit did not fail to leave a mark upon the religious conscience of the city, that certain sections of the community were to some extent infected with his doctrines, and the fact that in later days the Swiss uplands became a centre of evangelical opinions is not without significance for a continuity of ideas and traditions. Further than this we cannot go. It is worse than useless to endeavour to trace a direct and concrete continuity where the evidence is of such a fragmentary kind.

As to the personal aspect of the problem there can be little hesitation. In Zürich Arnold was pre-eminently a religious reformer—as he remained at heart to the end of his days—summoning both clergy and laity to a tardy amendment of their sinful lives, and urging the Church's

---

[1] Hausrath, p. 170, n. 11. This would account for the curious fact that Rudolf's name is placed first in the list. If Ravensburg and Bodmen are correct, both were near neighbours of the Bishop of Constance.

[2] Bern. Ep. 195, op. cit.

crying need of a return to the primitive poverty of the Apostolic Age. There is not a single trace of his having adopted the rôle of political demagogue characteristic of his later days at Rome. Of his relations with Cardinal Guido there is nothing further to tell. As we have indicated,[1] it is not even known for certain if he remained with the legate for any length of time.[2] But the silence of our authorities, particularly the abrupt cessation of St Bernard's frantic letters, together with the sequel of the reconciliation at Viterbo with Bernard's friend and pupil, Eugenius III, would seem to imply that Arnold discreetly refrained from further excursions into the field of action. Possibly this unexpected tranquillity was prompted more by circumstances than by a real change of heart.[3] Whether or no this be the true explanation, it must be admitted that his career would have been incomplete, even inconsistent, had he sacrificed his convictions at this point and acquiesced in a state of affairs which he honestly believed to be wrong. His mission was still unfulfilled. No substantial success had as yet come his way. But now the path to Rome lay open before him. "An inner necessity", writes Gregorovius, "drew him to the spot where the root of the evil lay. If Arnold had not gone to Rome, had not ended his life here, he would have been an incomplete figure of his age."[4] His keen instinct for the practical

[1] See ante, pp. 91–2.

[2] Breyer (p. 146) holds that Arnold never went to Guido at all and cites as evidence St Bernard's "Arnaldus de Brixia...fertur esse vobiscum...si tamen verum est quod vobiscum hominem habeatis" etc., Ep. 196, loc. cit. ante. Despite the doubt implied by the use of these phrases it is difficult to believe that Bernard would have written the legate so bold a letter had he not received fairly conclusive evidence of Arnold's whereabouts. Cf. Hausrath, p. 174, n. 4. Probably the doubt is only rhetorical.   [3] Cf. Hausrath, pp. 88–9.

[4] Gregorovius, IV, p. 547. Cf. Giesebrecht, p. 17: "Erst mit Arnolds Rückkehr (nach Rom) beginnt jene Wirksamkeit, die ihm einen Platz in der Weltgeschichte gewonnen hat".

divined in the situation at Rome a more favourable environment for the propagation of his mission. But this was
not all. Forces stronger than he knew were drawing him
thither. The magic spell of the Eternal City was cast upon
him, and the voice of antiquity sounding from her walls
awoke a response from the romantic strain inherent in his
nature. Nor was this attribute peculiar to Arnold; it was
the subconscious motive of the revolution under Innocent
II with which Arnold's fortunes were henceforward to be
closely knit.

Chapter VII

THE ROMAN REVOLUTION

THE full significance of the Roman Republic of the twelfth century cannot be understood apart from the unique position which Rome occupied in the mediaeval world. The aspiration articulate in the slogan *Roma capitale* is no new product of the nationalism of the Risorgimento. In a deeper, more mystical sense it is the heritage of the Middle Ages. Rome was a microcosm of the universe, the terrestrial counterpart of that archetypal heavenly city, the New Jerusalem, and in mystical metaphor her walls were figured as the *flammantia moenia mundi* of the pagan poet's fancy. She was the centre of Western Christendom and to the shrines of the martyrs flocked pilgrims from every land, chanting at their first glimpse of her the traditional paean to her praise.[1]

Yet if to the pilgrim stranger Rome was pre-eminently the Christian metropolis, to the native Latin she was also a visible memorial of classical antiquity. Even though "the shattered columns of the Forum" bore melancholy witness to the ravages of Time and the wanton destruction of barbarian invader, still she stood proud of her past,

"crowned by all Time, all Art, all Might
the equal work of Gods and Man,"

mutely imploring her degenerate sons for a worthy recognition of the grandeur of their inheritance.

[1]   "O Roma nobilis, orbis et domina
          Cunctarum urbium excellentissima,
          Roseo martyrum sanguine rubea,
          Albis et virginum liliis candida;
          Salutem dicimus tibi per omnia,
          Te benedicimus—salve per saecula."
                    Oxford Book of Mediaeval Latin Verse, p. 39.

It was, therefore, not unnatural that the twelfth-century Roman should cherish the ambition of restoring those ancient offices and institutions, to which by a curious perversion of history men attributed Rome's greatness in the past. But this was not the only incentive; to this potent conservatism was now joined a liberal impulse, the desire to secure a measure of civic independence comparable with that which the Lombard cities were beginning to achieve. Republicanism was in the very air breathed by the Italian of that epoch.[1] Unhappily for Rome several factors rendered the success of such an enterprise difficult if not impossible. First may be set the special relationship in which she stood both to the Teutonic Emperor beyond the Alps and to the Pope within her walls. Rome was something more than the chief city of Italy; she was also the capital of the Holy Roman Empire wherein each succeeding Emperor must be crowned, and the seat of the Holy Father, the head of the Western Church. She thus owed a double allegiance; her natural development was crushed between the upper and the nether millstones of Papacy and Empire. Even when she was not torn by the divergent policies of the twain, she was not free like the Lombard cities to develop along lines of her own choosing; her civic destiny was sacrificed to the dominant idealism of mediaeval political theory.[2]

This is well illustrated by an examination of the powers assigned to the Prefect (*praefectus urbis*), the most prominent official in the papal government. The Prefect was charged with supreme criminal jurisdiction within the

[1] Gregorovius, IV, pp. 478 seq.

[2] Cf. Paolucci, *R.S.I.* IV, p. 681: "Roma...non era una città come le altre, non era un semplice Comune particolare ma la sede dell' Impero, la fonte della libertà, la signora del mondo. Quello che per un' altra città sarebbe stato ordinamento locale, per Roma acquistava importanza mondiale; chi governà questa città doverà nello stesso tempo reggere il mondo".

city; he was prosecutor, judge and executioner in one.[1] He had also certain less clearly defined powers of civic magistracy, which seem in practice to have been resolved into the duties of giving audience to litigants, citing defendants, summoning the judges and pronouncing sentence.[2] Though accounts differ it seems fairly clear that in the twelfth century at least the Prefect was the nominee of the Pope, to whom he did homage and was responsible for his conduct.[3] Yet Gerhoh of Reichersberg, an authoritative writer, maintains that the Prefect was also bound by oath to the Emperor, at whose hands he received investiture.[4] In this view he was the joint representative of Pope and Emperor. No doubt we are on safe ground with M. Halphen in rejecting this explanation and concluding that the Prefect was primarily a papal officer.[5] Yet, however this may be, if Gerhoh's statement contains a modicum of truth, there is no denying that the prefectorial office was a valuable constitutional link between papal and imperial

[1] L. Halphen, *Études sur l'administration de Rome au moyen âge*, p. 19.
[2] Ibid. p. 21.
[3] See John of Salisbury's account, *Hist. pont.* cap. xxvii, p. 60: "Nam ille prefecture maximus et antiquissimus honor ab ecclesia habens auctoritatem iuris dicendi usque ad centesimum lapidem et utens gladii potestate ad inane nomen redactus erat".
[4] Gerhoh of Reichersberg, *De Investigatione Antichristi*, cap. xxxvii; *Lib. de lite*, III, pp. 344–5: "Etenim prefectus Urbis accepta a Romano pontifice super causas civiles judicandi potestate simul cum beneficio vel stipendio eidem potestate pertinente vindictarum, quae sanguinis dumtaxat effusionem poscunt, faciendarum potestatem ab imperatore per gladium evaginatum accipit, quod suum est utrique potestati recognoscens". Cf. *Com. in Psalm.* lxiv, pp. 440 seq. For a full discussion of the problem see Halphen, pp. 22–7. Cf. also Poole, Preface to *Hist. pont.* pp. lxvi seq.; Gregorovius, IV, p. 366; Gibbon, VII, p. 228. Gerhoh's account gives point to the fact that ecclesiastics could not deal (officially) with cases involving shedding of blood.
[5] Halphen, p. 27. It has also been argued that he was in the first instance chosen by the Roman people. Gregorovius, IV, loc. cit. But this view is entirely based on the election of Prefect Peter in 1116. This, however, is an isolated instance occurring in a moment of civic disturbance. Poole, Preface, p. lxvii.

authority,[1] a fact which the leaders of the revolution of 1143 were quick to recognise.

Of the remaining institutions of papal Rome there is little to tell. The ancient Senate had long ceased to function and, though the title of Senator survived, it seems to have implied membership of a social order, the new aristocracy of Carolingian origin, and not a definite office. A similar fate had overtaken the consulate. After the Byzantine era "consul" became a mere honorific title.[2] But the eleventh century saw the rise of a new type of consuls, the *consules Romanorum*, successors of the *duces* of the Ottos, drawn for the most part from noble families. They formed a special class of papal officials, and their duties consisted in aiding the Prefect to bring criminals to justice and in superintending the execution of sentence upon them.[3]

Such were the chief elements of Roman administration before the institution of the commune. It was an effete and incoherent system scarcely comparable with the highly mechanised, rigid constitution of the Republic which followed. The Prefect alone had anything in the nature of definite ordered functions attached to his office. Naturally the citizens had no voice in the government. Their political activities were limited to membership of the civic militia and the various gild-companies to which they belonged by virtue of their trade or profession.[4] They had thus no political institution in which their ripening political instinct could find expression. Their only hope of obtaining a share in the government of the city lay in overturning the papal régime and erecting upon its ruins a self-governing commune modelled on those of the Lombard cities.

But just here arose a second difficulty. The backbone of the Lombard commune was invariably that strong and numerous class of artisans which had risen to power and

[1] Vacandard, p. 73.   [2] Halphen, p. 31.
[3] Ibid. pp. 34 seq.   [4] Gregorovius, IV, p. 456.

prosperity through the extension of trade and the development of manufactures. At Rome there was no such class, and little industry or commerce to promote its existence. Both her historical antecedents and geographical position precluded the possibility. The total population was surprisingly small for her size and the burgher class which usually provided the most effective bulwark for the commune was of no outstanding numerical strength. In fact the initial revolt against the Pope was due to a coalition between the burghers and the lesser nobility. It is exceedingly doubtful whether the former could have struck so severe a blow unaided.[1]

The revolution had its origin in a dispute between the Romans and the neighbouring town of Tivoli occasioned by the papal schism of 1130. The Tivolese remained to the end staunch supporters of Anacletus, whilst in 1137 the Romans had become reconciled to the mild rule of Innocent II. In 1140 the smouldering jealousy between the two towns flared up into open war. For some unexplained reason Tivoli rejected the Roman claim to suzerainty. In June 1142 a Roman force sent to reduce the obdurate city to submission suffered an ignominious defeat at the hands of the rebel townsmen. Smarting under the indignity Innocent II despatched the year following a second and larger army. This expedition was successful. Tivoli was compelled to submit, but the astute Pope, with an eye to future needs, granted generous terms and refused to permit the destruction of the city's walls and a wholesale massacre of its inhabitants for which the Romans clamoured. At news of this concordat the fury of the Romans knew no bounds. Rushing to the Capitol the citizens renounced the papal authority, set up a new government with an order of Senators and prepared to resume the war

---

[1] Gregorovius, IV, p. 461. Paolucci, op. cit. pp. 671–2.

against Tivoli.[1] Innocent found himself powerless to stem
the tide of revolution and retired to the Lateran, where he
died the same year (24th September 1143) in vexation of
spirit.[2] It was an inglorious ending to a more than usually
troubled reign. Celestine II in his short pontificate
(September 1143 to March 1144) did nothing to quell the
revolt, and soon after the accession of Lucius II the
revolution was consummated by the abolition of the office
of Prefect and the appointment of a *patricius* (June 1144).
To this office was elected Jordan, son of Peter Leonis and
nephew of the anti-Pope Anacletus.[3]

The Roman Republic was inaugurated. It was a formidable blow aimed at the temporal power of the Popes,
similar in a general way to the step by which the Lombard
cities had won freedom from the temporal power of
bishops. Yet the resultant situation at Rome was vastly
different. There the bishop was also Pope and his claim to
political sovereignty rested on something more than a mere
feudal contract initiated in the chaos of the Dark Ages. It
had the imposing tradition of a supposedly sacred origin,
fortified by an honoured pedigree tracing itself back
through the historical Donations of Charles the Great and
Pippin to the mythical Donation of Constantine. Such was
the strength which the papal claim drew from the roots of
the past, and its validity seemed to be confirmed by contemporary political theory. It was an age when men conceived of the spiritual and the secular not as two separate, if
contingent, societies but as one and the same *Respublica*

[1] Otto of Freising, *Chron.* lib. VII, cap. xxvii (S.G.U.S. pp. 352–3).
Boso, "Vita Innocentii II" in Watterich, *Pont. Roman.* II, p. 179.
Godfrey of Viterbo, *Pantheon*, Muratori, Script. VII, p. 460.

[2] Jaffé-Loewenfeld, I, p. 911.

[3] Otto of Freising, *Chron.* lib. VII, cap. xxxi, p. 359. Romuald
Salern. *Chron.* VI, M.G.H. XIX, col. 424. *Hist. pont.* cap. xxvii, p. 60.
It is interesting to note the election of a noble to this office, thus
preserving a continuity of civic traditions. See p. 105, n. 2.

Christiana, wherein Pope and Emperor acquired each in his respective office the indelible sanction of Divine authority. Whence it followed that any attempt to subvert the Pope's temporal power equally threatened the prerogative of the Emperor. Further, looking at the question from the lower plane of political expediency, no Emperor of statesmanlike vision could view with equanimity the institution of a republican régime in his capital. Mediaeval political theory abhorred a republic much as Nature in the eighteenth century was said to abhor a vacuum. It is indeed remarkable that the leaders of the movement failed to recognise this unpalatable truth and clung pathetically to the hope that the Emperor would intervene on their side. The first acts of the new government were not calculated to bring this hope nearer to realisation. For the abolition of the Prefect and the establishment in his place of a *patricius*, invested with the temporal rights and prerogatives of the Popes (*regalia beati Petri*),[1] and thus made an office with definite functions attached instead of being largely a titular dignity as hitherto,[2] were significant of the lofty claim to political independence which the new régime upheld.

It cannot be said that our information for this early stage of the movement is as complete as could be

---

[1] *Hist. pont.* p. 50. Cf. Otto of Freising, *Chron.* op. cit.: "Omnia regalia ejus (pontificis)...ad jus Patricii reposcunt".

[2] The title "patricius" was customarily bestowed on a certain class of officials under the Roman Empire, notably provincial governors. It was retained on the break-up of the Empire in the West, being held *ex officio* by the Byzantine Exarchs of Ravenna. It was then extended as a token of honour to various barbarian chieftains, e.g. Odoacer, Theodoric and Clovis. Under the style of *patricius Romanorum* it was conferred by the Popes on Pippin and Charlemagne. See Ducange, *Gloss. ad Script.* VI, col. 214 seq.; Bryce, *Holy Roman Empire*, pp. 40 seq. It was usurped by Crescentius in 985 and by his son, John, in 1002. In 1046 Henry III annexed the title to the Imperial dignity. Gregorovius, III, p. 400, IV, pp. 5, 56, 64–6.

desired. Nor is the case improved by Otto of Freising's account in the *Gesta Frederici*, where Arnold of Brescia is made the protagonist and real author of the republican constitution.[1]

The charge is plainly baseless; on chronological grounds alone it is impossible for Arnold to have taken part in this purely political movement. At the time when the structure of the republican constitution was being raised, Arnold, as we have seen, was away beyond the Alps enjoying the patronage of Cardinal Guido. Otto wrote far removed from the scene of strife and in all probability some years later than the events he purports to record.[2] Further, in the larger and more substantial account of them found in his other work, the *Chronica*, Arnold's name is nowhere mentioned.[3] Moreover, there is the significant fact of St Bernard's silence in two letters of the date 1145 or 1146 which were occasioned by the Roman troubles, one addressed to the Roman people and the other to Conrad III.[4] It is scarcely credible that the zealous saint would have neglected to proclaim the latest crime of his enemy had he any suspicion that Arnold was in the slightest degree implicated in the movement.[5] Finally, the precision of John of Salisbury's narrative of the reconciliation at Viterbo, coupled with the established fact that he was at

[1] "His diebus Arnaldus...urbem Romam ingreditur ac senatoriam dignitatem equestremque ordinem renovare ad instar antiquorum volens totam pene urbem ac precipue populum adversus pontificem suum concitavit"—*Gesta Fred.* lib. I, p. 44. Cf. ibid. lib. II, cap. xxviii, p. 134.

[2] The *Gesta Fred.* is carried down to the date 1156; the continuation is by Rahewin.

[3] Otto of Freising, *Chron.* lib. VII, caps. xxxi and xxxiv, pp. 357–60, 367. This work is carried down to January 1146, and may therefore be regarded as a contemporary narrative. Cf. Poole, Preface, p. lxiv; Giesebrecht, p. 19.

[4] Bern. Ep. 243, 244. The allusion to Arnold made in Migne's heading to Ep. 243 is not warranted by its contents. Poole, loc. cit.

[5] Cf. Giesebrecht, p. 20; De Castro, pp. 360 seq.

this time in the papal employ,[1] disposes of the charge altogether.

Meanwhile with every passing month the revolution gained ground and Pope Lucius II—a man of prudence and power—so his biographer terms him,[2] found himself impotent to retrieve the papal fortunes. Already before the establishment of Jordan Pierleone as *patricius* Lucius had made a vain appeal for aid to the German king.[3] Conrad of Hohenstaufen, faced with disaffection and rebellion at home, was in no position to undertake an arduous Italian expedition, even had he been so minded. Overtures, which the Pope opened with the Norman king, Roger of Sicily, met with a more favourable response.[4] Fortified with a band of Sicilian mercenaries Lucius and the dispossessed nobles thought to crush the commune by armed force (February 1145), but the expedition miscarried badly. The papal army besieging the Capitol was decisively repulsed by the citizens and, according to one account, the Vicar of Christ himself was mortally wounded by stones hurled at him during the battle.[5]

---

[1] See Appendix I, pp. 207–8.

[2] "Vir prudens et fortis"—Boso, "Vita Lucii II", Watterich, II, p. 279. Cf. Otto of Freising, *Chron.* pp. 357 seq.; "Vir pro mansuetudine et humilitate sui officio sacerdotali dignus."

[3] The letter is no longer extant. The fact of the appeal is known from Otto of Freising, op. cit.; Jaffé-Loewenfeld, *Regesta*, No. 8684.

[4] Romuald Salern. loc. cit. ante.

[5] "Lucius secundus itaque intendens senatum extinguere, cum ingenti militia Capitolium Romae conscendit, ut sedentes ibi tunc senatores cum dedecore removeret. Senatus autem Populusque Romanus ad arma conversus, Papam cum suis omnibus a Capitolio in momento repellunt. Ubi Papa (sicut tunc audivimus) lapidibus magnis percussus, usque ad obitus sui diem, qui proxime sequutus est, non sedet in sede"—Godfrey of Viterbo, Muratori, Script. VII, col. 461. Other chroniclers (e.g. Boso, "Vita Lucii", op. cit.; Sigebert, *Continuatio Praemonstratensis*, M.G.H. Script. VI, p. 453), though they record the attack on the Capitol, give no indication that Lucius died other than a natural death. Godfrey's account is to be received with great caution in view of his qualifying *ut dicitur* phrase.

His successor, Eugenius III, was the Cistercian monk, Bernard of Pisa, now Abbot of St Vincent and St Anastasius. He was one of St Bernard's best beloved pupils, and by his elevation to the Holy See the reforming ideas of the Abbot of Clairvaux gained control of the administration of the Church. Yet at a time so critical many doubted the wisdom of the cardinals' choice.[1] The situation seemed to them to call more for an experienced statesman than for a scholar or a saint. And Bernard of Pisa was a monk of simple graces and unaffected piety, wholly unversed in the art of politics. He had resigned his position as *vice-Dominus* to the Bishop of Pisa on the double ground of a supposed ineptitude for the work of episcopal administration and the desire for a life of prayer and contemplation within the cloister. Men might well ask how a man who had felt himself unable to manage diocesan affairs could be expected to cope with the difficulties and dangers of ecclesiastical politics. Even St Bernard, whilst legitimately gratified that a member of the Cistercian Order had at last attained the papal throne, echoed the prevailing sentiments. In his letter to the cardinals upon receipt of news of the election the saint expresses grave doubts as to the wisdom of their choice. How is it possible, he asks in effect, for a man of mild and angelic disposition, with a taste for spiritual meditation, who has once renounced the vanities and perplexities of the world, to fulfil the arduous task of the care of all the churches and the administrative duties of the Apostolic See? Like the man going down from Jerusalem to Jericho he will fall among thieves. Yet the saint comforts both himself and his readers with the reflection that this hasty act may prove to be a miracle, comparable with

[1] The election of a comparatively unknown man came as a surprise to all. A curious parallel is found in the election of Celestine V in 1294. Yet the choice was unanimous. Cf. Boso, " Vita Eugenii ", Watterich, II, p. 281 : " Hic electus est . . . ex insperato concorditer. " Bern. Ep. 237, col. 426.

that of old when God took David from among the sheep-folds to set him as king over Israel.[1]

If not indicative of a miracle, the history of Eugenius' pontificate certainly dispelled all gloomy forebodings, and proved incidentally that St Bernard had understood the Pope's character no better than other observers. Eugenius is an excellent example of a man of average ability who, when summoned to high office in the Church, managed to fill it not unworthily by judicious exercise of his talents and careful husbandry of his resources. He made no pretence to genius; he excelled neither as an administrator nor as a theologian. Too often in practical affairs he was inclined to trust to his own opinion when it would have been more prudent to have followed the guidance of experts. Yet he was saved from numerous blunders by his natural shrewd-ness. His judgment of men was seldom at fault and he in-stinctively chose the right man for a post. Add to this a tenacity of purpose, which remained unshaken by succes-sive defeats and disappointments, and his remarkable success becomes a little more intelligible. Above all he was wise enough to profit by his own experience, and this trait counteracted to a considerable degree the initial dis-advantage accruing from his lack of political training. His private virtues were doubly conspicuous in an age when the corruption of Roman administration was becoming proverbial among the Transalpine Churches. Upright and loyal, gentle and forbearing, he practised amidst the worldly environment of the Curia that self-denying piety which he had learned within the cloister. His personal fame remained unsullied to the last, and, though he was never canonised, his memory was cherished with affection by all who dreamed of reviving the primitive simplicity of Apostolic times.

In one respect Eugenius was more fortunate than his

[1] Bern. Ep. 237, col. 425 seq.

predecessors, for it was to him that St Bernard dedicated his "golden book, *De Consideratione*", a kind of political text-book for Popes.[1] It is not easy to gauge how far Eugenius' general policy was moulded by the reforming ideas contained in this work. The frequency of personal intercourse between Pope and abbot, maintained unbroken to the end of the pontificate, is a clear indication of a definite interaction of ideas and opinions. Moreover, the popular view of the relationship was so mistaken that men spoke openly of the Pope as a mere puppet in the hands of the Cistercian Order, ascribing to the Abbot of Clairvaux the real authorship of papal policy. So much we learn from Bernard's own remark. "They say", he writes to Eugenius, "that it is I who am Pope not you, and all who have business crowd in on me from every side."[2] It was scarcely an exaggeration; Clairvaux became for a time almost a department of the Curia.[3]

The desperate situation, with which the Papacy was faced, called for a high degree of statesmanship, and Eugenius was not found wanting. With rare insight he perceived that the Roman commune was no mere transient expression of the spirit of revolution, but a well-organised constitutional movement based on public opinion, and that in consequence any attempt to subdue it by force of arms was foredoomed to failure. The fact was that the Papacy as a political institution had forfeited the respect of its subjects. Untold damage had been dealt to its prestige by the long and sordid struggle between Innocent II and Anacletus. Till this was in a measure repaired there could be no prospect of security for the Temporal Power. Certainly the cause was not well served by the spectacle of the

[1] Gregorovius, IV, p. 492.
[2] "Aiunt non vos esse Papam, sed me: et undique ad me confluunt, qui habent negotia"—Bern. Ep. 239, col. 431.
[3] Vacandard, *St Bernard*, II, p. 260.

Vicar of Christ, the *servus servorum Dei*, at the head of an army of mercenaries, bent on the recovery of his patrimony like any secular lord dispossessed of his demesne. That had been the mistake of Lucius II. Eugenius' plan was to restore the fallen dignity of the papal chair by the subtler yet surer weapon of diplomacy, to adopt wherever possible a conciliatory attitude, to widen the cleavage already visible in the ranks of the republicans, and to win over the more moderate men to his side by a discriminating liberality of favours and timely appeals to their own interest. The traditional maxim *Divide et impera* provides a not un-fitting epitome of his policy. But this was not all. He strove to counterbalance weakness at home by a close alliance with the friendly monarchs beyond the Alps, more particularly with the French king.

On the very day of his election a fresh tumult broke out in Rome. The militant citizens demanded from him a formal renunciation of his temporal rights and the re-cognition of the commune. The Pope gave an indignant refusal, but on the third day the threatening attitude of the populace forced him to retire secretly to Farfa where his coronation took place.[1] Two months later (15th April 1145) he removed to Viterbo whence he issued a ban of excommunication against Pierleone, the *patricius*, and con-cluded an alliance with Tivoli and the barons of the Roman *contado*.[2] Meanwhile at Rome a veritable reign of terror was in progress. The infuriated mob sacked the palaces of the cardinals and the castles of the nobles, and the churches were the scene of frightful sacrilege. Pilgrims were robbed of their offerings and even slain in the porches.[3] These excesses could hardly fail to alienate the more

[1] *Annales Casinenses*, M.G.H. XIX, col. 310.
[2] Boso, Watterich, II, pp. 282 seq. Otto of Freising, *Chron.* p. 360. Jaffé-Loewenfeld, II, p. 22.
[3] Otto of Freising, op. cit.

moderate men in the commune, and in face of the formidable coalition which Eugenius had gathered round him
the Republic found it expedient to come to terms. A compromise was effected whereby the Pope agreed to recognise
the Senate subject to its members acknowledging their
powers to be dependent upon him, and on condition that
the Romans abolished the *patricius*, restored the Prefect
and admitted the validity of the Temporal Power.[1] A
treaty embodying these provisions was drawn up and signed
in December 1145, and before Christmas Eugenius was
able to return to Rome. His procession to the Lateran was
something of a triumph. A vast multitude assembled to
greet him, strewing branches of trees before him, amidst
every sign of genuine welcome.[2] But the prospect of a
peaceful residence within the city proved an illusion.
Within a month the old Roman hostility towards Tivoli,
the papal ally, rekindled into flame the smouldering embers of the revolution.[3] In March 1146 the unhappy Pope
was again a fugitive at Sutri[4] and the republican institutions
were fully restored.

It was at this critical juncture that the indefatigable
Abbot of Clairvaux, in whose hands the pen was truly
mightier than the sword, placed his inimitable power of
rhetoric at the service of his papal protégé. His famous
letter of 1146 addressed to the Roman people[5] is possibly

---

[1] "At Eugenius cum Romanis hoc tenore pacem fecit ut patriciatus
dignitatem exfestucarent et prefectum in pristinam dignitatem re-
ciperent, senatores vero ex ejus auctoritate tenerent"—Otto of Freising,
Chron. p. 367.
[2] Boso, Watterich, II, p. 283.
[3] Otto of Freising, op. cit.
[4] Jaffé-Loewenfeld, 8895.
[5] Bern. Ep. 243, col. 437 seq. It is not easy to fix the date with
certainty. Vacandard (*St Bernard*, II, pp. 261 seq.; *R.Q.H.* loc. cit.
pp. 77 seq.) places it in 1145 before Eugenius' first return to Rome.
Gregorovius (IV, p. 506) and Hausrath (pp. 94 seq.) following Migne
give 1146, subsequent to Eugenius' second flight to Sutri.

the most extraordinary document in all his correspondence. The letter opens in a strain of mock humility and fulsome flattery[1] which, though to some extent it should be discounted as a convention of the age, scarcely prepares the reader for the penetrating analysis of the crimes and follies of the Romans given in the body of the letter. Here the saint piles Pelion upon Ossa in an endeavour to exhaust the catalogue of their offences. The city, which their ancestors made mistress of the world, they, the Romans of to-day, hasten to make a by-word.[2] They have driven Peter's heir from Peter's See; they have laid sacrilegious hands on the prerogatives and privileges of the Holy See, when it should properly have been their pride and their duty to defend them against the whole world. Now Rome is a headless trunk, a face without eyes, a darkened countenance; for was not the Pope their head, and the cardinals their eyes? And it is to be feared that this is but the beginning of evils and that worse is to come.[3] On their heads alone be their iniquities; the rest of the world is guiltless of their blood. Now is taught more plainly the truth of Our Lord's prophecy that a man's foes shall be they of his own

[1] "Sermo mihi est ad te, popule sublimis et illustris, cum sim vilis exiguaque persona, ac nullius pene momenti homuncio. Id quidem verecundum atque onerosum mihi consideranti quis quibus scribam, simulque quam aliter hoc alius judicare possit...sane non vereor, quamvis verecundia reluctante pro mea ignobilitate scribere de longinquo ad populum gloriosum, atque his litteris transmontanis sui ipsorum periculi atque peccati commonere Romanos si forte audiant, et quiescant....Ita nunc quoque, etsi adolescentulus sum ego et contemptus (adolescentulus dico, non annorum paucitate, sed meritorum), potens est tamen Deus dare etiam voci meae vocem virtutis, per quam fiat ut et is populus, quem nihilominus constat esse seductum, ad judicium revertatur"—Bern. Ep. 243, col. 438.

[2] "Patres vestri Urbi orbem subjugaverunt, vos Urbem properatis facere fabulam"—Bern. loc. cit. col. 439.

[3] "Nonne ille caput, et illi oculi tui erant? Quid ergo Roma, nisi sine capite truncum corpus, sine oculis frons effossa, facies tenebrosa?...Verum initia malorum haec: graviora timemus"—Bern. loc. cit.

household. There follows a series of passionate entreaties. Let the scattered sheep return to their pastures, to the Shepherd and Bishop of their souls. Let them be reconciled to their true princes, Peter and Paul, whom, in the person of their vicar and successor, Eugenius, they have driven from hearth and home. Let them be reconciled to the thousands of martyrs who are with them, yet against them because of the enormity of their sins, and to the whole company of saints whom they have scandalised by such conduct. Otherwise the very page of his letter will rise up as witness against them.[1]

As the Abbé Vacandard finely remarks, "la lettre s'achève dans un sanglot et une prière".[2] It is scarcely credible that the hearts of the Romans could remain untouched by such plaintive eloquence. Yet we search in vain for any concrete results, and Bernard himself laboured under no illusion as to their true character. In his letter of the same year to Conrad, the German king, appealing for military aid in the restoration of the Pope's temporal power, he uses language of a very different order, describing them as men whose pride and arrogance far exceed their courage, an accursed and turbulent people, which knows not how to measure its forces, to reflect upon its object or to weigh an issue.[3] Even more outspoken is the characterisation given of them in the *De Consideratione* —"What shall I say concerning this people?" he writes to Eugenius. "It is the Roman people. Impossible to express more briefly or plainly what I feel about your flock. What is more widely known than the impudence and pride of the Romans? It is a people unacquainted with

[1] "Alioquin pagina ista contra te in testimonium erit"—Bern. loc. cit. col. 440.

[2] Vacandard, *St Bernard*, II, p. 264.

[3] "Superbia et arrogantia Romanorum plus quam fortitudo eorum ...populus hic maledictus et tumultuosus qui suas nescit metiri vires, cogitare finem, considerare proventum"—Bern. Ep. 244, col. 442.

peace and accustomed to violence, a savage and unruly people,...hateful to earth and heaven, lifting up hands against both, impious towards God and heedless of sacred things, seditious among themselves, envious of their neighbours and inhuman towards strangers, loving no man and winning no man's love, desiring all the world to stand in awe of them they must needs fear all the world, unable to endure the rule of others, yet knowing not how to rule themselves, faithless to their superiors, insufferable towards their subjects. Their speech is of great things but their deeds are trifling. Bountiful in promises and niggardly in performance, wheedling flatterers and biting slanderers, open dissemblers and malignant traitors."[1] There can be no doubt that these two passages taken together give a sure index of the saint's real opinions.

Meanwhile in the East a calamity far greater than the destruction of the Pope's temporal power had befallen the Church. The loss of Edessa to the Moslems in 1144 opened the eyes of Christendom to the new peril confronting the Latin kingdom of Jerusalem, and fears were entertained for the Holy City itself. Preparations were hastily set on foot for a new Crusade. St Bernard went on a great missionary tour in France and Germany, and in March 1147 Eugenius III, following in his steps, departed

---

[1] "Quid de populo loquar? Populus Romanus est. Nec brevius potuit, nec expressius tamen aperire de tuis parochianis quod sentio. Quid tam notum saeculis, quam protervia et fastus Romanorum? Gens insueta paci, tumultui assueta, gens immitis et intractabilis.... Hi invisi terrae et coelo; utrique injecere manus, impii in Deum, temerarii in sancta, seditiosi in invicem, aemuli in vicinos, inhumani in extraneos; quos neminem amantes amat nemo, et cum timeri affectant ab omnibus, omnes timeant necesse est. Hi sunt qui subesse non sustinent, praeesse non norunt, superioribus infideles, inferioribus importabiles....Docuerunt linguam suam grandia loqui, cum operentur exigua. Largissimi promissores et parvissimi exhibitores; blandissimi adulatores, et mordacissimi detractores; simplicissimi dissimulatores et malignissimi proditores"—*De Consid.* lib. IV, cap. ii, col. 773 seq. Cf. *Hist. pont.* cap. xl, p. 82.

to France to superintend the recruiting of the crusading armies.[1] This enterprise absorbed the greater part of the Pope's energies for the next two years and in Rome the commune was left in undisputed control.

The new constitution is a curious illustration of the confusion present in the minds of the mediaeval Romans. New institutions and new offices, which sprang naturally from the administrative needs of the day, were given titles which suggested a continuity with those of the Republic of classical times. Such was the prevailing ignorance of Rome's past history that the authors of the new constitution may have believed the continuity to be true. Or possibly the choice of such names was intended to strengthen the new government by placing it on a supposedly historic foundation. If so it was a poor attempt. "In this curious phantom of ancient times", writes Gregorovius, "the name alone was Roman, the character was new."[2] The keystone of the edifice was the Senate. Its members were the chief officers of the commune, and as a body it was vested with legislative, executive and judicial powers, the right of making war or peace and of coining money.[3] It was not, however, absolute sovereign, since it was ultimately responsible for its actions to the whole body of citizens assembled in the *parliamentum*, by whom its decrees required ratification. The latter had merely the right to accept or refuse *in toto* and not to debate or amend proposals. In addition there was a smaller council (*concilium urbis*) whose function was largely probouleutic and thus acted in some degree as a check on hasty legislation.[4] The majority of senators sprang from the burgher class, and this gave the institution a democratic cast, which it succeeded in retaining despite a steady influx of nobles, who from policy or ambition threw in their lot with the com-

[1] Jaffé-Loewenfeld, II, p. 39.
[3] Halphen, op. cit. pp. 61–2.

[2] Gregorovius, IV, p. 496.
[4] Ibid. pp. 63–4.

mune.[1] The number of its members remained variable throughout the twelfth century. In 1151 there were fifty, but by the end of the century the number seems to have been fixed at fifty-six.[2] Every year, apparently in November,[3] a fresh election took place, the members being chosen by the vote of the citizens. They were divided into two groups, senators-in-ordinary (*senatores*) and senator-councillors (*senatores consiliarii*), the latter a small group, twelve in number, forming a kind of executive committee and renewed in personnel every six months.[4] Connected with the Senate were a number of permanent officials engaged in administrative work, of whom the chancellor was chief. There was also a *Curia Senatus* composed of legal experts and charged with the administration of civil justice.[5]

It will be seen at once from this account how greatly the powers claimed and exercised by the Senate entrenched on the authority of the Prefect,[6] and doubtless it was for this reason that the Popes strained every nerve to secure the restoration of that office, a feat accomplished by Eugenius III in his concordat with the Romans in 1145. In general the new constitution resembled those of the contemporary republics of Lombardy far more than that of ancient Rome. It was grounded on the political independence of the burgher class and not on the traditional privileges of the aristocracy. Not till the succeeding century did the nobles acquire a monopoly of political power; in its origin the Republic was the concrete expression of a democratic

---

[1] Gregorovius, IV, pp. 496–7.
[2] Halphen, p. 66.
[3] "Innovationem senatorum qui in kalendis Novembribus urbis regimen accepturi sunt"—Joannis Saresber. Ep. 261, col. 302, M.P.L. 199. Halphen, pp. 68–9.
[4] Halphen, pp. 67 seq.
[5] Gregorovius, IV, p. 499.
[6] Cf. H. K. Mann, *Lives of Popes in Middle Ages*, IX, p. 150.

impulse. Yet it was a forced, artificial plant rooted in alien soil rather than one of natural growth. Unlike the northern communes it was not a product of a historical necessity; it had no root in past traditions and, though some of its features maintained a stubborn existence for a long period, they were kept alive more by a mere negative antagonism to the temporal power of the Popes than by a positive aim or a true creative instinct. Consequently with the removal of the particular local circumstances responsible for its inception it fell an easy prey to the combined onslaught of Pope and Emperor.

Before this, however, it enjoyed a glorious, if brief, career with which Arnold's name is inseparably connected. In effect the coming of Arnold to Rome gave it a coherence of form and a unity of purpose which, it is safe to hazard, it would otherwise have lacked.

Chapter VIII

ARNOLD, THE PAPACY AND THE
ROMAN REPUBLIC

IT would be far easier to form a satisfactory judgment on Arnold's Roman career if more were known of the terms of his reconciliation with Eugenius III at Viterbo. John of Salisbury is our sole witness to the fact, and concise and lucid though his narrative is, it leaves one or two points of interest and importance unexplained. "Returning to Italy", writes John, "he promised satisfaction and obedience to the Roman Church and was received by the Lord Eugenius at Viterbo. A penance of fasting, vigils and prayers in the holy places of Rome was imposed on him, and this he agreed to fulfil. Further, he swore a solemn oath of obedience."[1] We are not told, be it observed, what were the errors for which Arnold made satisfaction, whether they were the proscribed tenets of Abailard, which he had sponsored at Sens, or his own doctrine of evangelical poverty, which he had tried to impose on the clergy at Brescia. The ban of Sens, however, was now lifted and the returned prodigal received back into the bosom of the Church.

We are next faced with a problem regarding the oath which John mentions in connection with the episode. What actually did it imply? Did Arnold forswear his previous opinions on the nature of the Church and his teaching on the incompatibility of spiritual functions with material possessions? If so there is no escaping the fact

---

[1] "Reversus est in Italiam et promissa satisfactione et obediencia Romane ecclesie a domino Eugenio receptus est apud Viterbum. Iniuncta est ei penitentia, quam se in ieiuniis, vigiliis et orationibus circa loca sancta que in urbe sunt professus est esse facturum et quidem de servanda obediencia sollempne perstitit iuramentum"—*Hist. pont.* loc. cit. ante.

that his subsequent actions constitute a grave breach of faith, since it cannot be maintained that there is in principle any difference between his teaching in Rome and that of former days in Brescia or on the Mont Ste Geneviève. Yet there is sufficient room for doubt whether this is a correct interpretation of John's remark. Two considerations suggest that it is not. First, so complete a surrender of his convictions seems quite out of keeping with what we know of Arnold's character. It is almost incredible that the man, who had willingly suffered banishment rather than subscribe to the decree of Sens, should now suddenly, and with no immediate advantage to be gained, make an abject submission to papal authority. Such a view would only be tenable by postulating with the Abbé Vacandard Arnold's definite "conversion" during his stay with Cardinal Guido,[1] but his subsequent history points to a decisive rejection of this hypothesis. Secondly, it is equally inconceivable that his enemies would have let slip such a tempting opportunity as this of heaping further opprobrium upon his character. Yet nowhere, not even in the rescript of 1148, which Eugenius despatched to the Roman clergy, do we get the slightest hint that a charge of perjury was afterwards laid against him. No doubt John is correct in ascribing to Arnold some form of oath, but there is no proof that its terms bound him to forswear his cardinal tenets on Church reform.[2]

The date of Arnold's arrival in Rome is unknown, but, since a pilgrimage to the churches there formed part of his penance, it may be conjectured that he repaired thither immediately after his reception at Viterbo. This provision, it may be observed, is one of the few impolitic acts of Eugenius during his difficult and stormy pontificate. It was at the least imprudent to facilitate Arnold's presence

[1] Vacandard, p. 71.
[2] Cf. Breyer, op. cit. pp. 149 seq. on the subject.

in Rome at a time when the city was seething with discontent. At first, however, the reformer seems to have confined himself to the scrupulous fulfilment of the papal
injunctions,[1] and not till Eugenius went to France in 1147
do we find him taking any part in affairs. Then he appears
as an itinerant preacher with a large personal following
known as the "heresy of the Lombards", which took him
as a pattern in works of piety and asceticism. In particular
he gained for adherents certain women of a devout turn of
mind, and the nascent faith of these simple believers was
nourished by frequent sermons on the Capitol and public
disputations.[2]

It is clear from John of Salisbury's account that Arnold
was not at first even remotely connected with the republican movement. As Dr Poole puts it: "Arnold did not
at that time work as a political agitator but as a religious
teacher".[3] But he was not for long content to preach his
gospel by his own example.

Once again fervid appeals for a return to apostolic
poverty were mingled with inflammatory tirades against
the iniquity of prelates. In particular he launched a
scathing attack on the Pope and the College of Cardinals.
The latter, he taught, filled with pride and avarice, with
hypocrisy and every kind of vice, was not the Church of
God, but a house of merchandise and a den of thieves,
harassing Christian men like the scribes and Pharisees of

---

[1] It is not clear what Gregorovius (p. 502) means by his assertion
that Arnold "lived in concealment".

[2] "Dum sub optentu penitentis Rome degeret, urbem sibi con-
ciliavit, et domino papa agente in Galliis liberius predicans hominum
sectam fecit que adhuc dicitur heresis Lumbardorum. Habuit enim
continentie sectatores, qui propter honestatis speciem et austeritatem
vite placebant populo sed maximum apud religiosas feminas invenie-
bant subsidium. Ipse frequenter in Capitolio et in publicis contionibus
audiebatur"—*Hist. pont.* p. 65. "Religiosas feminas" may denote
nuns or members of a sisterhood.

[3] Preface, *Hist. pont.* p. lxiv. Cf. pp. lxviii and lxix.

old. The Pope himself, far from being as he professed a
man of apostolic life and a shepherd of souls, was a man of
blood who gave sanction for acts of incendiarism and
murder, the torturer of the churches and oppressor of innocence, whose sole concern was to glut his appetite and
to fill his coffers by draining those of others. Furthermore,
since the Apostolic Vicar had so far fallen away from the
Apostles' example and teaching, men ought no longer to
pay him obedience or reverence.[1]

Such teaching, it must be confessed, came perilously
near a total rejection of papal authority. It was but a short
step from the denial of the Pope's claim to temporal power
to a refusal of obedience to him as spiritual overlord.
Indeed this was the logical outcome of Arnold's earlier
teaching at Brescia on the sinfulness of monks and secular
clergy who held property and of bishops who retained the
regalia. It is a matter for deep regret that John of Salisbury's concise résumé of Arnold's tenets breaks off abruptly
at this point, so that we have no means of observing his
transition from expounding a gospel of reform to acquies-
cence in the political programme of the Roman commune.[2]

One significant factor in the situation deserves notice
here. The movement which Arnold inaugurated in Rome

[1] "Iam palam cardinalibus detrahebat dicens conventum eorum ex
causa superbie et avaricie ypocrisis et multimode turpitudinis non esse
ecclesiam Dei sed domum negociationis et speluncam latronum qui
scribarum et Phariseorum vices exercent in populo Christiano. Ipsum
papam non esse quod profitetur apostolicum virum et animarum
pastorem, sed virum sanguinum qui incendiis et homicidiis prestat
auctoritatem, tortorem ecclesiarum, innocentie concussorem, qui nihil
aliud facit in mundo quam carnem pascere et suos replere loculos et
exhaurire alienos. Dicebat quod sic apostolicus est, ut non apostolorum
doctrinam imitetur aut vitam et ideo ei obedientiam aut reverentiam
non deberi"—*Hist. pont.* op. cit.

[2] "Deshalb ist es durchaus falsch, in Arnold den Führer dieser
Revolution oder gar den Urheber derselben zu sehen.... Arnold war
nicht der Urheber der Revolution, er war aber von bestimmendem
Einfluss auf den Gang der selben"—Breyer, p. 160.

was not exclusively lay in character. The sequel proves that he derived substantial support from the ranks of the lower clergy. In this respect Rome witnessed a repetition of a prominent feature of the Patarin strife in Lombardy. Once again the raising of the standard of reform ranged the lower clergy against the hierarchy. As Gregorovius has pointed out, the factor chiefly responsible for the division of parties along these lines was Arnold's proclamation of the spiritual equality of the priesthood.[1]

Meanwhile in June 1148 Eugenius had returned to Italy,[2] and while halting at Vercelli the rumour of Arnold's latest exploit and the defection of the Roman clergy reached his ears. By easy stages he removed to Brescia, and from thence, Arnold's own city, he issued a bull in which the reformer was again branded as a schismatic and the Roman clergy forbidden to enter into relations with him on pain of loss of benefice and deprivation of priestly office.[3] The effect of this rescript on its recipients is not fully known. It is conceivable that the Pope's timely warning, coupled with the dire penalties threatened at the close, succeeded in detaching from Arnold's party a few of the more moderate men among the Roman clergy. Be that as it may, for Arnold's own position the publication of the edict was an event of the first magnitude, the decisive

[1] Gregorovius, IV, p. 505.
[2] Jaffé-Loewenfeld, 9271.
[3] "Fallax et invidus humani generis inimicus per Arnaldum schismaticum, quasi per membrum proprium hoc effecit, ut quidam capellani unitatem Ecclesiae, quae sectionem non patitur, quantum in eis est, dividentes, ipsius Arnaldi sequantur errorem, et cardinalibus atque archipresbyteris suis obedientiam et reverentiam promittere et exhibere debitam contradicant...igitur...per praesentia vobis scripta mandamus atque praecipimus quatenus praefatum Arnaldum tanquam schismaticum modis omnibus devitetis. Quod si aliqui clerici, Dei et sanctae Ecclesiae contemptores, ejus errorem post praesentium acceptionem sequi praesumpserint, scire volumus quia tam officio quam beneficio ecclesiastico reddemus eos penitus alienos"—M.P.L. 180, col. 1358.

factor determining the future direction of his policy. Casting scruples to the winds and forsaking the spirit of compromise, which so ill suited his character, he boldly crossed the Rubicon of his career. The two movements, which had hitherto existed side by side but independent one of the other, now coalesced into one. The agitation for ecclesiastical reform born of Arnold's vigorous preaching came to reinforce the original revolt of the commune against the Pope as temporal overlord.[1] Henceforward Arnold himself assumed a dual rôle of religious teacher and political demagogue, and it was in the second capacity rather than the first that he was a menace to the peace of the Church.[2]

There is much in Gregorovius' description of Arnold as "a popular tribune in the habit of the priest",[3] and it is easy to show that from this time forward his teaching becomes more and more entangled in the web of politics. Yet this is largely because of the impossibility of separating the religious issue from the secular. To assert that the former is entirely dwarfed by the latter would rob his career of any measure of consistency and vitiate the attempt to form an accurate judgment of his policy. It should also be remembered that during his alliance with the commune he had continually to re-shape his programme in order to keep abreast of the rapid changes in the political situation.

The Republic was by now in dire straits. In 1149 it had with difficulty withstood yet another attempt to subdue it by armed force. For once Eugenius abandoned his policy of conciliation and endeavoured to take the city by

[1] "Seitdem ging Arnold und der Senat, die kirchliche und die politische Revolution in Rom Hand in Hand"—Giesebrecht, p. 21. Cf. De Castro, p. 421.

[2] Doubtless Arnold considered himself freed from his oath at Viterbo by the papal sentence of excommunication. *Hist. pont.* p. 63.

[3] Gregorovius, IV, p. 480.

storm. Possibly he concluded that the desperate character of the situation called for heroic measures, or possibly this was one of the rare occasions when he allowed his better judgment to be overridden by his counsellors in the Curia.

In April 1149 he had moved from Viterbo to Tusculum where preparations were made for an assault on Rome. At great expense he contrived to raise an army, which was reinforced by Sicilian auxiliaries sent by King Roger. The command of the papal militia was bestowed on Cardinal Guido, nicknamed *Puella*.[1] But the enterprise proved a failure with small return for vast expenditure,[2] and besides tasting the bitterness of defeat the Pope had to endure much criticism both from the Abbot Gerhoh of Reichersberg and from St Bernard for resorting to weapons of war.[3]

Nevertheless by the end of November Eugenius was able to conclude a truce with the victorious Republic and was once more safely lodged in the Lateran.[4] But it was

[1] *Hist. pont.* pp. 60, 61.

[2] "Infeliciter pugnabatur. Ecclesia namque fecit sumptus maximos et profectum minimum"—*Hist. pont.* loc. cit.

[3] Gerhoh, Ep. 17, *ad Alexandrum papam*, M.P.L. 193, col. 568–9. Related in form of an anecdote: "Cum essem Viterbii apud sanctae recordationis Papam Eugenium et ille familiari alloquio mihi retulisset de sua vexatione, in qua Tiburtinis contra cives Romanos favens multas pecunias expenderat, et tandem satis miseram pacis compositionem fecisset, ego respondi:—Licet sit misera pretio multo coempta pax ista, melior tamen est quam pugna vestra, quia cum Romanus pontifex praeparet se ad bellum per milites conductos agendum, videor mihi videri Petrum evaginantem gladium ferreum. Sed cum ei sic pugnanti vel pugnaturo non bene cedit, videor mihi audire Christum...Petro dicentem, '*Mitte gladium tuum in vaginam*' (*Joannes XVIII*)". Bern. *De Consid.* lib. iv, cap. iii, col. 776: "Quid tu denuo usurpare gladium tentes, quem semel jussus es reponere in vaginam?...Tuus ergo et ipse, tuo forsitan nutu, etsi non tua manu evaginandus". From date of composition, it would seem that the saint had the expedition of 1149 in mind.

[4] *Hist. pont.* p. 63. Jaffé-Loewenfeld, 9359.

soon evident that this was only a temporary lull in hostilities.
All attempts at negotiating a permanent peace failed, and
in June 1150 the Pope, unable longer to endure the
tyranny of the citizens, quitted the city and travelled south
to Anagni to treat with Roger of Sicily concerning certain
ecclesiastical grievances in his dominions.[1]

The chief obstacle to a cordial *rapprochement* between
Pope and commune was undoubtedly the person of Arnold.[2]
Eugenius demanded his expulsion from the city; the Republic could do no less than protect its sworn ally. For
under stress of a common danger the tacit understanding
between Arnold and the Senate had been consummated in
a formal treaty of alliance, whereby the reformer bound
himself by oath to aid the Republic in return for the
latter's protection against all his enemies and in particular
against the Pope.[3] This was a purely defensive alliance
based on political expediency and designed to provide
mutual safeguards against a papal *coup d'état*. Arnold
needed the armed protection which the commune alone
could give him, and the Republic gained an ally invaluable
for his ascendancy over the citizens in the not unlikely
event of the new government losing its popularity. But
apart from this primary advantage the key to the alliance
is a common antagonism to the Pope's temporal power.
True, each approached the problem from an opposite
angle; Arnold from that of its bearing upon the Church as
an institution, the Senate from that of its effect on the
civic government of Rome. Both, however, were agreed

---

[1] *Hist. pont.* p. 65. Poole, Preface, p. xvii.

[2] Cf. Giesebrecht, p. 23: "Der Papst und Arnold beisammen in
Rom: das waren unverträgliche Gegensätze".

[3] "Sed pacem tum multa prepediebant, tum maxime quod eicere
nolebant (Romani) Ernaldum Brixiensem, qui honori urbis et rei-
publicae Romanorum se dicebatur obligasse prestito iuramento, et ei
populus Romanus vicissim auxilium et consilium contra omnes homines
et nominatim contra dominum papam repromisit"—*Hist. pont.* op. cit.

on the prime necessity of its annihilation. But while for Arnold this was but the first step towards a larger scheme of ecclesiastical reform, the aim of the Republic did not travel beyond this point. Yet this in itself was a sufficiently big objective and involved a revolution in the Church's constitution no less than in the administrative system of the city.

Furthermore, the revolution had now ceased to be a local phenomenon; it was being drawn into the web of Imperial politics. The Roman Republic was in danger of becoming a pawn on the political chess-board. Eugenius was away at Anagni and only prevented from concluding a military alliance with the Norman king by the fear of alienating Conrad of Hohenstaufen, Roger's hereditary enemy. Conrad had but lately (May 1149) returned from the disastrous Crusade, and both Pope and commune cherished hopes of his intervention on their behalf.

From 1149 onwards the German court was flooded with letters from both camps containing urgent appeals for aid. Two communications despatched by the Senate are particularly interesting for the light which they throw on the political theory of the makers of the commune.

The first[1] is addressed "To the most illustrious and renowned Conrad, Lord of the city and the whole world, by the grace of God King of the Romans, ever Augustus, from the Senate and people of Rome, health and a happy and glorious rule over the Roman Empire". After

---

[1] Jaffé, *Mon. Corb.* Ep. 214, pp. 332 seq. Cf. Ep. 215 sent in the name of Sixtus, Nicholas and Guido, Councillors of the Republic, where certain phrases reappear word for word (e.g. "Omni clericorum remoto obstaculo") and the generality of the sentiment bears a striking resemblance. Both letters should be dated, following Gregorovius (IV, p. 513 n.), not later than November 1149. See Wibald, Ep. 252, p. 378, for proof that they were received by Conrad in January 1150. Hence Migne, Mansi and Martène are in error in giving 1150 as date of composition.

expressing surprise that their earlier letters have been left
unanswered, and reaffirming their loyalty to the Imperial
crown, the writer proceeds, "Imbued with the desire to
exalt and extend the kingdom and empire entrusted by
God to your governance, it is our earnest and united endeavour to restore the same to its ancient position under
Constantine and Justinian, who by the powerful arm of
the Senate and the Roman people held in their hands the
government of the whole world. Wherefore to this end,
and by the grace of God, we have restored the Senate and
crushed most of those who rebelled against your rule, in
order that you may possess the things which rightly belong
to Caesar. We have made a good beginning and laid a
solid foundation. We keep peace and justice for all who
seek them. We have seized the strongholds of the civic
nobility, who, together with the Sicilian (Roger of Sicily)
and the Pope, were preparing to defy your authority, and
these we either hold in trust for you or have razed to the
ground. But because of all these things which we have
done out of loyalty to you, the Pope, the Frangipani and
the sons of Peter Leonis, liegemen and allies of the
Sicilians (with the exception of Jordan our standard-
bearer), Tolomaeus and many others hem us in on every
side; nor will they allow us, as is fitting, to place the
Imperial crown on your royal head. Meanwhile, though
we suffer much hardship, we bear it gladly out of love and
honour to you, since no labour is too heavy to those who
love. For we know that we shall receive from you the
reward due from a father but the enemies of the Empire
your chastisement". In the same pompous and patronising
strain the writer goes on to warn Conrad against the evil
slanders of their common enemies, who seek only to rejoice
at the discord between them and to encompass their ruin
by craft. They bid him call to mind what great harm the
papal Curia and their former fellow-citizens have wrought

his predecessors. "And now with Sicilian aid they have sought to do further injury. Nevertheless with Christ's help we stand firm in our loyalty." Let him therefore bring speedy succour to his faithful subjects, for the whole city is at his feet. Let him dwell in Rome, the very capital of the world, whence he may rule the whole of Italy and the German kingdom more securely than almost any of his predecessors, since every clerical hindrance has been removed (*omni clericorum remoto obstaculo*).[1] Finally they inform him that they are engaged in rebuilding the Milvian Bridge, so long a handicap to the Emperors, in order that his army may cross and enter Rome without fear of the Pierleoni and their allies, the Pope and the Sicilian, entrenched in the castle of St Angelo. The letter closes with some execrable lines presumably intended to form a summary of its contents.[2]

The letter is a prolix and cumbrous effusion, showing no sign that Arnold had any part in its composition,[3] though the general tenour of its political principles points to a certain infiltration of his teaching. At any rate it affords a piquant illustration of the confusion present in the minds of the Romans. Having evolved a constitution which they fondly imagined to be a copy of that of the ancient Republic, in this epistle they are continually harking back to the glories of the Roman Empire. Thus a pious aspiration for a return of the "golden age" of Constantine

---

[1] Cf. Ep. 215, p. 335.

[2]　　"Rex valeat, quidquid cupit obtineat super hostes,
　　　　Imperium teneat, Romae sedeat, regat orbem,
　　　　Princeps terrarum, ceu fecit Justinianus.
　　　　Caesaris accipiat Caesar quae sunt sua Praesul,
　　　　Ut Christus jussit, Petro solvente tributum."
　　　　　　　　　　　　　　　　　　Wib. Ep. 214, p. 334.

[3] Gregorovius, p. 513 n. Clavel, *Arnauld de Brescia*, p. 164: "Une chef d'œuvre d'inconséquence, de vanité et d'ignorance".

and Justinian is coupled with a claim to sovereignty and the right of bestowing the Imperial crown.

The second letter, despatched the following year, is a document of a very different order.[1] The author describes himself as a "faithful adherent of the Senate" (*quidam fidelis senatus*) and there has been much discussion as to his identity. Three different views have been put forward, each possessed of some degree of plausibility. First came Jaffé's suggestion that the author was a Roman Senator,[2] and this was followed by Giesebrecht's conclusion that it was none other than Arnold himself.[3] Dr Breyer, taking the whole context of the superscription,[4] interprets the phrase "a faithful adherent of Conrad's in the Senate" in contrast with the extreme republicans, Arnold's supporters.[5] But this ingenious hypothesis is, as we shall see, hardly sustained by an examination of the contents of the letter. More recently Dr Hampe has reopened the question.[6] While he comes to no definite conclusion, he is inclined to accept Giesebrecht's view. Certainly this interpretation would fit Arnold's case, bound to the Senate as he was by the strongest of ties. And even if this identification be mistaken, there can be no doubt from the sentiments expressed in the concluding lines that the writer had drunk deep of the spirit of Arnold's teaching. Throughout, the frank and open tone of the epistle stands in marked contrast with the stilted bombast of the earlier. Conrad is urged to undertake with all speed an expedition to Rome, to regulate the affairs of the city and so to limit ecclesiastical authority that no Pope shall be consecrated without his order and consent, and the world be no longer polluted

---

[1] Jaffé, *Mon. Corbei.* Wib. Ep. 216, p. 335.   [2] Ibid.

[3] Giesebrecht, p. 23.

[4] "Quidam fidelis senatus servorum regis fidelissimus, quidquid tanto domino servus"—Wib. Ep. 216, loc. cit.

[5] Breyer, pp. 162 seq.

[6] Dr K. Hampe, *Hist. Zeitschrift*, 130 (1924), pp. 58 seq.

with priestly carnage and murder.[1] The succeeding sentence might almost be termed an epitome of Arnold's doctrine on the Church. "For", the writer says, "it is not the priest's function to bear both the sword and the chalice, but to preach the word of God, to confirm his teaching by good works, and by no means to stir up wars and strife throughout the world."[2]

All depended on Conrad's view of the Imperial dignity[3] and his attitude to the Papacy. Notwithstanding his theoretical obligation towards the latter, there were two factors suggesting the advisability of contracting an alliance with the Roman Republic. First, the eclipse of the papal power provided a splendid opportunity for reviving the waning prestige of the Empire. The proud position of arbiter between Pope and Romans, which Henry III had exercised before the days of Hildebrand, might again fall to the German king. Secondly, as the ally of the Eastern Emperor Conrad had heard with misgiving of the negotiations between the Pope and the Sicilian king for a military alliance, a combination which might prove dangerous in certain contingencies. It might well seem that these considerations would conduce to a favourable reception of the Roman Republic's advances

That so happy a prospect never came to pass was to a

---

[1] "Regali prudentiae consulo, ut sine mora Romam veniatis...et ita facere, ut sine vestra jussione ac dispositione numquam de cetero apostolicus in Urbe ordinetur...ne per sacerdotes bella fiant aut homicidia in mundo"—Wib. Ep. 216, pp. 335 seq.

[2] "Nam non licet eis sacerdotibus ferre gladium et calicem, set predicare, predicationem vero bonis operibus confirmare, nequaquam bella et lites in mundo committere"—ibid.

[3] Though Conrad was never crowned Emperor, proof that he considered himself such in the fullest sense is obtained from the superscription of a letter sent by him to Manuel, the Byzantine Emperor: "Conradus Dei gratia vere Romanorum Imperator". Otto of Freising, Gesta Fred. p. 41. Cf. Giesebrecht, Geschichte der deutschen Kaiserzeit, IV, pp. 215–16, also note on p. 468.

large extent due to an interesting personality. Conrad's
chief adviser in politico-ecclesiastical affairs was Wibald,
Abbot of Stablo and Corvey.[1] Born in Lorraine in 1098
Wibald entered the Benedictine Order in 1117. In 1122
he was first brought into touch with the Imperial court.
Journeys to Rome on diplomatic missions gained him
friends among the cardinals, of whom Cardinal Gerhard
of Bologna, afterwards Pope Lucius II, and Cardinal
Conrad of St Sabina, afterwards Pope Anastasius IV, may
be specially mentioned. In 1130 he was appointed Abbot
of Stablo and became confidential adviser to the Emperor
Lothaire and his agent in negotiations with the Papacy.
On the death of Lothaire he played a prominent part in
securing the election of Conrad of Hohenstaufen and in
1146 he was recompensed for his labours by the grant of
the abbacy of Corvey. Thenceforth he was universally
recognised as the Emperor's most influential counsellor.[2]
His influence was decisive in securing the rejection of the
Italian policy which appeared to offer Conrad such
tempting advantages.

In his view of the relations between the spiritual and
temporal powers Wibald was a child of his age. Pope and
Emperor were natural allies by virtue of their complementary positions in the Divine scheme for the world's
governance. In the matters of lay investiture and secular
interference in ecclesiastical elections he was a rigid
Gregorian,[3] and to a limited extent belonged to the ultra-

---

[1] Biographies by J. Janssen, *Wibald von Stablo und Corvey* (1854),
and L. Mann, *Wibald von Stablo und Corvei nach seiner politischen
Thätigkeit* (1875). Good short account given in Guibal, *Arnaud de
Brescia et les Hohenstaufen*, pp. 79–100.
[2] Hauck (*Kirchengeschichte Deutschlands*, IV, p. 206) thinks his
ability has been overrated: "Trotz aller seiner Klugheit und Gewandt-
heit war er kein politisches Talent. Er war der Mann der kleinen
Mittel".
[3] Mann, *Wibald*, p. 60.

Gregorian party which was profoundly dissatisfied with the incompleteness of the restrictions imposed by the Concordat of Worms.[1] It has indeed been claimed that he was in reality little more than a papal agent attached to the Imperial court.[2] His policy was certainly in line with that of the Curia, but there is no evidence that it was in the first instance inspired by it. It would seem rather to have grown independently out of the peculiarities of the political situation, which produced an identical policy for both Wibald and the Curia. Hence to remark that Wibald is first and foremost a supporter of the Papacy and only secondarily of the Empire is to effect a separation of interest which, if we look behind and beyond the immediate circumstances, is no fair representation of the facts.[3] Further, it is highly improbable that he would have been appointed co-regent for the young prince Henry during Conrad's absence from Germany on Crusade, had his policy been recognised as dependent on "instructions from Rome".

Together with the letters of the Romans Conrad had also received an urgent appeal from Eugenius, wherein the latter besought his aid in restoring "peace and tranquillity to the Christian people",[4] or, to put it more

[1] Janssen, *Wibald*, p. 34.

[2] "Es wird aber aus der ganzen vorhergehenden Darstellung klar geworden sei, dass Wibald in der Politik überhaupt keine selbständige Stellung einnimmt, sondern überall von der Curie abhängt und von ihr seine Instructionen einholt"—Mann, p. 81.

[3] Mann, p. 75. Cf. Janssen, p. 189: "Das muss uns ein Beweis sein, wie wenig er bei obwaltenden Zerwürfnissen zwischen beiden Gewalten eine Parteistellung eingenommen, wie sorgfältig er eben so wohl die Rechte des Reiches, als die der Kirche zu wahren gewusst".

[4] "Desiderium siquidem nostrum est, ut ea, inter aecclesiam et regnum quae a predecessoribus nostris et tuis statuta sunt, inter nos et maiestatem tuam ita Domino auxiliante firmentur quatenus sponsa Dei universalis aecclesia suo iure quiete fruatur imperium debitum robur optineat et christianus populus iocunda pace et grata tranquillitate letetur"—Wib. Ep. 272, Jaffé, *Mon. Corb.* pp. 399 seq.

bluntly, the temporal power of the Pope. Kept in touch with the Roman situation through his correspondence with Cardinal Guido,[1] Wibald was able to exert sufficient pressure on the unstable Conrad to procure the sending of an embassy to treat with the Pope at Ferentino.[2] A complete agreement was reached and preparations were set on foot for the Italian expedition. But Conrad's failing health and renewed dissension in his German dominions caused yet another postponement. In September of the following year (1151), however, fresh envoys, of whom Wibald himself was one, were despatched to Rome to make the final arrangements for the coronation.[3] With them they carried Conrad's reply to the letters of the Senate.

To the latter the Imperial response was disappointing if not disquieting. The letter entirely ignored its existence and was addressed to "the Prefect of the city; the consuls, the captains and the whole Roman people". Its tone was unmistakably hostile. After explaining that he had but lately returned from the Holy Land and thanking them for their expressions of good-will towards himself, Conrad announced his forthcoming expedition to Italy, when he would undertake the pacification of his dominions and dispense justice to all his subjects, rewarding the loyal and punishing the rebels.[4]

But the long deferred "Römerzug" was destined never to be carried out. In February 1152 Conrad died suddenly

[1] Cardinal Deacon of St Mary in Porticu, not to be confused with Cardinal Guido Puella, or the legate to Bohemia, Arnold's protector. For his correspondence with Wibald see Martène and Durand, Ampliss. Collect. II inter Wibaldi epistolas.

[2] The embassy consisted of the Bishops of Basle and Constance. The latter was the same Herman who had given shelter to Arnold years earlier. See ante, p. 87.

[3] Wib. Ep. 346, Jaffé, *Mon. Corb.* p. 480.

[4] "Ad res et urbes Italicae pacandas et firmandas sic transeamus, ut tam fidelibus gratiam quam rebellibus poenam Deo adjutore retribuere valeamus"—Wib. Ep. 345, Jaffé, op. cit. p. 479.

at Bamberg while maturing his plans. He was succeeded
by his nephew, Frederick Barbarossa, the Duke of Swabia,
a man with exalted notions of the Imperial dignity and
very unlikely to regard with equanimity the presence of a
republican government in his capital. Yet the Senate clung
blindly to the hope that the young monarch would protect
it, and a letter was sent inviting him to come to Rome
without delay to receive the Imperial crown.

This letter, the work of one, Wetzel, is a document of
some length and of more than ordinary interest.[1] It
illustrates to what a remarkable degree the popular government was permeated with Arnold's opinions. The letter
begins by congratulating Frederick on his accession, but
deplores the fact that he has neither recognised "the sacred
city of Rome, the mistress of the world, the maker and
mother of all the Emperors" as the source of his authority,
nor sought from her confirmation of his election. In like
manner the writer laments that Frederick has followed the
example of his predecessors by obeying the summons of
the "Julianists, to wit, heretics, apostate clergy and false
monks, who degrade their office by exercising dominion
against the Gospel precepts, the Apostles' exhortations and
the Canon Law, in contempt of laws human and divine,
and to the grievous hurt both of the Church of God and of
the civil powers".[2] Then follows a trenchant attack on the
Roman hierarchy. Copious citations from the Scriptures
serve to expose the unapostolic character of their lives.
They are those of whom the Apostle writes, "false teachers
who in covetousness make merchandise of you, abounding
in lasciviousness, and revelling in their banquets with you,
having eyes full of adultery, by reason of whom the way
of truth shall be evil spoken of" (2 Peter ii, 1, 2, 13 and 14).
How can such men say with Peter, "Lo! we have left all

[1] Inter Wib. Ep. 404, Jaffé, pp. 539 seq.
[2] Ibid.

and followed Thee"? And again, "Silver and gold have I none"? How can they hear from the Lord's lips, "Ye are the light of the world, ye are the salt of the earth"? Rather are they the salt which has lost its savour and is good for nothing but to be trodden under foot of men—or of swine. To Peter and the vicars of Peter the Lord saith, "As My Father hath sent Me, even so send I you". But the manner of His sending by the Father He expresseth saying, "If I do not the works of My Father, believe not in Me". If Christ Who did no sin was not to be believed without works, how are those to be believed who not only do evil but that openly? "How", the writer continues, "can men who covet all manner of riches bear to hear that first commandment of the Gospel—'Blessed are the poor in spirit', when they are poor neither in spirit nor in fact?"[1] The theme is carried yet further by a series of quotations from St Jerome and Pseudo-Isidore[2] designed in like manner to show how grievously the Church has strayed from the teaching of Christ and the practice of the Apostles. At length the climax of the argument is reached in the author's summary treatment of the Donation of Constantine. He does not mince his words but openly denounces it as "a lie and a heretical fable; so thoroughly exposed is it in Rome that even hired labourers and women make game of it, confuting the most learned on the subject, so that the Pope and his cardinals dare not show their faces for shame".[3]

What follows this remarkable outburst is something in

[1] Wib. Ep. op. cit. pp. 539 seq.

[2] The passage in question is ascribed to St Clement of Rome. Wib. Ep. op. cit. p. 541.

[3] "Mendacium vero illud et fabula heretica, in qua refertur Constantinum Silvestro imperialia symoniace concessisse, in Urbe ita detecta est, ut etiam mercennarii et mulierculae quoslibet etiam doctissimos super hoc concludant, et dictus apostolicus cum suis cardinalibus in civitate prae pudore apparere non audeat"—Wib. Ep. op. cit. p. 542.

the nature of an anti-climax. The writer makes a clumsy attempt to reconcile the juristic conception of the Emperor as the source of law, formulated in the tag "Quod principi placuit legis habet vigorem" here quoted, with the lofty claim that the Imperial dignity lay in the gift of the Roman people.[1] This last observation was scarcely calculated to commend the writer's cause to Barbarossa. Finally Frederick is bidden to send envoys and legal experts to Rome so that the Empire may be established on a true legal foundation.

Who was this man who dared thus to lecture the haughty Barbarossa? Here, as in the case of "the faithful friend of the Senate", we are left in ignorance of his identity. The older view, propounded by Gregorovius and accepted by Giesebrecht and Hausrath, was derived from the peculiar character of the name, Wetzel, which appeared to indicate a person of Teutonic extraction. Whence it was assumed that the writer was one of Arnold's Swiss followers, who had accompanied him on his return to Italy.[2] Some measure of support for this theory is to be found in the names of the three men commended to Frederick at the close of the letter, all of whom are known to have been dwellers in the diocese of Constance.[3] The whole argument depends on whether or not the name is authentic, and in his recent monograph Dr Hampe argues ingeniously against this hypothesis, holding on the contrary that "Wetzel" is a mere pseudonym covering Arnold himself.[4] Internal evidence lends strong support to this novel interpretation. The letter is in any case the work of an able man, a man of some learning and a fair dialectical skill—witness

[1] Wib. Ep. op. cit.; cf. p. 539.
[2] Gregorovius, IV, p. 519, n. 1. Giesebrecht, p. 24. Hausrath, pp. 120 seq., 178, n. 2. Breyer, p. 164, n. 6.
[3] See ante, pp. 95–6.
[4] K. Hampe, op. cit. p. 61.

his knowledge of the Fathers, of Pseudo-Isidore and of Roman Law, and the masterly character of his exposition. Further, there is something to be said for the view that the passionate conviction which underlies the argument and the spirited eloquence which carries it forward betray the hand and mind of the Brescian reformer. It would seem impossible to arrive at a definite solution of the problem; much might be said in favour of either view. What, however, is tolerably certain is that we have here a typical expression of Arnoldist principles, an example of "reasoning after the characteristic Arnoldist method".[1] This is shown most clearly in the author's treatment of the Donation of Constantine. It is one of the earliest attempts to discredit the legend, though it must be remembered that its authenticity is denied, not because the writer doubts its historicity or was capable of disproving it, but solely because it formed the chief bulwark of the temporal power of the Pope. It is also noteworthy that the grounds upon which the attack is based are themselves equally fictitious.[2]

A clear-cut issue faced the new monarch. Either he must follow the traditional lines of Imperial policy and work in harmony with the Pope, or he must acquiesce in the demand of the Roman Republic for recognition as an independent political entity under the suzerainty of the Emperor. There was really little doubt as to his choice. Political tradition and the bent of his own mind alike impelled him to side with the Pope. Nevertheless, he was not altogether devoid of sympathy with the Arnoldist teaching on the Church. Possibly he shared to some degree the view that the root of the trouble lay in the Temporal Power. At any rate he was quite capable of appreciating the force of Wetzel's arguments. Yet he could not but regard with wholehearted contempt the fantastic claim of

[1] E. Scott Davison, *Forerunners of St Francis*, p. 147.
[2] Cf. Döllinger, *Fables respecting the Popes of the Middle Ages*, p. 142.

the Romans to the right of bestowing the Imperial crown. This cut at the very roots of his political creed.

During these early years of his reign his policy was governed by the paramount need of securing the Imperial title. No one but the Pope could perform the ceremony of coronation. Frederick's attitude to this particular question is of a piece with his whole political outlook. He was a rigid conservative, it might almost be said a blind traditionalist, with something of the obscurantism of the legalist superadded. His ecclesiastical policy was static if not reactionary. His principal aim was to regain for the Empire the proud position it had enjoyed in the palmy days of Henry III and the Ottos. Despite his contest with Adrian IV and Alexander III he was not at heart an opponent of the Papacy as an institution. On the contrary, his political theory was as theocratic as that of Gregory VII or of Innocent III. Above all he was wholly estranged from that spirit of political separatism, which, as it slowly gathered power, marked the passing of the old feudal order of society and the dawn of a new age. Hence just as in later years he failed to realise the value of the Lombard communes as a potential ally in his struggle with Alexander III, so now at the beginning of his reign he was blind to the advantages offered by a treaty with the Roman Republic.[1]

His first steps were cautious beyond expectation. Polite exchanges with the Pope, in which he expressed his goodwill and reverence towards the Holy See, did little to allay the natural anxiety of Eugenius.[2] Moreover from Wibald, who was not at first one of the new monarch's chief advisers,[3] came the disquieting news that the lay coun-

---

[1] Cf. Hauck, *Kirchengeschichte Deutschlands*, IV, p. 216; *Friedrich Barbarossa als Kirchenpolitiker* (1898), pp. 9, 23; Simonsfeld, *Jahrbücher des Deutschen Reiches unter Friedrich I*, I, p. 327.
[2] Ep. 372 inter Wib. Ep. pp. 499 seq.   [3] Ep. 377, p. 507.

sellors of the Empire were urging a postponement of the projected Italian expedition on account of the unstable condition of affairs in Germany.[1] Accordingly in May 1152 Eugenius wrote to Frederick in cautious tones reminding him of the obligations to the Church inherent in his sacred office and exhorting him to maintain an earnest regard for her welfare.[2] At the court Wibald continued to work manfully for the papal cause and, in proportion as he regained something of his old ascendancy, Frederick inclined more and more towards a resumption of Conrad's policy.

Meanwhile in Rome the situation underwent changes of which the exact nature is not very clear to us. From this time forward the materials for the history of the Roman Republic become scantier than ever. Documents are few and fragmentary, chronicles meagre or biased. That part of the *Historia Pontificalis* which remains extant ceases abruptly at the year 1152, and although Otto of Freising's *Gesta Frederici* gives a wealth of information on Frederick's Italian expedition, it is plainly written from the German standpoint and by no means compensates for the loss of John of Salisbury's discriminating and impartial judgment. Especially is this the case when we are concerned with the change in Arnold's fortunes, and attempt to trace the successive stages in the decline of his power. We can only fix on the salient events and guess darkly at the hidden forces responsible for the trend of affairs.

From 1148 onwards the perils threatening the commune were augmented by internal dissension. Parties and factions emerge, and there is no longer a common purpose or a common agreement save perhaps on fundamental principles, and even that is doubtful. Certainly a serious

[1] Ep. 375, p. 504. Cf. Ep. 396, p. 529.
[2] Eug. Ep. 504, M.P.L. 180, col. 1523 or inter Wib. Ep. 382, pp. 513–14.

cleavage of opinion is manifest in matters of policy. The Senate, composed mainly of the more moderate men, desired an accommodation with the German king, and its arm was still nerved by the hope of securing his aid against the Pope. In this direction, it believed, lay the commune's sole prospect of maintaining a permanent existence. Very different was Arnold's view. His ideal was a free self-governing commune, modelled on the Lombard type, yet incorporating those peculiar features judged at the time to be characteristic of the ancient Roman Republic. Senate and Capitol Arnold found already renovated on his arrival. Just what changes in the constitution were accomplished through his agency or by his inspiration it is difficult to tell. Twice in the *Gesta Frederici* Otto of Freising speaks of his having procured the restoration of the equestrian order.[1] Yet in view of the patent confusion of events in Otto's narrative we can by no means be sure that this had not been done earlier. It would seem, however, that Arnold cherished the ambition of reviving, at least in name, the old social order of patricians and *quirites* and the office of tribunes of the plebs. Not that the members of these orders were to be endowed with political functions. Ample provision for the administration of the city was to be found in existing institutions. But Arnold was probably right in thinking that some sort of class distinction was necessary if the delicate mechanism of the new constitution was to work without friction. The crown of the edifice was the Emperor; without a titular monarch Rome as a political entity was inconceivable. But the Emperor might rightly take no share in the government; rather he was to stand as a symbol of civic unity and civic aspiration. In this respect Arnold's scheme differed vitally from that of the Senate, to whom the Imperial office was not a mere honorific title,

[1] Otto of Freising, *Gesta Fred.* lib. I, cap. xxviii, p. 44; lib. II, cap. xxviii, p. 134. Cf. Gunther, *Lig.* col. 371, lines 330 seq.

but an integral part of the constitution. Nor was it essential with Arnold that the office should be identified with the alien monarch beyond the Alps, who bore the customary title of King of the Romans. That would depend on the latter's disposition towards the Republic and the demands of the local situation. In fact by 1152 Arnold had given up all hope of obtaining protection from this quarter. Therefore it lay within the province of the citizens to pass over the claims of the German king in ordering the affairs of the commonwealth, and to proceed to the election from among themselves of a new Emperor, who should receive the crown from their hands and reside permanently in Rome, who, in short, should be Roman in fact as well as in name.[1]

Such a policy depended for success on the wholehearted support of all sections within the commune. In particular the basis of the constitution needed broadening in order to allow of the representation of the lower classes, among whom were numbered Arnold's more fanatical admirers. Such in outline was the reformer's project; a visionary and impracticable scheme, it must be confessed; visionary in that it cut across the traditions of the past and ignored the plain facts of contemporary politics, impracticable since its author no longer commanded the allegiance of the mass of the citizens.

Ever since the publication of the bull of 1148 Arnold's influence in politics had been on the wane. Reasons are not far to seek. No doubt the instability of temperament and vacillation of purpose, which St Bernard years before had singled out as the distinguishing marks of the Roman character, counted for much. Like the Athenians of old they were ever eager to hear some new thing, and Arnold's gospel had by now lost the attraction of novelty. Nothing could damp the ardour of his more enthusiastic followers, "the sect of the Lombards", but even in the ecclesiastical

[1] Paolucci, *R.S.I.* IV, p. 682.

sphere his prestige had dwindled. He was now little more than leader of a purely lay party. The clergy as a body were definitely estranged. The menaces of the papal bull had succeeded in their object only too well. The situation counselled prudence, but prudence was not one of Arnold's virtues. Instead he risked all in a last despairing effort to regain control of the ship of State, and engineered a *coup d'état*. Our knowledge of the plot is derived from a letter sent by Eugenius to Wibald and dated the 20th September 1152. According to this account Arnold, backed by the country-folk (*rusticana turba*) but without the knowledge of the nobles and the chief men of the city, was conspiring to secure by armed force the return of a hundred of his adherents as life-senators at the forthcoming elections in November. Moreover, he had also determined to appoint two consuls and to elect an "emperor".[1]

Unfortunately we have no means of ascertaining what exactly lay behind this last allegation. We have no guarantee that Eugenius' account of the plot is strictly accurate. It is not unlikely that he purposely exaggerated the gravity of the situation. But whatever Arnold's real intention may have been, the hatching of this conspiracy was the greatest mistake of his career. It enabled Eugenius to represent him as a rebel against the authority of the Emperor, a tactical advantage which the astute Pope was quick to seize. It was in fact this startling report which finally convinced Frederick of the need for an alliance with the Pope.[2] In March 1153 the Treaty of Constance

[1] "Ad hec sanctitati tuae quaedam notificamus quae faciente Ar(noldo) heretico, rusticana quaedam turba absque nobilium et majorum scientia nuper est in Urbe molita. Circiter enim duo millia in unum sunt secretius conjurati, et in proximis Kalendis Novembris centum perpetuos senatores malorum operum et duos consules... disponant....Unum autem quem volunt imperatorem dicere, creare disponunt"—Eug. Ep. inter Wib. Ep. 403, Jaffé, p. 538.
[2] Cf. Vacandard, p. 93; Breyer, p. 167.

between Pope and Emperor marked the triumph of Wibald's policy. By the terms of this concordat Frederick
undertook the recovery and defence of the Temporal
Power, whilst Eugenius in return agreed to crown him
Emperor in Rome and uphold his authority to the best of
his ability.[1]

By this time Eugenius was back in Rome. Arnold's plans
had miscarried badly. The senatorial elections resulted in
the return of the moderate party by a large majority, and
on the 9th December 1152 Eugenius made yet another
triumphal entry into the city. The terms of the agreement
doubtless included a renewal of his recognition of the
commune, and warned by past experience he took immediate steps to consolidate his position. By a liberal use
of money he succeeded in winning over to his side all but
the most fanatical of Arnold's adherents.[2] Yet the continued presence of the arch-enemy within the city rendered
the need for an understanding with the Emperor all the
more urgent. Hence the arrangements concluded at Constance. But the triumphant pontiff was not destined to
reap the fruits of his hard-won victory. He was engaged
in subjugating the barons of the Campagna when he died
suddenly at Tivoli on the 8th July 1153.[3] It is impossible
to say what he might have accomplished had not death
removed him at this juncture. Such at least was the
opinion of Romuald of Salerno, who says that with the aid
of the people he would have gone on to deprive the Senate

---

[1] Ep. 407, inter Wib. Ep. Jaffé, p. 546. Watterich, *Pont. Rom.* II,
pp. 318 seq.

[2] "Interea Eugenius Papa apud Tusculanum aliquanto tempore
demoratus, pacem cum Romanis fecit, et a senatoribus et ab universo
populo Romano cum summo est honore susceptus. Hic autem adeo
universum populum sibi beneficiis et eleemosinis alligavit, quod bene
pro majore parte Urbem poterat pro sua voluntate disponere"—
Romuald Salernit. *Annales*, M.G.H. Script. XIX, p. 425.

[3] Watterich, II, p. 320.

of its newly acquired functions.[1] Even so, considering the
magnitude of the task confronting him, a remarkable
degree of success had attended his efforts. "Quiet sub-
tilty", writes Gregorovius, "succeeded in achieving what
weapons had not been able to accomplish."[2] We may add
that his successors on the papal throne were deeply his
debtors. By his patient endurance and dogged pertinacity
he accomplished much towards retrieving the political fortunes of the Papacy. By his private virtues he contributed
not a little to the repair of the damage wrought to its
spiritual prestige by the selfish and worldly lives of his
immediate predecessors. Gerhoh of Reichersberg pays
him a tribute none the less fitting in that it comes from one
who had known him intimately.[3] "Departing this life", he
writes, "he left behind him a fragrant memory [*dulcem
memoriam*] in the whole Church. Many grieved that after
him none was found in the Apostolic See like unto him",
and the worthy abbot himself sighs that Elijah has found
no Elisha to receive his mantle.[4]

Notwithstanding his success, in respect of Roman
affairs the task which Eugenius bequeathed to his successors was truly no light one. The wings of the arch-enemy
of Brescia had been clipped, but stronger hands than those
of Eugenius were needed if the dragon of revolution was
to be scotched.

---

[1] "Nisi esset mors emula, que illum cito de medio rapuit, senatores
noviter procreatos populi amminiculo usurpata dignitate privasset"—
Romuald Salernit. loc. cit. ante. Cf. the letter in which Hugo, Bishop
of Ostia, announced the death of Eugenius to the Cistercian chapter.
"Jam fere enim senatum adnihilaverat"—inter ep. Bern. Ep. 488, col.
695. The letter is an eloquent panegyric on the virtues of the deceased
pontiff.   [2] Gregorovius, IV, p. 522.
[3] For Gerhoh's relations with contemporary Popes see his *Com.
in Psalm.* cxxxiii (*Lib. de lite*, III, p. 502; M.P.L. 194, col. 896): "Liber
de gloria et honore Filii hominis" (*Lib. de lite*, III, pp. 396 seq.; M.P.L.
194, col. 1077). Ep. 17, M.P.L. 193, col. 567.
[4] *Com. in Psalm.* lxv (*Lib. de lite*, III, p. 493).

But Gerhoh's gloomy prognostication proved unfounded; the hour was destined to produce the man. In the person of the Englishman, Nicholas Breakspear, Arnold found a more vigorous and ruthless enemy in the papal chair than the mild and pacific Eugenius.

Chapter IX

ARNOLD'S LAST DAYS. THE FALL
OF THE REPUBLIC

THE day following the death of Eugenius the cardinals met in conclave and on the 12th July elected unanimously Conrad, Cardinal Bishop of Sabina, to the vacancy. The new Pope, who adopted the style of Anastasius IV, was a Roman by birth and under Eugenius had been papal vicar in the city. He was known for a benefactor of the poor and a great builder of churches. In one respect his election augured well for the maintenance of the alliance between Papacy and Empire, for he was a close and trusted friend of Abbot Wibald. But this advantage was neutralised by his great age and infirmity. A man of nearly ninety years could scarcely be expected to undertake the subjugation of the Roman Republic. Actually very little is known of his relations with the commune. The Senate seems not to have disputed or interfered in any way with his election and, though the papal biographer, Boso, hints that the Pope suffered no little inconvenience from Arnold's faction,[1] he contrived to pass his pontificate in Rome undisturbed. The Republic gained a brief respite, which proved only to be the proverbial calm before the storm.

On the 3rd December 1154 Anastasius died full of years and honour. His successor was the Englishman, Nicholas Breakspear,[2] one of the most remarkable men of his age.

---

[1] Boso, "Vita Adriani IV" in Watterich, II, p. 324.

[2] The chief authorities for his early life are the *Historia Rerum Anglicarum* of William of Newburgh, lib. II, cap. vi, R.S. (ed. R. Howlett), pp. 109 seq. and the *Gesta Abbatum Monasterii Sancti Albani* ascribed to Matthew Paris, R.S. (ed. H. T. Riley), pp. 112–13, 124–5. Of these William of Newburgh's account alone is contemporary and to be preferred in cases of discrepancy. See also Boso, "Vita Adriani IV" in Watterich, II, pp. 323 seq. It is almost certain

His rise to eminence had been meteoric even for the Middle Ages, when ecclesiastical promotion was wont to be rapid. His father had become in later life a monk of St Albans and the young Nicholas was brought up in close connection with the monastery. When in due time he aspired to enter the community he was refused owing to his failure to pass the test of learning prescribed. Such is the account of Matthew Paris, who adds that deeply chagrined he betook himself to Paris (c. 1130) and applied himself diligently to study.[1] Thence wandering down into Provence he entered the Abbey of St Rufus, a house of Canons-regular at Avignon, becoming Abbot in 1137.[2] Complaints against the severity of his rule brought him to the notice of Eugenius III, who in 1149 raised him to the cardinalate as Bishop of Albano.[3] And thus, says Fuller, it came to pass "that he who was refused to be Monachus Albanensis in England became Episcopus Albanensis in Italy".[4] From 1152 to 1154 he was absent on a legatine mission in Scandinavia (in gentes ferocissimas).[5] There he did work of permanent value, restoring order in the dis-

that Boso, himself an Englishman, was Adrian's secretary and papal chamberlain; cf. Watterich, Preface, p. lxxviii. Modern biographies by A. H. Tarleton, *Nicholas Breakspear, Englishman and Pope* (1896), and H. K. Mann, reprinted 1914 from the author's *Lives of the Popes in the Middle Ages*, IX, pp. 236–40. See also R. L. Poole, "The early lives of Robert Pullen and Nicholas Breakspeare", in *Essays in Med. History presented to T. F. Tout* (1925).

[1] Matt. Paris, *Gesta Abbatum*, p. 112, cf. p. 125. William of Newburgh (p. 109) records that his father, ashamed of his indolence, drove him out with bitter taunts. If Matthew Paris' statement concerning the visit to Paris can be accepted (Dr R. L. Poole, op. cit. pp. 65–6, is decidedly sceptical on the point) it was possibly then that Nicholas met John of Salisbury, an acquaintance which ripened into a firm and lasting friendship. Cf. *Joannis Saresberiensis Metalog*. lib. IV, cap. xlii, § 945 b.

[2] William of Newburgh, p. 110.
[3] Poole, p. 67.
[4] Fuller, *Worthies of England* (1811 ed.), I, p. 428.
[5] William of Newburgh, p. 111.

tracted churches of Norway and Sweden and promoting missions to the still heathen parts of those lands. So great was the reputation he acquired that on the death of Anastasius, a few months after his return to Rome, he was unanimously elected Pope as Adrian IV.[1]

By sheer merit the poor wandering outcast of St Albans had climbed to the highest rung of the ecclesiastical ladder. True, he owed much to Eugenius III, who with his usual shrewdness had remarked his uncommon abilities and secured his services for the Papacy. But Adrian was not only endowed with great practical ability; he was also a man of outstanding personality and high character. Energy and resolution were perhaps his dominant characteristics, both of them qualities indispensable for a successful Pope in the twelfth century. But this was not all. He had a softer side to his nature; so at least it appears from Boso's characterisation of him as kind, patient and gentle, slow to anger, swift to pardon, a cheerful giver and prodigal of alms. The same writer speaks also of his eloquence and learning,[2] and there can be no doubt from John of Salisbury's account of conversations with him that he was a man of culture and possessed both the interests and the instincts of the scholar.[3] Other authorities mention his dignified bearing and handsome person,[4] and in this respect at least he was not inferior to his illustrious

[1] Boso, Watterich, II, p. 324.

[2] "Erat enim vir valde benignus, mitis et patiens, in anglica et latina lingua peritus, in sermone facundus, in eloquentia politus, in cantilena praecipuus et praedicator egregius; ad irascendum tardus, ad ignoscendum velox, hilaris dator, in eleemosynis largus et in omni morum compositione praeclarus"—Boso, loc. cit. ante. Cf. William of Newburgh, p. 110: "prudens in verbis, ad injuncta impiger...acris ingenii et linguae expeditae, frequenti et studiosa lectione ad scientiam atque eloquentiam multum profecit". *Gesta di Fed.* line 658: "Vir doctus clemens facundus moribus ingens".

[3] *Policraticus*, passim.

[4] "Corpore elegans vultu jocundus"—William of Newburgh, loc. cit. ante; Matthew Paris, p. 112.

contemporary, Barbarossa. Such was the character of the sole Englishman who has attained the papal chair, and in him Arnold of Brescia found a foeman worthy of his steel.

At the outset Adrian showed the Romans that he had no intention of adopting the temporising policy of his predecessors. The Senate had declined to admit the validity of his election, and he on his side refused to recognise the Republic. Further, he demanded the unconditional expulsion of Arnold and his faction before he would even discuss the question of terms. The Senate, still trusting in the hope of aid from the German king, ignored his demands. It seemed indeed that Adrian was scarcely in a position to translate his resolute language into action. He was more or less a prisoner in the Leonine city, unable even to gain possession of the Lateran.[1] For weeks on end Rome was given over to street brawls and riots. The atmosphere was heavy with the sense of an impending calamity.

The climax came when Guido, Cardinal-priest of St Pudentiana, was attacked in the streets while on his way to an audience of the Pope by men of Arnold's faction, wounded and left half-dead. Adrian, however, saw in this the means of bringing the recalcitrant citizens to heel and of obtaining Arnold's expulsion. He instantly placed the city under an interdict.[2] The sequel justified the gravity of the measure. Never before had this terrible weapon been employed against the Holy City, never till now had Peter's vicar dared to outlaw the site of Peter's tomb. It was Holy Week and no spiritual consolation could be afforded the devout. The prospect of Easter dawn without the ban being lifted plunged the whole populace in terror. When four days had passed and no Mass had been said,

[1] Boso, Watterich, II, p. 325.
[2] For a graphic picture of conditions under an interdict see Radulph de Coggeshall, *Chronicon Anglicanum*, R.S. pp. 112–13. Cf. Milman, V, pp. 250 seq.; Gregorovius, IV, p. 527.

the frenzied citizens compelled the reluctant senators to seek terms from the Apostolic Father. Adrian replied with a peremptory demand for Arnold's submission or expulsion. Yielding to pressure from the mob the Senate tamely gave way, and the alliance between Arnold and the Republic was shattered.[1] His followers were scattered abroad and he himself forced to fly the city. He managed to reach the Tuscan border, but at Bricole in the valley of the Orcia he was surprised and taken by Cardinal Odo of St Nicholas, a fellow-townsman but a bitter enemy. He was imprisoned in a monastery of the Camaldulenses, till a timely rescue was effected by the Viscounts of Campagnatico who lodged him in one of their castles and treated him with the reverence due to a prophet.[2] Meanwhile Adrian had removed the interdict and on Maundy Thursday entered the Lateran in triumph, where he kept Easter amid the jubilation of his people.[3]

His victory was well-nigh complete, a victory all the more impressive in the eyes of contemporaries in that it was obtained by the exercise of his spiritual prerogative. With one bolt from his ghostly armoury Adrian had shattered the link uniting the Romans and the Brescian reformer in a common bond of enmity towards the Papacy The dangerous demagogue, who had so long troubled the peace of the Church and menaced the Temporal Power, had been driven into exile shorn of his power and in a measure discredited in character. And the final failure of Arnold's plans was also a signal that the commune's days were numbered. Since the reformer's fatal attempt to overrule the Senatorial elections the republican constitution had to all intents and purposes ceased to function. The

---

[1] Boso, p. 324.

[2] "Tanquam prophetam in terra sua cum honore habebant"— Boso, p. 320. Cf. Otto of Freising, *Gesta Fred.* p. 134.

[3] Boso, pp. 324–5.

Senate itself still remained, but the bewildered senators, abandoned by the fickle-minded populace and divided in counsel, knew not where to turn for help. Fortunately for them the expected advent of Barbarossa gave a brief respite to their shadowy power, since it prevented the Pope from administering then and there the *coup de grace*.

Frederick indeed was now marching through Tuscany en route for Rome. In October 1154 he had crossed the Brenner Pass, and descending into the Lombard plain held a Diet at Roncaglia. Many of the cities made their submission at once, but Milan and her allies stoutly resisted the Imperial demand for homage. After wasting sixty days in the siege of Tortona, which he finally took and razed to the ground, Frederick received the iron crown of Lombardy at Pavia (17th April 1155). Flushed with success he now pressed on to Rome for the Imperial coronation in St Peter's. The report of the ruthless treatment meted out to the Lombard cities filled all hearts in Rome with consternation. So little was known of his disposition or intentions that both Pope and Senate had cause for anxiety as to the future. Adrian, alternating between hope and fear, judged it prudent to retire to Sutri (17th May). A fortnight later he moved further north to Viterbo, whence he despatched envoys to treat with the victorious monarch.[1] The letters they carried contained a request for the surrender of Arnold to the Pope.[2] Doubtless Adrian intended this to be a test of the Emperor's good-will. Frederick on his part was only too eager to accommodate the Pope in the matter. To him the sacrifice meant little; it was an act of grace whereby Adrian's suspicions might be mollified. For all Frederick's actions at this time were governed by

[1] Jaffé-Loewenfeld, 10073. The legation consisted of three cardinals, Guido of St Pudentiana, now healed of his wound, his namesake of St Mary in Porticu and John of SS. John and Paul.

[2] "Litteras...in quibus continebatur inter cetera ut redderet eisdem cardinalibus Arnoldum hereticum"—Boso, loc. cit. ante.

his ambition of securing the Imperial crown, and to this end a friendly understanding with the Pope was a political necessity. Furthermore he was moved by anxiety to prevent a repetition of the alliance between the Pope and the Sicilian king, which had been a thorn in the side of his uncle Conrad. These two kindred motives were largely responsible for the complaisance which marked his dealings with Adrian from 1152 to 1155. Although Arnold was not at the moment in Frederick's hands it was not difficult to comply with the Pope's request. By the simple expedient of sending troops to seize one of the friendly viscounts and holding him as a hostage, Frederick speedily obtained the surrender of Arnold's person. The unfortunate reformer was thereupon handed over first to the papal legates and by them to the Prefect to await trial and sentence.[1]

Assured of Arnold's safe custody the legates now pressed Frederick for a confirmation of the Treaty of Constance. After a delay occasioned by the absence of news from his own ambassadors to the Pope, Frederick gave the required guarantees, and arrangements for the coronation were completed. Satisfied with the monarch's friendly disposition Adrian rode out from Civita Castellana to greet him. They met at Campo Grasso in the neighbourhood of Nepi where Frederick had pitched his camp (9th June). But an untoward incident marred the spectacle. The king neglected to perform the customary service of holding the papal stirrup as Adrian dismounted. The cardinals, mindful of the unhappy fate of Paschal II at the hands of Henry V and fearing a repetition of that act of violence, turned and fled in a panic to Civita Castellana,[2] leaving the Pope alone in the German camp.

In high dudgeon Adrian refused Frederick the kiss of peace and rode back to Nepi. The weight of tradition lay

---

[1] Boso, loc. cit. Otto of Freising, *Gesta Fred.* p. 134.
[2] "Turbati et valde perterriti"—Boso, p. 327.

clearly on the Pope's side, and the remonstrances of Frederick's older and more experienced counsellors, many of whom had seen Lothaire perform a similar lowly office on his coronation journey, finally banished the monarch's scruples. Accordingly on the following day the ceremony was re-enacted, and on this occasion no hitch occurred in the programme. With due reverence Frederick approached on foot to greet the Pope, and after leading his horse for a distance of a stone's throw, held the stirrup firm for the Holy Father to dismount. Thus amicably the incident was closed, and with united forces Pope and King set out for Rome.[1]

An even more dramatic interlude followed hard upon this. The joint cavalcade was met by a deputation from the Roman Senate. Their leader proceeded to inflict on Frederick a bombastic harangue reminiscent of the letter addressed to Conrad in 1149.[2] Mirrored in the prose of Otto of Freising it is a remarkable illustration of the fantastic character of the political theory of the Roman republicans. Frederick was bidden to hearken with all humility to the voice of the peerless city, the "Mistress of the world". "Thou wast my guest; I have now made thee a citizen. What was mine by right I have now bestowed upon thee." A formal offer of the Imperial crown was made to Frederick on condition that he pledged himself to uphold the laws and customs of the city and agreed to pay a subsidy of five thousand pounds in silver to the officials of the Republic. At first Frederick listened with mingled contempt and amusement to this singular oration, but, as the pompous imbecilities were babbled forth, his tolerant mood changed to one of open indignation. At the mention

---

[1] Boso, loc. cit. ante. Gregorovius (p. 531) treats the whole proceeding as a farce, and his spirited account is thus marred by his constitutional inability to appreciate the mediaeval attitude towards religion which the incident symbolises. Cf. Mann's *Lives of Popes*, IX, p. 261, n. 1.   [2] See ante, pp. 127 seq.

of the indemnity a paroxysm of wrath seized hold of him. Silencing the unhappy spokesman with an imperious gesture he loosed a torrent of scornful eloquence at the heads of the startled deputies. Branding them as the degenerate successors of a people once eminent for wisdom and renowned for valour, he bluntly proclaimed that these noble virtues had long since departed from them and were now lodged among his own kinsfolk, the Germans, having been transmitted to the Franks together with the dignity of Empire. "With us are thy Consuls, with us thy Senate, here are thy legions. To the wisdom of the Franks and the sword of their chivalry thou owest thy preservation." Hereupon he launched into an elaborate disquisition on the meaning of the Imperial dignity and its relationship to the city of Rome. He ended with a flat refusal to parley with them or to discuss the terms of his entry into the city.[1] Awed and discomfited the envoys returned post-haste to Rome with the evil tidings, and the citizens hastily shut the gates of the city in preparation for a siege. Adrian, who had witnessed the scene with ill-concealed amusement, urged Frederick to secure immediate possession of the Leonine and the castle of St Angelo, prefacing his counsel with the malicious observation that the king had as yet scarcely begun to fathom the depths of Roman guile.[2]

In the dawn of the 18th June the coronation ceremony was performed in St Peter's with all wonted pomp and magnificence. The enthusiasm of the Germans knew no bounds. At the climax of the ceremony their shout of triumph "cleft the air like a thunderbolt".[3] Too late the Romans awoke to the situation. Springing to arms they

[1] Otto of Freising, *Gesta Fred.* pp. 135 seq. Gregorovius (p. 537) regards Frederick's speech as "the manifesto of the Hohenstaufen coronation programme". [2] Otto of Freising, p. 139.

[3] "Statim tam vehemens et fortis Teutonicorum conclamatio in vocem laudis et laetitie concrepuit, ut horribile tonitruum crederetur de caelis subito cecidisse"—Boso, p. 330.

pressed forward in a body to attack St Peter's. For a
while Adrian stood in peril of his life, but Frederick and
his troops managed to effect his rescue. A bloody battle
followed and raged till nightfall. At first the issue was
doubtful, but in the end the superior valour and discipline
of the Germans turned the scale. The Romans were driven
out of the Leonine with great loss and ultimately routed.
Otto of Freising, who tells the story, displays an excess of
patriotic zeal wholly out of keeping with his episcopal vocation. "Our soldiers", he writes, "were seen smiting the
Romans as if they would say, 'Take, ye Romans, German
steel for Arabian gold. This is the money your Prince gives
for your crown. Thus is empire bought by the Franks'."[1]

On the morrow Adrian, genuinely distressed at the
grievous slaughter of his subjects, obtained from Frederick
the release of the prisoners, now in the custody of the
Prefect.[2] Despite the decisive character of the victory the
Emperor's position remained full of anxiety. With an
army weakened in numbers, straitened by lack of provisions
and a prey to the inevitable scourge of malaria, Frederick
reluctantly abandoned the idea of entering the city. That
very day, the 19th of June, he struck his camp and re-
treated in the direction of Tivoli, destroying the castles of
the nobles of the Campagna as he passed.[3] At Tivoli he
took leave of the Pope and by the end of September he
had recrossed the Alps and was safely back in Germany.[4]

Thus amid torrents of blood had Frederick come by the

[1] "Cerneris nostros tam immaniter quam audacter Romanos
cedendo sternere, sternendo cedere, ac si dicerent; Accipe nunc Roma
pro auro Arabico Teutonicum ferrum. Haec est pecunia quam tibi
princeps tuus pro tua offert corona. Sic emitur a Francis imperium"
—Otto of Freising, p. 141.

[2] Boso, pp. 330 seq. Otto of Morena (M.G.H. Script. XVIII,
p. 597) speaks of many drowned in the Tiber.

[3] *Gesta di Fed.* lines 754 seq.

[4] Otto of Freising, pp. 143 seq. Giesebrecht, *Geschichte der deutschen Kaiserzeit*, v, p. 72.

coveted dignity of Holy Roman Emperor. The expedition had by no means fulfilled expectations. He had asserted his power in no uncertain manner, but at the cost of an unenviable reputation for cruelty and the permanent hatred of the Italians. Yet in one respect the expedition was decisive. The Roman Republic as an independent, self-governing entity was overthrown and upon its ruins the edifice of the temporal power of the Papacy was gradually rebuilt.[1] Under the strong hand of a succession of able pontiffs Rome entered on a period of quiet, ordered government broken only by spasmodic outbreaks of the revolutionary spirit. The sole remaining vestige of its political autonomy was the Pope's formal recognition of the offices of the commune. But these became little more than titular dignities bereft of political significance, and, when the commune was revived as a political unit by Brancaleone and Rienzo successively, passage of time and changed conditions wrought for it a new civic ideal and modifications in its constitution.

The extinction of the Republic was accompanied by the death of its most distinguished citizen. After being condemned by an ecclesiastical tribunal in accordance with canonical procedure Arnold was reserved to the judgment of the secular arm. Beyond this nothing is told us of his trial. Merely the fact and mode of his execution receive a casual mention. He was first hanged, his corpse being afterwards burnt and the ashes thrown into the Tiber, lest, says Otto of Freising, they should become an object of the people's veneration.[2] Fortunately we are able to supplement this bald and frigid statement by a graphic description from the pen of the Bergamasque poet. From this it

[1] The process was not completed till Innocent III in 1198 succeeded in getting the appointment of a single Senator in his own hands. Gregorovius, v, pt. 1, pp. 21–5.

[2] "Principis examini reservatus est, et ad ultimum a praefecto Urbis ligno adactus, ac rogo in pulverem funere redacto, ne a stolida

is clear that Arnold died, as he had lived, in quiet confidence in the justice of his cause and with the courage of his convictions unshaken. Asked on the scaffold whether he would abjure his heretical opinions and confess his sins, he replied that his teaching seemed in all things good and true, and that he was not afraid to suffer death for it. He begged only for an interval to confess his sins to Christ, but refused the offices of a priest. Tears sprang to the eyes of the bystanders and even the executioners were moved with compassion as with upraised hands and closed lips he knelt and commended his soul to God.[1]

Such was the poignant close of Arnold's career. His melancholy fate appears to have occasioned singularly little attention among his own countrymen; only one Italian chronicle gives the event a passing notice, and even here the reformer's name is wrongly entered.[2]

Our knowledge of the particular circumstances is indeed woefully incomplete. A great many points of details are left unexplained. We are unable, for example, to fix either the date or the scene with any certainty. It is even difficult

plebe corpus ejus veneratione haberetur in Tyberim sparsus"—Otto of Freising, loc. cit. ante.

> "Judicio cleri nostro sub principe victus,
> Adpensusque cruci flammaque cremante solutus
> In cineres, Tyberine, tuas est sparsus in undas
> Ne stolidae plebis quem fecerat, improbus error
> Martyris ossa novo cineresve foveret honore."
>
> Gunther, *Lig*. col. 371, lines 344 seq.

"(Arnoldus) suspendio neci traditus, quin et post mortem incendio crematus atque in Tybrim fluvium proiectus est, ne videlicet Romanus populus quem sua doctrina illexerat sibi eum martyrem dedicaret"— Gerhoh of Reichersberg, *De Invest. Antichristi*, lib. I, cap. xlii, *Lib. de lite*, III, p. 347. See also Appendix III.

[1] *Gesta de Fed.* lines 832–49. See Appendix III for text. For credibility of this account see Appendix I, p. 209.

[2] *Annales Mediolanenses Minores*, M.G.H. XVIII, p. 393: "A.D. 1155. De Mense Februarii Fred. rex cepit obsidere Terdonam et iam rediderunt die 24 April. *Et Arnulfus combustus est*". For brief notices of Arnold's fate in German chronicles see Appendix III.

to resolve whether it preceded or followed Frederick's coronation. The balance of probability, however, inclines us to place it about ten days later at a convenient halt in Frederick's retreat from the capital.[1] At any rate it is exceedingly improbable that it occurred in Rome, where in the event of a possible revulsion of feeling on the part of the Romans an ugly situation might have arisen.[2] More probable alternatives are Civita Castellana, as Giesebrecht first suggested,[3] or Monte Rotondo, about ten miles north of Rome.[4] The Tiber flows through both places, so that Otto of Freising's statement concerning the disposal of Arnold's ashes would apply equally as well as to Rome.

Upon whose head lies the guilt of Arnold's blood? The question is not easy to answer. Though the Prefect was the actual instrument of vengeance, the ultimate responsibility rests upon Emperor, Pope and Senate alike, and if discrimination is to be made, the two latter must divide between them the major portion of the blame. Doubtless it would not be just entirely to exonerate Frederick for his part in the unhappy business. Yet in his case, though the execution proved in the long run to be a disastrous political mistake, the excuse of a supposed political necessity may justly be pleaded in extenuation. Frederick understood neither the problem itself nor the issues involved in his own

---

[1] Hampe, p. 67. Otto of Freising and the *Ligurinus* place the event a little before the coronation, the *Gesta di Fed.* afterwards.

[2] Sismondi (*Histoire des républiques italiennes du moyen âge*, 2nd ed. II, 1826, pp. 64–5) gives a graphic description of the reformer's death in Rome before the Porta del popolo, depicting him being burned alive and the glare of the flames from his funeral pyre awakening the sleeping citizens, who thereupon rushed in a body to effect his rescue and finding themselves too late collected his ashes as relics. All this is pure fantasy, unsupported by any evidence. But the statement is slavishly copied by Francke (p. 196) and Clavel (pp. 306–7). Even Hefele (p. 872) commits himself to this assertion.

[3] Giesebrecht, pp. 29–30.

[4] Hampe, pp. 67–8. Vide ibid. pp. 61 seq. for a minute examination of the evidence.

action.[1] Arnold was a sacrifice on the altar of political idealism, the dominant mediaeval concept of the relationship between *sacerdotium* and *regnum*.

The position of the Pope was more distinctly compromised. It can hardly be a mere accident that Boso, whose account of Arnold's latter days is in other respects so full, is silent as to his ultimate fate. As papal secretary Boso occupied an official position in the Curia, and the omission would appear to indicate official anxiety to gloss over an episode which brought little credit, and concerning which awkward questions were already being raised. Such objections were met in two ways. On the one hand, efforts were made to place the responsibility on the Prefect; on the other, stress was laid on the view that Arnold was punished as an ecclesiastical renegade. Such a plea will not for a moment bear examination; there is no escaping the fact that Arnold's execution was dictated by an ulterior and purely political motive. The reformer's existence threatened the Temporal Power, and to safeguard this the Papacy did not scruple to deal through Arnold's martyrdom a crushing blow at all who shared his general convictions on the need for a return to apostolic poverty as the cardinal principle of the Church.

Especially interesting from this point of view are the comments made on the matter by Gerhoh of Reichersberg, a detached and fair-minded critic, who was willing to acknowledge Arnold's genuine zeal for reform, although he deplored the evil effects of his teaching.[2] Writing in 1162

---

[1] The author of the *Gesta di Fed.* asserts that in later years Frederick expressed regret for his part in bringing Arnold to the scaffold. "Sed doluisse datur super hoc rex sero misertus"—line 850.

[2] "Ne doctrine ejus prave que, et si zelo forte bono, sed minori scientia prolata est...videar assensum prebere"—*De Invest. Antichristi*, p. 348. The inference which De Stefano (p. 54) draws from this passage that Gerhoh had "a great admiration" for Arnold appears quite unwarranted.

he openly regrets that the death penalty was meted out to the misguided reformer, affirming that in his judgment a sentence of exile or imprisonment would more justly have met the needs of the case. More particularly he disapproves the part played by the Pope and Curia in the execution and shows himself acutely sceptical of the attempt to evade responsibility. He foresees the dangers liable to arise from a participation of the spiritual authority in the purely secular function of shedding blood.[1]

But if the conduct of Pope and Curia invites a strict condemnation, that of the senators deserves the utmost contempt. It matters little that petty differences concerning ways and means had arisen between them and Arnold or that the newly elected members discountenanced his radical programme. Wisely or unwisely Arnold had chosen to dedicate his talents to the cause of Roman independence, and at the height of its power the commune had taken him under its wing. The Senate in its corporate capacity had given a solemn pledge to protect him against his enemies. In a moment of panic that pledge was broken, and the man, whose courage and vision could alone have saved the Roman Republic from imminent destruction, was summarily handed over to the vengeance of a reactionary hierarchy. Not even the straitened circumstances which compelled acceptance of Adrian's terms can mitigate the guilt incurred by so shameless a breach of faith.

[1] "Quem ego vellem pro tali doctrina sua quamvis prava vel exilio vel carcere, aut alia pena preter mortem punitum esse vel saltim taliter occisum, ut Romana Ecclesia seu Curia, ejus necis questione careret. Nam si, ut aiunt absque ipsorum scientia et consensu a Prefecto Urbis Romae de sub eorum custodia, in qua tenebatur, ereptus, ac pro speciali causa occisus ab eius servis est, maximam siquidem cladem ex occasione eiusdem doctrinae idem prefectus a Romanis civibus perpessus fuerat—quare non saltem ab occisi crematione ac submersione eius occisores metuerunt, quatenus a domo sacerdotali sanguinis questio remota esset, sicut David quondam honestas Abner exequias providit atque ante ipsas flevit, ut sanguinem fraudulenter effusum a domo ac throno suo removeret?"—Gerhoh of Reichersberg, pp. 347–8.

Speculations on this topic, however, are at best of doubtful value. It is even possible to maintain that some such fate as that which Arnold met lay in the logic of history. The only confident judgment we dare make at this stage of our enquiry concerns the immediate effect of the reformer's death on the movement he had led and the ideals which had created it. In this respect the verdict admits of no qualification. As a religious reformer no less than as a political leader Arnold of Brescia had ostensibly failed. His conviction that the root of all evil in the Church lay in the anomaly of the Temporal Power impelled him to enter the arena of politics, and the utter failure of his appeal to the sword did much to make impossible that spiritual reformation which, in common with many other reformers of his time, he held to be the ultimate objective. Thus, despite its prominence, at a superficial glance his career would seem to have left little impress upon his age. The enquiring student may with some justification ask, "Why, if this be all, does Arnold of Brescia occupy a key-position in the history of the Mediaeval Church?" Yet, notwithstanding diversity of interpretation and judgment, all modern writers from Gibbon to Giesebrecht, who have dealt with his career, are agreed on its significance for the development of the ecclesiastical framework of the mediaeval polity. The solution of the problem is to be found not in what Arnold succeeded or failed in accomplishing but in the inspiration of his example and the intensity of his zeal. If his own life must be writ down a failure, the very manner of that failure gave a greater impetus to the growth of the cause for which he fought than any partial success could have done. And the legacy he bequeathed to Christendom was simply the vision of a "poor Church", bereft of temporal power and confining its energies to spiritual ministration.

In the two closing chapters of this essay an attempt will

be made to work out in greater detail the two major problems arising out of Arnold's career, first the implications of his teaching for his own time, and secondly, the way in which the "evangelical idea" was put into practice by the sect which bore his name.

Chapter X

THE TEACHING OF ARNOLD

THE most fervent of Arnold's admirers could scarcely claim for his teaching the merit of originality. Viewed broadly its principal elements may be reduced to two: insistence on the practice of apostolic poverty, and the restriction of the Church's interests and activities to the spiritual sphere. Neither of these principles was in essence new, for both were born of those cognate ideals, the "poor" Church and the "other-worldly" Church, which were perennial sources of inspiration for the mediaeval reformer, whether founder of a new monastic movement or apostle of some new sect, which too often found itself at variance with the Church's dogma and ultimately banished from her fold.

The first, the principle of evangelical poverty, was one of the cardinal tenets of the Patarini, and with them took practical shape in scathing, and often scurrilous attacks on worldly and simoniacal priests. The second, prompted by dissatisfaction with the increasing secularisation of the Church, led ultimately to the conviction that the Pope's temporal power was the root-cause of the Church's malady. This belief also boasted a pedigree, which may be difficult to trace but can be proved to exist through the intermittent raising of the problem from the days of Hildebrand onwards. It is a far cry from the sober reasoning of the *York Anonymous* to the impassioned rhetoric of Arnold of Brescia, yet, divergence of method and medium apart, their criticism under this head is fundamentally the same.[1] Some idea of Arnold's opinions on these twin

---

[1] Extracts from the *York Anon.* are given in the Appendix to Böhmer, *Kirche und Staat in England und in der Normandie im XI und XII Jahrhundert* (Leipzig, 1899) and in the Monumenta Germaniae series, *Lib. de lite*, III. See especially Tract XXX, Böhmer, pp. 482

themes—for the second cannot be dissociated from the first, since in practical affairs the two problems are found constantly overlapping—may be gleaned from the foregoing narrative of his life. It will be well, however, to attempt here a closer scrutiny of his principles with a view to ascertaining his proper position in the movement for ecclesiastical reform.

Let us take first the ideal of the "poor Church" and examine its practical application in Arnold's teaching. It was his firm conviction that the major part of the Church's troubles arose out of increasing preoccupation with secular interests. An insatiable greed for riches on the part of individual clerics and of the Church corporately in the Curia gave plausibility to this view. Nor was this diagnosis peculiar to Arnold; it was confirmed by all the more enlightened churchmen of his day. The Brescian reformer was no voice crying in the wilderness for the restoration of the primitive Christian ideal, when men "had all things in common", when, in effect, material benefits were regarded as a Divine trust and an opportunity of service instead of an inalienable and imprescriptible right to self-indulgence.

But Arnold, unlike St Bernard or Gerhoh of Reichersberg or John of Salisbury, was not content with registering ineffectual protests against what were acknowledged to be flagrant abuses; he went one stage further and called in question the validity of a system which allowed these abuses to creep in and corrupt the Church's life. And it was in the system itself that he found the root of the evil. To him the corporate wealth of monasteries and the temporal dominion of bishops were alike a negation of Christian principles, a betrayal of the Master's teaching. For Christ

seq. and *Lib. de lite*, pp. 661, 683. For discussion of authorship, Böhmer, pp. 182–98, 259–65. For estimate of the author's general position, ibid. pp. 255–9.

had lived on earth as a mendicant, having nowhere to lay His Head, and had straitly charged His disciples to forego scrip and purse whilst preaching the Gospel. And since for Arnold the true Christian life was a perpetual missionary campaign it followed that to covet this world's goods was in all men reprehensible, and in the clergy in the highest degree criminal, amounting to an apostasy from their sacred calling. From thence he drew his fundamental principle that for clerks and monks the possession of property was a barrier to salvation,[1] and it would seem to have been this doctrine which John of Salisbury had in mind when he characterised the reformer's teaching as in strict accord with Christian principles but scarcely suited to everyday life.[2]

The reformer's teaching under this head, however, was not confined to the mere statement of a principle which, if acted upon, must of necessity profoundly alter both the status of the clergy and the institutional development of the Church. His consuming passion for righteousness drove him to condemn anything falling short of the exalted standard of conduct which he himself had set up as the true Christian ethic.[3] Anything which even faintly resembled worldly indulgence aroused the full measure of his wrath. Alike at Brescia, on the Mont Ste Geneviève and later in Rome he thundered against the avarice and immorality of the hierarchy.[4] Judging from the account

---

[1] Otto of Freising, *Gesta Fred*. loc. cit. ante. Gunther, *Lig*. loc. cit. ante. [2] *Hist. pont*. loc. cit. ante.

[3] Cf. *Gesta di Fed*. lines 768 seq.:

> " Iste sacerdotes pariter populosque minores
> Carpebat dampnans; se solum vivere recte,
> Ast alios errare putans, nisi qui voluissent
> Eius dogma sequi ".

[4] Ibid. lines 781 seq.:

> " Namque sacerdotes reprobos Simonisque sequaces
> Eius qui precio voluit divina tenere
> Omnes censebat, vix paucos excipiebat ".

left us by the Bergamasque poet, there can be little doubt that in general Arnold had something of the puritan temperament and the puritan's outlook on life.[1] Certainly the pithy phrases used by Otto of Freising to describe the tone of the reformer's preaching read like a report of Savonarola's feverish impatience with the pomps and vanities of the fifteenth-century Italian.[2]

Yet it must not be supposed that Arnold's attitude in these matters was utterly unreasonable. He was quite prepared to admit the legitimacy of tithes and free-will offerings as contributions towards the revenue of the clergy. This indeed was in perfect harmony with his conception of a Church that "lived of its own". Furthermore, if the poet of Bergamo is to be believed, the reformer reserved one of his keenest strictures for laymen who misappropriated tithes.[3]

Arnold's teaching on the vexed question of the *regalia* was equally explicit. First, be it noted that Otto of Freising mentions bishops who held *regalia* as included in Arnold's anathema.[4] For in the latter's view the Church had no right to lands held of the secular power on feudal tenure. These, like the corporate property of monastic houses,

---

[1]   "Usuras raptusque omnes et turpia lucra,
         Bella simultates luxus periuria cedes
         Furta dolos turpesque thoros, carnalia cuncta
         Ut Scriptura docet, vite referebat obesse.
         Nullum palpabat vitium; resecans languencia membra
         Ut fatuus medicus, cum lesis sana trahebat."
                                        Gesta di Fed. lines 775 seq.

[2] "Omnia lacerans, omnia rodens, nemini parcens"—Otto of Freising, *Gesta Fred.* p. 133. Cf. *Gesta di Fed.* loc. cit.: "Mordebat graviter, parcebat denique nulli".

[3] "Pro decimis laicos damnabat quippe retentis"—*Gesta di Fed.* line 774. The passage is ambiguous. On the one hand it might be taken to refer to lay refusal to pay tithe; on the other hand it may mean lay acquisition of revenue from tithe. The context affords no clue as to which the poet meant. See Appendix III, p. 218.

[4] Otto of Freising, loc. cit.

should belong to the laity. Hence the restoration of these lands and profitable rights of jurisdiction was an integral part of his reforming programme.[1] Nor did this appear such a revolutionary proposal to Arnold's contemporaries as it sounds to us.

As far back as the early days of the Investiture contest Gregory VII had discerned with eagle eye the close connection subsisting between the *regalia*, lay investiture and simony. All were successive links in the feudal chain which bound the Church, and from which it was his ambition to set her free. While, however, he toiled manfully to eradicate simony and to abolish lay investiture, he left the problem of *regalia* untouched, and in practice he approved of bishops exercising secular jurisdiction. Possibly he was right in thinking that the investiture question was of primary importance. If the idea of feudal contract could be banished from this transaction, the secular power would no longer exercise control over the *regalia*, and the anomaly attached to the latter would be removed. In any case Gregory would certainly have rejected the idea of surrendering it as impracticable and calculated to involve the Church in even greater difficulties. And from the point of view of political expediency the unhappy sequel to Paschal II's attempt to cut the Gordian knot entirely justified Gregory's decision.

Arnold, however, had no responsibility of office to act as a check upon his temperamental *intransigeance* and, where the Christian life was concerned, was ever wont to make short shrift of political expediency. Nor did he stand alone in his radical opinions on the subject. Whatever the damage wrought to the Church's immediate well-being and prestige by Paschal's gesture of temporal renunciation there can be no two opinions as to its ultimate effect. In fact it gave a tremendous impetus to the growth of the ideal of apostolic poverty and kindled the faith that in

[1] Vacandard, pp. 60 seq.

happier circumstances that ideal might be translated into fact.[1] Yet the hope that the Holy See itself might initiate a further step in this direction was doomed to disappointment in face of the succession of mediocre and worldly Popes, which the election of Innocent II inaugurated. For a while hope ran high when under Eugenius III the banner of reform was again unfurled, and in this respect the exhortations of St Bernard in the *De Consideratione* are indicative of the sanguine expectancy nourished in a few faithful hearts. But once again hope flattered to deceive. A combination of domestic and international troubles conspired to prevent Eugenius from undertaking any practical measures of reform, and the opportunity of leading the "evangelical crusade", once missed by the Papacy, was never again vouchsafed to it.

No better illustration of Arnold's relationship to the reforming ideas of his age could be sought than that afforded by an examination of the life and principles of Gerhoh of Reichersberg.[2] And the comparison will be found the more fruitful, since Gerhoh was typical of a way of thinking

[1] Cf. Hausrath, p. 2: "Praktische Folgen hat der Vertrag von Sutri deshalb nicht gehabt, aber es hatte doch einen ungeheurn Eindruck gemacht, dass ein Papst das Aufgeben aller weltlichen Herrschaft und ein Leben apostolischer Armuth für den kanonisch richtigen Stand der Kirche erklärte", and Gregorovius, IV, pp. 481–2.

[2] Earlier works published in Migne, P.L. 193 and 194. Critical edition, M.G.H. *Lib. de lite*, III.

Biographies by J. Bach in *Oesterreichische Vierteljahrschrift für katholische Theologie* (Vienna, 1865) and H. Nobbe (Leipzig, 1880).

For his writings W. Ribbeck, "Gerhoh von Reichersberg und seine Ideen über das Verhältnis zwischen Staat und Kirche" (*Forschungen zur deutschen Geschichte*, XXIV (1884) and XXV (1885)); K. Sturmhoefel, *Der geschichtliche Inhalt von G.'s von R. erste Buche über die Erforschung des Antichristi* (Leipzig, 1887); *G. von R. über die Sittenzustände des zeitgenossischen Geistlichkeit* (Leipzig, 1888); and H. Grisar, "Die Investiturfrage nach ungedruckten Schriften G.'s von R." (*Zeitschrift für kathol. Theologie*, IX (1885)).

For G.'s general position A. J. Carlyle, *History of Mediaeval Political Theory*, IV, pp. 342–83; Hauck, *Kirchengeschichte Deutschlands*, IV, pp. 367–8, 456–8; and W. Wattenbach, *Deutschlands Geschichtsquellen im Mittelalter*, II, pp. 308–14 (Berlin, 1894).

which numbered many exponents among the German clergy, including Archbishop Eberhard of Salzburg, Gerhoh's correspondent and literary patron, Otto of Freising, who looked for reform through the secular power, and Rupert, Abbot of Deutz († 1135), who held decided opinions on simoniacal priests.[1] These men, together with Gerhoh, formed the nucleus of a strong party of reform, and their principles received a fair measure of support from the party of Cardinal Hyacinth in the Curia.[2]

Born in 1093 at Polling in Upper Bavaria, Gerhoh was educated at Hildesheim and became later a teacher in the cathedral school at Augsburg. In early manhood he was a strong supporter of the Imperialist party in the question of investitures. Deeper reflection on the issues at stake produced a change of front, but to the end of his days he remained essentially a "moderate" of the school of Ivo of Chartres. Driven from Augsburg on account of his opinions he found shelter for a time in the Augustinian house of Raitenbuch. After the Concordat of Worms he was recalled to Augsburg and the following year was present at the First Lateran Council. In 1124 he returned to his cloister at Raitenbuch and in 1127 was ordained priest. Henceforward his chief object in life was to secure a stricter observance of the so-called Rule of St Augustine in the German houses of that Order, and if possible to extend its jurisdiction over all cathedral clergy.[3] His strenuous labours in this direction won for him the protection and patronage of Bishop Kuno of Regensburg, and in 1132 he was appointed prior of the canons of Reichersberg. Here he prosecuted his cherished scheme of conventual reform with conspicuous success. From 1145 onwards he

---

[1] Gerhoh, *De clericis saecularibus et regularibus*, *Lib. de lite*, III, pp. 219 seq. or M.P.L. 194, col. 1397 seq.

[2] Gerhoh, Ep. 19, 22, M.P.L. 193, col. 573 seq., 586.

[3] Sturmhoefel, *Gerhoh von Reichersberg über die Sittenzustände der zeitgenossischen Geistlichkeit*, pp. 5 seq.

was in close touch with Eugenius III, and found in the latter a sympathetic confidant of his hopes and fears for the Church's future. In 1150 Eugenius appointed him papal legate to Hungary but for a variety of reasons, mainly political, the mission was never carried out. With the accession of Adrian IV his influence at Rome was considerably diminished, and the outbreak of the schism between Alexander III and Victor IV in 1159 ushered in troublous days both for the German Church and Gerhoh personally.[1] Long in doubt as to the true Pope, Gerhoh finally decided in favour of Alexander III and in consequence was driven from his office by the Imperialist clergy. It is only fair to add, however, that this misfortune was not solely due to political causes; Gerhoh's position was also complicated by his participation in a theological controversy concerning the Person of Christ.[2] After an exile of some years he was allowed to return to Reichersberg, cleared of the suspicion of heresy, but destined soon to die (1169).

Notwithstanding the manifold range of his activities and the practical reform which he advocated, it is as an ecclesiastical publicist that Gerhoh lives in history.[3] His total literary output is large and of a mixed character, but from our present standpoint the most valuable treatises are those written between the Concordat of Worms and the outbreak of the contest between Barbarossa and Alexander III in 1167.[4]

The dates given in the foregoing sketch of Gerhoh's life

[1] For Gerhoh's relations with contemporary Popes see ante, p. 145, n. 3.

[2] Nobbe, op. cit. pp. 29 seq. Hauck, op. cit. pp. 457 seq.

[3] A. J. Carlyle, op. cit. p. 342.

[4] The principal works are the *De Edificio Dei* (1126–32); the *De Ordine Donorum Sancti Spiritus* (1142–3); the *Commentarium in Psalm.* lxiv (1151); the *De Novitatibus huius Temporis* (1155–6); the *De Investigatione Antichristi* (1161–2); and the *De Quarta Vigilia Noctis* (1167). All these are printed in the *Lib. de lite*, III.

are sufficient indication that he was roughly Arnold's contemporary, and a comparative study of their respective
teachings and principles will serve to elucidate the kind of
problem which reformers had to face and the divergent
solutions they advocated or adopted.

In nearly all his works Gerhoh is much occupied with
the sources of ecclesiastical revenue, though, when he
comes to deal with *regalia*, his conclusions are not always
consistent. At the outset he distinguishes between *regalia*
and property derived from purely ecclesiastical sources,
mainly from tithe and alms.[1] He is at one with Arnold in
pronouncing the latter to be legitimate, but condemns the
uses to which they were being put in his own day. For
even tithes had been enfeoffed for secular purposes, an
abuse of Church revenue which Gerhoh holds to be
nothing less than sacrilege.[2] Accordingly he puts forward
a scheme for the distribution of tithes, dividing them into
four parts: the first to be given to the clergy, the second
to be used in building and restoring churches, a third to
be distributed in alms to widows, orphans and the destitute,
and a fourth to be expended on the provision of lodging and
entertainment for pilgrims. Soldiers and secular princes
are not included in this category unless they are *bona fide*
pilgrims.[3]

---

[1] "Patet aecclesiarum facultates trifariam esse distinctas; in deci-
marum videlicet oblationes, et agrorum possessiones, necnon regales aut
publicas functiones"—*De Edificio Dei*, cap. xxv, *Lib. de lite*, III, p. 154.

[2] "Et de decimis quidem nulla est contradictio, quin eas laici
possideant cum sacrilegio"—*De Edificio Dei*, loc. cit. Cf. *De Novitatibus hujus Saeculi*, *Lib. de lite*, III, p. 298: "Portionem sacerdotum
in decimis eatenus in usu ecclesiastico qualitercumque habitis dimi-
nuunt atque in laicas abusiones transferunt, sacrum de sacro con-
ferentes atque in hoc sacrilegium grande committentes". Cf. Grisar,
op. cit. p. 539.

[3] "Debetur enim pars una clericis, altera ecclesiarum edificationibus
et reparationibus, tercia viduis ac ceteris in hoc mundo consolationem
non habentibus, quarta episcopo, non ut inde cum militibus convivetur,

Gerhoh's treatment of *regalia* requires fuller discussion. It was an intricate problem which he never solved to his own satisfaction. At any rate his later works show a marked change of front on the subject. This, together with the qualifications and reservations which habitually clog his arguments, gives some ground for Hauck's charge that he was in reality a trimmer.[1] Yet his continual preoccupation with the difficulty[2] proves that he regarded it as being of vital significance and was sincerely anxious for an equitable and permanent solution.

In his earliest treatise, the *De Edificio Dei*, he complains that in the present state of affairs the *regalia* and ecclesiastical property in general are so confused and intermixed that the bishop cannot secure for the Church her legitimate rights without appearing to defraud the secular power.[3] There follows a long argument on the expediency, or even the possibility of surrendering the *regalia*, culminating in the proposal that the Church should make this heroic sacrifice rather than suffer herself to be involved in secular affairs.[4] Though Gerhoh patently has in mind the example of Paschal II's effort at a settlement in 1111, the treatment is inclined to be a little academic. At the outset he states

sed peregrinis et hospitibus quod sibi suisque cubiculanis superesse poterit ita largus dispensator impendat, ut omni viatori ostium suum pateat....Inter quos hospites, milites ac principes non numerantur, nisi forte cum de terra sua peregrinantur"—*De Edificio Dei*, cap. xvii, p. 149.

[1] "Bald auf dem rechten Fuss zu stehen, bald auf dem linken"—Hauck, IV, p. 215.

[2] The matter is treated of in all the works above mentioned. See ante, p. 171, n. 4.

[3] "Sic etenim confusa sunt regalia et aecclesiastica, ut iam videretur episcopus regnum spoliare, si aecclesiae facultates militibus vellet denegare"—*De Edificio Dei*, cap. xiv, pp. 144–5.

[4] "Publicas autem functiones non curat aecclesia multum defendere; non curat Rachel vestem suam ad eas tegendas extendere, quoniam spirituales viri malunt carere talibus, quam ex eorum occasione implicari negotiis secularibus"—ibid. cap. xxv, p. 154.

the problem fairly enough but then proceeds to shirk the difficulties connected with it.

By 1142 Gerhoh has changed his ground. He is not now prepared to advocate surrender of the *regalia*, but recommends that it should be wisely regulated and administered by the bishops,[1] adding to this counsel a condemnation of the customary practice of exacting from bishops homage or fealty for ecclesiastical property.[2] Very similar is Gerhoh's treatment of the question in his *De Novitatibus huius Temporis* (1155–6). Here he has no hesitation in pronouncing in favour of the Church's retaining the *regalia*, because of the insuperable difficulty of separating it from other ecclesiastical property, and "what God has joined together no man should put asunder".[3] And for Gerhoh the hand of the Almighty is plainly visible in the matter, since Our Lord Himself in the presence of Herod and Pilate wore successively the white robe of priestly office and the purple of kingship in token of His dominion over all the kingdoms of the world.[4] In this illustration Gerhoh

---

[1] "Si quid enim de regalibus pertinentiis donatum est ecclesiis a regibus piis et catholicis, non licet ab aecclesiis denuo abalienari, sed hoc ab ecclesiarum rectoribus convenit sapienter dispensari"—*De Ordine Donorum Sancti Spiritus*, pp. 278 seq.

[2] "In proximo futurum speramus, ut et illud malum de medio fiat, ne pro regalibus, immo iam non regalibus, sed ecclesiasticis dicendis facultatibus ab episcopis hominium [sic] fiat vel sacramentum, sed sit episcopis liberum res ecclesiarum possidere de iure concessionis antiquae, sicut mater aecclesiarum Romana ecclesia possidet quae de iure oblationis vel traditionis antiquae tenet"—*De Ordine*, p. 280.

[3] "Illud quod ibidem copiose tractatum est et nunc succincte perstringendum videtur de regalibus ecclesiae collatis. De his enim quem alii contendant, ecclesiis eadem occasione talium periclitantibus auferenda, alii vero, ea semel ecclesiis collata in usus earum tenenda, posterior magis placet sententia, quia sic ipsa regalia bona ecclesiasticis interserta sunt, ut vix ab invicem discerni valeant. Huc accedit quod quae Deus conjunxit homo separare non debet"—*De Novitatibus*, p. 296.

[4] Ibid.

finds conclusive proof of the truth of his argument.[1] The sole deviation he makes from his previous position is concerned with the question of fealty. He now, somewhat reluctantly, permits the bishop to take an oath of fealty to the secular monarch as the price of his retention of the *regalia*.[2] Gerhoh's caution on this point is the more intelligible since the Concordat of Worms had left open the distinction between fealty and homage. Homage, indeed, was almost universally regarded as an invasion of spiritual prerogatives.[3]

In the *De Investigatione Antichristi*, a work rich both in illustration of the Church's wretched plight and in proposals to amend it,[4] Gerhoh traverses the whole field of relations between *sacerdotium* and *regnum*. In the course of his peregrination he has much to say on the *regalia*. A vivid, though not strictly accurate account of the controversy between Paschal II and Henry V affords him an opportunity of recounting the arguments used on either side.[5] And while perhaps his perspective is not quite a true one, his lengthy disquisition illustrates most clearly how the practical difficulty of ecclesiastical revenues came vitally to affect the theoretical balance between the spiritual and the secular powers.

It is, in fact, a characteristic of Gerhoh's later writings

---

[1] "Respondeo plane mihi placere, ut reddantur quae sunt Caesaris Caesari, et quae sunt Dei Deo, sed sub ea cautela, ut non vastetur ecclesia vel nudetur saltem veste alba, si nimis incaute abstrahitur ei purpura"—*De Novitatibus*, p. 297.

[2] "Verum tamen ut insolentia non crescat ultra modum contra imperium, ex necessitate jusjurandum (licet hoc ipsum sit a malo) interponitur, ut sibi fidem servent mutuo pontifices et reges....Ergo sicut illi (Abraham et Abimelech) sibi mutuo juraverunt, sic adhuc reges jurant justitiam, ecclesiae cum consecrantur et coronantur, et episcopi quoque regalia tenentes regibus jurant fidelitatem salvo sui ordinis officio"—ibid.

[3] Grisar, op. cit. p. 542.

[4] Sturmhoefel, op. cit. passim.

[5] *De Invest. Antichristi*, caps. xxv and xxvii, pp. 333–4, 336 seq.

that he shows himself more fully conscious of the practical issues at stake and less careful of the theoretical basis of his argument. Hence in this particular question of the *regalia* he is now concerned more for its effect on the Church's life than for abstract justice. He would seem at last to have recognised his inability to grapple with the ethics of the problem, and abandons the attempt to judge it by *a priori* values in favour of an argument developed along utilitarian lines. The only specific judgment he allows himself to make is a condemnation of unlawful and improper use of *regalia*,[1] followed by a plea for the distribution of its revenues after an apocryphal example of Gregory the Great.[2]

This absence of a clear and definite statement of his own position makes it extremely difficult to discover how far Gerhoh had moved from the rigid standpoint taken in the *De Edificio Dei*. The one sure fact to be gleaned both from the *De Investigatione* and his few remarks on the same subject in the *De Quarta Vigilia Noctis* (1167)[3] is that Gerhoh now finally rejects the idea of the Church's renunciation of the *regalia*. Secularisation of all lands held in fee of the lay power still remained for him the ideal solution, but he had learned from experience that it was quite beyond the bounds of practical politics. Accordingly he is now content with propounding schemes for the amelioration of existing evils.

[1] "Non enim condemno ecclesiam Dei vel ecclesiarum praesules regalia possidentes et eis licite ac modeste utentes, licet laboriosas eorum curas et occupationes molestas sexagenarie illi domus Dei celsitudini assimilare mihi visum est. Quod vero plerique sacerdotes vel episcopi toto se studio secularibus negotiis vel actibus impendunt, obliti quae sacerdotii sunt"—*De Invest. Antichristi*, cap. xl, p. 348.

[2] Ibid. cap. lxix, pp. 388 seq.

[3] "Teneat ergo episcopus ecclesiae sibi commissae data regalia, salva sui ordinis et officii libertate, quae non debet saecularibus negotiis implicari aut serviliter subiugari"—*De Quarta Vigilia Noctis*, p. 518.

We have dwelt at some length on the topic of *regalia*, because it is by choosing a particular issue and comparing Arnold's treatment of it with that of Gerhoh and like-minded reformers that the significance of his teaching can be best appreciated. Above all a problem like this, where the ultimate solutions of the two men were diametrically opposed, helps in the long run to determine at what point Arnold departed from the programme of the more conservative school of reformers. To complete the investigation, however, we need to examine certain important aspects of the Church's life where Arnold and Gerhoh started from a common basis of agreement.

We have seen how in Rome Arnold's general indictment of the hierarchy was augmented by a venomous diatribe on the Pope and Curia. According to John of Salisbury he even indulged in a gross libel on Eugenius III, defaming him as "a man of blood, a torturer of the churches and an oppressor of innocence"[1]—terms that can only be regarded as a cruel caricature of the Pope in question. In this connection it is interesting to observe the evolution of Gerhoh's opinions. For him also the field of enquiry came in course of time to be narrowed down to Rome. In his earlier treatises (the *De Edificio Dei* and the *Commentarium in Psalm.* lxiv), while attacking luxury, avarice and simony among the secular clergy, he passes lightly over the Curia. He can even stop to give an unexpected eulogy of the Roman Church,[2] a fact to be accounted for partly by his personal reverence for Eugenius and partly by the encouragement given by the authorities to his own scheme for reforming the German canons. This favourable judgment was greatly modified in his later writings. In the

[1] *Hist. pont.* loc. cit. ante.
[2] "Prioribus temporibus persecutionum Roma Babylonia potius erat appellanda. Nunc vero ipsa urbs urbium Roma recte Syon dicitur ...cum sit aula pudicitiae, sedes iusticiae, asylum religionis canonicae ac monasticae"—*Com. in Psalm.* lxiv, p. 446.

De Investigatione Antichristi he finds the root of the evil in the Roman Curia. All the discords prevalent in the churches spring from its grasping, avaricious policy. The burden of avarice (*avariciae detestabile malum*) is the constant refrain in all Gerhoh's later works.[1] The Roman Church is no longer God's temple but a den of thieves and the synagogue of Satan.[2] For simoniacal and incontinent priests are members of Antichrist rather than disciples of Christ.[3] Gerhoh sighs for a new Elijah who shall teach the Romans not to destroy but to build up the power of the churches. The Pope's abuse of his authority for simoniacal purposes is the abomination of desolation standing in the holy place. The spectacle of "Avaritia" enthroned in Peter's seat is worse than the image of Caesar in the temple of Jerusalem.[4]

For this sorry state of things Gerhoh without hesitation blames the Church's immersion in secular affairs. Above all the Church should bear no part in the settlement of questions of property. Like Wetzel he reverts pathetically to the "golden age" of Constantine and Sylvester I. He even introduces a pointed contrast between Sylvester and Adrian IV, charging the latter with connivance in the corrupt practices of the cardinals and negligence in bestowing offices.[5] But unlike Wetzel he has no doubts what-

---

[1] *De Invest. Antichristi*, cap. lxxii, p. 391. *Epist. ad Card.* p. 400. *De Quarta Vigilia Noctis*, cap. viii, p. 506.

[2] "Non templum vel ecclesia Dei sed spelunca latronum et sinagoga Satanae"—*De Invest.* cap. iv, p. 314.   [3] Ibid. cap. lxxii, p. 391.

[4] "Quis enim locus in terris sede beati Petri apostoli sanctior, in quo videlicet claves regni celorum repositi sunt? At iam dicte, superius quoque notate desolationes in eodem sancto loco iam ex aliquanto tempore steterunt. Et abominanda quidem fuerit desolatio in loco sancto in templo Ierosolymis imaginem Caesaris vel aliquid aliud simulacrum manufactum stetisse, ego vero magis abominabile existimem in sede beati Petri avariciam, quae est simulacrorum servitus, fronte aperta residere"—ibid. p. 392.

[5] *De Quarta Vigilia Noctis*, cap. xviii, pp. 520 seq.

soever on the validity of the Donation of Constantine; on the contrary, he argues from it ingeniously that the Pope should not intervene in temporal affairs.[1] Gerhoh stands out as an uncompromising opponent of the increasing impetus towards centralisation of ecclesiastical administration in Rome, and it is from this point of view that he condemns the growth of appeals and exemptions.[2] The relations between Pope and Curia were the real cause of discord in the Church. Two things in the main were required of Rome—good counsel and right judgment. If these were followed all simony and avarice would be done away.[3]

Yet despite his high courage Gerhoh recognised that in reality the reforming measures he had outlined were little more than palliatives. At least he ends on a note of pessimism. The constitution of the Church has become so complex, the problems of ecclesiastical administration so intricate that the spirit of true Christianity is in danger of being extinguished. The Church has well-nigh ceased to be the vehicle of Christ's teaching and has become a political system. Faith has waxed dim and charity has grown cold, and the holy and immaculate spouse of God is tossed about with the winds of avarice and unrighteousness like the disciples' frail boat on the Sea of Galilee. For the Church, even as for them, the only hope of salvation in this fourth watch of the night is that the Master Himself will stretch forth His Hand to calm the tempest.[4]

Such was Gerhoh's diagnosis. Possibly his tempera-

---

[1] *De Quarta Vigilia Noctis*, cap. xvii, p. 517.

[2] *De Invest.* cap. xlviii, pp. 355–6, cap. lxiii, p. 379.

[3] "Sunt autem duo, que precipue in ea queruntur a suis filiis, videlicet bonum consilium et rectum iudicium....Quod si hec satisfactio requiritur ab avaris huius mundi, volentibus ad Deum converti maxime recognoscentibus ipsorum studio vel innocentes oppressos vel nocentes iniuste liberatos, quanto magis in ecclesia Dei, precipue in ecclesia Romana cavenda est hujuscemodi avaricia..."—*De Quarta Vigilia Noctis*, cap. viii, p. 506.

[4] Ibid. cap. x, p. 508.

mental pessimism gave him keener insight than his fellows into the dangers confronting the Church. At any rate, though generally representative of the conservative school of reformers, he stands nearer to Arnold of Brescia than any other writer of his age. So far as criticism of evil and injustice is concerned his language matches in vigour anything to be found in John of Salisbury's report of Arnold's discourses.[1] And in the substance of their criticism there is much common ground. Both found in simony and avarice cancers eating out the Church's life; both deprecated the bad examples set by Pope and Curia in this respect. Both reverted in imagination to the unfeudalised Church of earlier days, a Church independent of secular patronage and financially self-supporting, expending its surplus wealth in alms and deeds of charity. Both drew courage and inspiration from the example of Paschal II's attempt to release the Church from the bonds of feudalism. But here with the purely critical and analytical faculty the likeness ends. In framing constructive proposals the two men worked along widely divergent lines.

A rough generalisation will serve to make this plain. Gerhoh viewed the situation from a clerical, professional standpoint; Arnold, on the other hand, reflected the enlightened lay conscience of his day.[2] To the end Gerhoh remained at heart a faithful priest endowed with the ingrained dispositions and prejudices of his order, acutely conscious of the claims and sanctions of ecclesiastical authority, and accepting to the full the hierarchical doctrines of Gregory VII on the nature and function of the Church. Hence his constructive proposals were cast in a pre-eminently clerical mould. His plan was to leaven first

[1] Cf. the use of the scriptural phrase "spelunca latronum" in reference to the contemporary Church by Gerhoh (*De Invest. Antichristi*, p. 314), John of Salisbury (*Policrat.* § 676) and Arnold (*Hist. pont.* p. 65) alike.

[2] *De Stefano*, pp. 76 seq.

the Church and ultimately society with the higher morality of the Monastic Orders, and this he looked to accomplish by replacing where possible the corrupt secular clergy by regulars. As a last resort he placed his hopes in a drastic reform of the Church's administrative system along lines of departmental decentralisation. In this respect, no less than Arnold in others, he was striving to stem the prevailing currents of his age, but this, if he was conscious of it, in no wise deterred him from an ardent pursuit of his plan.

We have said that Arnold was an exponent of the layman's view of reform. Nowhere is the gulf between layman and ecclesiastic more marked than in the final judgments of Arnold and Gerhoh respectively on the character of the contemporary Church. Here, notwithstanding his keen and searching criticism, Gerhoh absolutely refused to accept the radical conclusion of the Brescian reformer. He would not bring himself to admit that a Church honeycombed with vices and immersed in secular affairs had ceased *ipso facto* to be the Body of Christ. On the contrary, this tenet of Arnold's he expressly and unequivocally repudiates.[1]

It is this vital distinction which makes Arnold's career of such outstanding significance, for it both separates him from his reforming contemporaries of the Hildebrandine school and connects him with the anti-sacerdotal teaching of the heretical sects of the succeeding century. Other elements in his teaching had roots in the past and links with his own day. His opinions on evangelical poverty were in substance derived from the Patarini of his native Lombardy.[2] All which he preached with fervent zeal concerning contempt of this world's goods and frank imitation of the lowly lives of Christ and His Apostles Ariald had

---

[1] *De Invest.* loc. cit. ante, p. 160, n. 2.
[2] Giesebrecht, pp. 9, 10. Poole, Preface, p. lix. Breyer, p. 127.

taught with equal vigour at Milan before him. But the ruthless logic, which led Arnold to assert that a Church thus far negligent of the Gospel precepts had forfeited all claim to Divine inspiration, was unknown to Ariald and the Patarini. In this respect Arnold was prophetic of the future.[1]

Further this doctrine of the apostate Church is Arnold's synthesis of the two principal elements in his teaching enumerated at the beginning of this chapter. For not only had the Church lapsed from the ideal of apostolic poverty; it had also become part of the political system and so lost its primitive spirituality.

Arnold's teaching on the Temporal Power is more concrete and practical than that on apostolic poverty. It was largely based on his experience and observation in the world of men rather than the product of abstract reasoning like the conclusions of the *York Anonymous* or, in the opposite camp, St Bernard and John of Salisbury. It was from this standpoint that Arnold had waged war against Bishop Manfred in his early days at Brescia, and, when he came to Rome, every circumstance which had prompted him to deny the validity of the Church's claim to temporal dominion was aggravated tenfold. If the secular power of bishops was a flagrant scandal, there were yet certain practical considerations which might be pleaded in extenuation. For in nearly all the provincial churches ecclesiastical property was bound up with the feudal organisation of society. At Rome this was not so. Here the temporal power of the Popes antedated the beginnings of feudalism by several centuries; it was based ultimately on a supposedly historic contract, the Donation of Constantine, the validity of which Arnold certainly impugned, that is, assuming we can credit him with opinions identical with those expressed in Wetzel's epistle.[2]

[1] Hauck, IV, p. 215.   [2] See ante, pp. 136, 138.

There can be no reasonable doubt that Arnold did utterly and unconditionally repudiate the Temporal Power. Unfortunately Otto of Freising and John of Salisbury give few details. Otto states that Arnold denied the Pope's claim to dominion over the city, restricting his authority to the exercise of purely ecclesiastical jurisdiction.[1] Presumably by this is meant matters included within the Canon Law. John tells us that Arnold taught that neither obedience nor reverence was due to the Pope as spiritual overlord; further he would not tolerate those who wished to put Rome, "the mistress of the world, the seat of Empire and fount of liberty" under the yoke of servitude.[2] This juxtaposition, in so careful and scrupulous a writer as John, can only mean that Arnold denied the papal claim to temporal dominion. Further evidence, however, is forthcoming, albeit of a secondary nature. Wetzel in his letter to Frederick speaks of apostate clergy who exercise temporal rule against the Gospel precepts and the Canon Law.[3] Moreover the proposition is attested by Arnold's political activities in the Roman commune, by his proposal to revive patricians, tribunes and *quirites*[4] no less than by his acceptance as a *fait accompli* of the abolition of the office of Prefect. Similarly it is the prime factor in his political theory.

This has been variously appraised. On the one hand Gregorovius and the majority of Arnold's Italian biographers represent him as rejecting alike the theocratic

[1] "Nichil in dispositione Urbis ad Romanum pontificem spectare, sufficere sibi aecclesiasticum iudicium debere"—Otto of Freising, p. 134.

[2] "Dicebat quod sic apostolicus est, ut non apostolorum doctrinam imitetur aut vitam, et ideo ei obedientiam aut reverentiam non deberi; praeterea non esse homines admittendos qui sedem imperii, fontem libertatis, Romam, mundi dominam volebant subicere servituti"—*Hist. pont.* pp. 65–6.

[3] Inter Wib. Ep. loc. cit. ante.

[4] See ante, p. 141.

principles of the Papacy and the Imperialist claim to sovereignty over the city of Rome.[1] The Abbé Vacandard, on
the other hand, has depicted him as a staunch Imperialist.[2]
Hausrath also seems to arrive at the same conclusion,
when, in reference to Arnold's teaching on the restoration
of property to the secular power, he terms Arnold's disciples "the earliest Italian Ghibellines".[3] More accurately
Giesebrecht, Hauck and Breyer regard Arnold's political
principles as incidental or subsidiary to his religious convictions, and wisely avoid the temptation to construct a
coherent and comprehensive political theory on such
slender foundations.[4] Certainly the attempt to include
Arnold in the ranks of a definite political party breaks down
for lack of evidence.

A comparison of Arnold's opinions on the Temporal
Power with the teaching of St Bernard and Gerhoh on the
same subject will do much to restore a correct perspective.
The clearest exposition of St Bernard's political theory is
to be found in the *De Consideratione*. Here Bernard starts
from the conception of the Church as the fountain of
Divine authority, the chosen instrument of the Divine Will
both in the spiritual and the temporal sphere of man's
activities. Both the spiritual and the temporal sword are
entrusted to her keeping. The spiritual sword is hers to use
directly, but the temporal may only be wielded by the
secular power, albeit solely when and where the Church
shall command.[5] Thus, although Bernard denies the

[1] Gregorovius, IV, pp. 480 seq., 547–8. Guerzoni, op. cit. pp. 30 seq.
Paolucci, pp. 679 seq.

[2] "Un impérialiste dans le sens le plus dur et le plus anti-libéral du
mot"—Vacandard, p. 111.

[3] Hausrath, *Die Arnoldisten* (Leipzig, 1895), p. 13.

[4] Giesebrecht, pp. 20–1. Hauck, IV, loc. cit. ante. Breyer, pp. 177–8.

[5] "Quid tu (Eugenius papa) denuo usurpare gladium tentes, quem
semel jussus es reponere in vaginam? Quem tamen qui tuum negat,
non satis mihi videtur attendere verbum Domini dicentes sic: *Con-
verte gladium tuum in vaginam* (Joannes xviii, 11). Tuus ergo et ipse,

Church direct exercise of secular power, he allows her the rights of sanction and of veto, a reservation of considerable importance in practical politics and, when logically pressed, capable of producing results destructive of Bernard's whole position. Had Arnold ever employed the current simile of mediaeval publicists, he would most certainly like Bernard have denied the Church's right to wield the temporal sword. But unlike Bernard he would not have tolerated its claim to control either the mode or the extent of its use.

Though Gerhoh of Reichersberg arrives at conclusions generally similar to those of St Bernard, the basis of his argument is somewhat different. Gerhoh starts not from the Hildebrandine conception of the Church as the ultimate authority, but from the Gelasian definition of the respective spheres of "church" and "state". In the *De Edificio Dei* he is deeply intent on the limitation of the spiritual and secular arms each to its proper sphere.[1] This *caveat* he repeats in the *Commentarium in Psalm.* lxiv, in the course of a spirited protest against the presence of bishops and clergy at secular tribunals (*iudicio et negotio sanguinis*), citing a decretal of Pope Nicholas I in support of his argument.[2] Elsewhere, however, Gerhoh reverts to the

tuo forsitan nutu, etsi non tua manu evaginandus. Alioquin si nullo modo ad te pertineret et is, dicentibus Apostolis, *Ecce gladii duo hic*: non respondisset Dominus, *Satis est* (Luc. xxii, 38) sed Nimis est. Uterqᵣe ergo Ecclesiae et spiritualis scilicet gladius et materialis, sed is quidem pro Ecclesia, ille vero et ab ecclesia exserendus: ille sacerdotis, is militis manu, sed sane ad nutum sacerdotis et jussu imperatoris"—Bern. *De Consid.* lib. IV, cap. iii, col. 776. Cf. Ep. 256, col. 463 seq.

[1] "Illa (regalia, etc.) per mundi principes, ista (decimae et oblationes) per pontifices antiquitus tractabantur, ea videlicet cautione ac distinctione, ut neque pontifex in his, quae erant ad saeculum, neque princeps in his, quae erant ad Deum preesset; sed uterque suo iure contentus, modum divinitus ordinatum non excederet"—*De Edificio Dei*, cap. xxii, p. 153. Cf. *De Ord. Don. S. Spiritus*, pp. 274–5.

[2] *Com. in Psalm.* lxiv, pp. 465–6.

Gregorian theory, employing the stock simile of the sun and moon in illustration of the relation between *sacerdotium* and *regnum* and arguing therefrom that kings should be subject to the priesthood. To judge from the context, it would seem that this is done with the sole object of rebuking the custom of exacting homage from ecclesiastics, whereby, reversing the Divine ordinance, priests were rendered subject to kings.[1] No problem of practical politics, however, can be found in explanation of a passage in the *Commentarium in Psalm.* lxiv where Gerhoh again accepts the Gregorian premise and uses the Gregorian simile of the two lights. As the sun rules the day and the moon the night, so the Pope is the ruler of light and the Emperor the ruler of darkness![2] Yet even this invidious comparison marks in reality no departure from Gerhoh's original position. Proof of this is to be found in an amplification of the simile of the two swords, which immediately follows, together with a delineation of the sphere of operation for each.[3] In the *De Investigatione Antichristi* this limitation of the Church's authority is made more stringent. Gerhoh reiterates his horror at the spectacle of ecclesiastics taking part in secular judgments. In view of Christ's own words: "Suffer ye thus far", there can be no room for doubt that the spiritual power is forbidden to wield the material sword.[4]

With this general principle Arnold would have found himself in full agreement, but he would have regarded it

[1] "Quibus dictis evidenter innuitur, quod reges gladio, id est de gladii ministerio viventes, debent servire sacerdotio, licet nunc fiat e contrario, dum sacerdotes regibus hominio (sic) subduntur, et sacerdotibus reges pro libito suo damnantur"—*De Ord. Don. S. Spiritus*, p. 282.

[2] "...duo luminaria magna, que Deus ita creavit et ordinavit, ut alterum preesset diei, alterum nocti, quia spiritualia, quibus preest domnus papa, diei, et temporalia, quibus preest domnus imperator, nocti comparantur"—*Com. in Psalm.* lxiv, pp. 440–1.

[3] Ibid. loc. cit.

[4] *De Invest.* cap. xxxv, pp. 343 seq., cap. lxxii, p. 392.

as in no way solvent of the problem. In practice this turned on where the line of demarcation between the spiritual and the temporal was drawn and on the nature of those secular affairs over which the Church should have no control. Was the temporal power of the Papacy included in the latter or had it any kind of spiritual sanction? Was it wholly the product of the worldly ambition of Popes or was it a legitimate part of the Divine scheme for the world's governance? In each case Arnold answered the first half of the question with a confident affirmative and the second with an equally decisive negative.

The *De Consideratione* provides us with Bernard's answer. In his view God is the source of all authority, whether spiritual or temporal. Hence it is an error to assume that the apostolic power is the sole power ordained of God. The text: "He that resisteth the power resisteth the ordinance of God", though applied principally to the Pope, is not exclusively so. The Pope's authority differs from that of others not in kind but in degree.[1] To Peter was committed the care of all the churches, not dominion over them; a proposition in support of which the saint quotes the Apostle's own words.[2] To Bernard, therefore,

---

[1] "Erras, si ut summam, ita et solam institutam a Deo vestram apostolicam potestatem existimas. Si hoc sentis, dissentis ab eo qui ait: *Non est potestas nisi a Deo.* Proinde quod sequitur, *Qui potestati resistit Dei ordinationi resistit*; etsi principaliter pro te facit, non tamen singulariter.... Non ergo tua sola potestas a Domino, sunt et mediocres, sunt et inferiores. Et quomodo quos Deus conjunxit, non sunt separandi (Matth. xix, 6): sic nec quos subjunxit, comparandi"— *De Consid.* lib. III, cap. iv, col. 768.

[2] "Quod habuit (Petrus), hoc dedit, sollicitudinem, ut dixi, super Ecclesias. Nunquid dominationem? Audi ipsum. *Non dominantes,* ait, *in clero sed forma facti gregis* (1 Petrus v, 3)....Planum est: Apostolis interdicitur dominatus"—*De Consid.* lib. II, cap. vi, col. 748. Cf. lib. IV, cap. vii, col. 788: "Consideres anti omnia sanctam Romanam Ecclesiam, cui Deo auctore praees, Ecclesiarum matrem esse non dominam; te vero non dominum episcoporum sed unum ex ipsis; porro fratrem diligentium Deum, et participem timentium eum".

the question is linked up with a greater, namely the functions of the priesthood.[1] And if by its very nature the priestly office disqualifies its holder from participation in secular affairs, how much more wrong was it for the Pope to take upon himself the status and attributes of a temporal prince!

This reads like an extract from the *York Anonymous*, and is not very far removed from the arguments of Arnold of Brescia. Thus from the *De Consideratione* alone it might appear that Bernard and Arnold were substantially in agreement on the question. Yet this is far from being the case. It is questionable whether on all points the views set forth in this work represent the saint's considered judgment. Certainly his treatment of the papal authority is mainly governed by his anxiety to impress on Eugenius III the spiritual nature of the papal dignity. Stimulated by the ardour of his zeal for reform and carried away by his own eloquence, consciously or unconsciously the saint delivered his oracle in extravagant language in which all reservations were swept away. In reality Bernard was too theocratically minded, too susceptible to the idea of the Pope's moral supremacy to contemplate a diminution in his worldly state. It was one of Bernard's limitations that he was more than usually blind to his own inconsistency. Just as he saw no incongruity in the spectacle of a protagonist of the conventual life spending half his days traversing Europe in the interests of the Papacy or of his own Order,[2] so he seems to have been oblivious of the discrepancy between his literary gospel and his public activities in support of the attempt to restore the papal monarchy in Rome.

Arnold and Bernard approached the problem from

[1] See Bernard's sketch of the model bishop in his *Tractatus de moribus et officio episcoporum*, M.P.L. 182, col. 817 seq.
[2] Cf. Dom. Berlière, *L'Ordre monastique*, p. 293.

opposite angles. Bernard's object was so to stress the spiritual vocation of the Church, so to wean her from secular pursuits that the essential superiority of her claims might be made manifest. Arnold dreamed of a Church bereft of secular power and confining its energies to spiritual ministration. Hence, while Bernard may be acclaimed a lineal descendant of Gregory VII, Arnold was a determined opponent of the Hildebrandine theory.[1]

Arnold's teaching marked a breach with the accepted political theory of his age at two salient points; first by his proclamation of the apostasy of the contemporary Church, secondly by his refusal to allow the Church the right to sanction or to veto the use of the temporal sword. The first was the logical outcome of his teaching on apostolic poverty, the second a deduction drawn from his view of the Church as a purely spiritual society.

[1] Cf. Giesebrecht, *Geschichte der deutschen Kaiserzeit*, IV, pp. 318–19; De Castro, p. 527; Tocco, op. cit. p. 241.

Chapter XI

THE LEGACY OF ARNOLD

IN the course of this study frequent comments have been made on the lack of materials, both for Arnold's personal history and for his peculiar tenets. Nor are matters improved in this respect when we come to examine the subsequent history of the reformer's opinions. It cannot be gainsaid that Arnold's teaching on apostolic poverty and the Temporal Power continued to be a potent factor after his death. The first provided a basis for the anti-sacerdotalism of the Arnoldists, the Waldenses and the Spiritual Franciscans in the succeeding century; the second was made the keystone of their political theory. How were these opinions transmitted? The attempt to answer this question gives rise to many others.

In the first place did Arnold leave any writings, or did he confine himself to oral methods in propagating his gospel? There is no clear evidence to warrant the assumption that Arnold ever at any time wrote books, and nearly all his biographers have answered the first part of the question in the negative. Guibal alone gives an affirmative,[1] basing his opinion on Innocent II's rescript of 1141 condemning Abailard and Arnold, where "the books containing their errors" (*libros erroris eorum*) were ordered to be burned. Yet it is not plain from the context[2] that

---

[1] Guibal, op. cit. p. 36.

[2] "Per praesentia scripta fraternitati vestrae mandamus, quatenus Petrum Abaelardum et Arnaldum de Brixia, perversi dogmatis fabricatores, et catholicae fidei impugnatores, in religiosis locis, ubi vobis melius visum fuerit, separatim faciatis includi, et libros erroris eorum, ubicumque reperti fuerint, igne comburi"—Mansi, XXI, col. 565. The only other shred of evidence bearing on the point is furnished by Walter Map, *De Nugis Curialium*, p. 39: "Hic Ernaldus ab Eugenio papa...absens condempnatus est, *non ex scripto* sed ex praedicatione". The ambiguity is patent and offers no solution of the problem.

any works other than those of Abailard are implied, and it is clearly uncritical to draw any further inference in the absence of direct confirmation from other sources. To the general question Giesebrecht has given a categorical denial and all subsequent writers have endorsed his verdict.[1]

We are, therefore, reduced to the alternative of oral discourse as the medium whereby Arnold chose to inculcate his opinions. It is significant in this respect that all our primary authorities stress the reformer's oratorical ability. Our chief source for the effect produced by his teaching on his disciples is the epistle of Wetzel. Whether the author was Arnold or some other[2] is immaterial for our present purpose. The important fact is that this is the only document from an "Arnoldist" source that has come down to us and may be taken as representative of the mentality of those who ranged themselves under the reformer's banner.

Equally difficult to resolve is the question whether Arnold was the founder of a definite sect or party. The author of the *Gesta di Federico* seems to imply that Arnold's teaching perished with him[3], and this conclusion is also reached by Giesebrecht.[4] It will be remembered, however, that John of Salisbury mentions in connection with Arnold's preaching in Rome a "sect of the Lombards" who looked to him as exemplar and guide.[5] But

[1] "Er (Arnold) selbst hat seine Lehren nicht durch Bücher verbreitet"—Giesebrecht, p. 34. Cf. Clavel, pp. 107–8; Guerzoni, p. 28; Breyer, p. 141, n. 1; Scott Davison, op. cit. p. 158.

[2] See ante, pp. 137–8.

[3] "Dogma perit, nec erit tua mox doctrina superstes"—*Gesta di Fed.* line 858.

[4] "Weitere Spuren sucht man vergebens; es ist kaum zu erwarten, dass Arnold mit seinem Geiste spätere Generationen beherrscht habe"—Giesebrecht, p. 34.

[5] *Hist. pont.* loc. cit. ante.

beyond a veiled reference in the *Ligurinus*[1] nothing further
is known of this body, and it is not included in the numerous heretical sects anathematised by the Church in the
twelfth and thirteenth centuries.

But a group of men known as Arnoldists[2] makes a series
of fugitive appearances in contemporary chronicles and
incurs repeated anathemas in the decrees of Church
Councils. Nothing is told us of the origin of this sect and
little respecting its constitution or doctrines. Otto Morena,
the historian of Lodi, recounting the siege of Crema by
Frederick Barbarossa in 1159, speaks of a vast company of
poor and needy folk, called in derision *filii Arnoldi*, who
took service in the Imperial host and struck terror into the
hearts of the besieged by their daring escapades.[3] There is
nothing to suggest that these mercenaries were in any way
connected with Arnold of Brescia, and Dr Breyer is inclined
to reject the identification.[4]

Further mention of Arnoldists is forthcoming in papal
and Imperial documents. In the synod of Cremona (1184)
Pope Lucius III issued a bull condemning as heretics
Cathari, Patarini, "those falsely called Humiliati or Poor
men of Lyons" and the Arnoldists.[5] Similar edicts were

[1]   "Unde venenato dudum corrupta sapore,
          Et nimium falsi doctrina vatis inhaerens
          Servat adhuc uvae gustum gens illa paternae."

Gunther, *Lig*. lines 310 seq.

[2] On the Arnoldists see Breyer, "Die Arnoldisten" (*Zeitschrift für
Kirchengeschichte*, XII, Gotha, 1891); Hausrath, *Die Arnoldisten*
(Leipzig, 1895); Tocco, op. cit. pp. 187 seq.; E. Scott Davison, op. cit.
pp. 163 seq. Hausrath's work is more ambitious than its title indicates,
since it includes chapters on the Waldenses, St Francis, Joachim of Flora
and the Spiritual Franciscans, Segarelli and Dolcino. The first chapter
alone deals with the Arnoldists proper and the treatment is a trifle sketchy.

[3] *Annal. Laudenses*, M.G.H. Script. XVIII, pp. 611 seq.

[4] Breyer, *Die Arnoldisten*, p. 391, n. 3.

[5] Mansi, XXII, pp. 492 seq. The description applied to the Humiliati
was designed to distinguish them from the true Humiliati who were
in no wise tainted with heresy and worked under the patronage and
protection of the Church. See Scott Davison, chap. v.

issued from time to time by Frederick II, who strove to vindicate his own orthodoxy by a cruel extirpation of heretical sects in his dominions,[1] and these measures were endorsed by a bull from Gregory IX in 1229.[2]

This list is little more than a catalogue and does nothing but prove the widespread existence of a sect of this name. Happily information of a more explicit nature may be gleaned from the writings of various Catholic apologists in the twelfth and thirteenth centuries. First may be taken the evidence of Arnold's strict contemporary, Gerhoh of Reichersberg. He tells how, when on a visit to Rome in 1149, he embarked on a controversy with a "certain very learned Arnoldist", the gist of which was put to writing and lodged in the papal archives, where probably if anywhere it lies hidden to this day. In view of this Gerhoh does not think it worth while to recapitulate the arguments used on either side,[3] and history is the poorer for this unfortunate concatenation of circumstances. The date of the event, however, leaves small margin for doubt that Gerhoh's opponent was one of Arnold's disciples, and the tribute paid to his learning is an interesting illustration of the intellectual prowess of some of Arnold's followers.

In the *Vitae Hereticorum* of Bonacursus, written in 1190, we first learn something of the doctrinal errors charged to the Arnoldists. Bonacursus was a convert from the Cathari and a zealous defender of Catholic doctrine against heretics. He represents the Arnoldists as teaching that the Church's sacraments were to be shunned because of the wickedness

---

[1] 1220, M.G.H. *Leges*, II, p. 244; 1232, ibid. pp. 287–8; 1238, ibid. pp. 326–8. The Arnoldists are included in each of the above.

[2] M.G.H. *Epist. saec.* XIII, pt. 1, p. 318.

[3] "Memini me cum fuissem in Urbe, contra quendam Arnoldinum valenter literatum in palatio disputasse, et ipsa disputatio monente papa Eugenio, reducta in scriptum pluribus auctoritatibus aggregatis, posita est in scrinio ipsius, ubi cum adhuc posset inveniri, non opus est iam scripta iterum scribi"—Gerhoh, *De Novitatibus*, p. 296.

of the clergy.[1] This is confirmed a century later by the canonist Durandus of Mende in his *Rationale divinorum officiorum*, a work completed in 1286. Among the heretical sects there dealt with are mentioned "the Arnoldists, perfidious heretics who assert that it is nowhere read that Christ committed the care of His spouse, the Church, to dissolute and unchaste ministers, neither gave He them the power to perform the sacred mysteries, the keys of Heaven, or the power to bind and loose. As saith Gregory, only those who deal righteously and hold the faith and imitate the life of the Apostles have this power of the Apostles conferred on them "[2]. Whence they drew the conclusion that the sacraments of unworthy priests have neither validity nor efficacy for salvation.[3] In another reference to the Arnoldists in the same work Durandus ascribes to them the opinion that the Holy Spirit is received not through baptism but through the laying on of hands.[4]

Taken in conjunction these two accounts from the twelfth and thirteenth centuries respectively are of the utmost importance. They make it clear that the Arnoldists held the Donatist tenet whereby the validity and efficacy of the sacraments were made dependent on the worthiness

[1] "Pro malitia clericorum sacramenta Ecclesiae dicunt esse vitanda" —Bonacursus, *Vitae Heret.* M.P.L. 204, col. 791. Cf. Döllinger, *Beiträge*, II, p. 328; Breyer, *Die Arnoldisten*, p. 398.

[2] "Arnoldistae tamen perfidi heretici dicunt nusquam legi, quod immundis et luxuriosis ministris Christus sponsam suam ecclesiam tradiderit custodiendam vel potestatem sacrorum misteriorum [sic] peragere vel claves regni vel potestatem ligandi et solvendi, quia illi soli, ut ait Gregorius, et justi in hac carne positi potestatem habent ligandi atque solvendi sicut apostoli, qui vitam vel fidem illorum cum eorum doctrina tenent"—Durandus, *Rationale divin. officiorum* (Mainz, 1459), lib. IV, fol. 26.

[3] "Unde, ut dicunt, a talibus sacramenta prestita nec valent nec proficiunt ad salutem"—ibid.

[4] "Arnoldistae...asserunt quod nunquam per baptismum aquae homines spiritum sanctum accipiunt, nec Samaritani baptizati illum receperunt, donec manus impositionem acceperunt"—idem, lib. I, fol. 16.

of the officiating priest. This does not imply that they rejected the institution of sacraments or dispensed entirely with them, but it does indicate their antagonism to the principle which confined the sacerdotal office to a priestly order. For them "no ministry can be a true one except through imitating the ministry of the Apostolic Age".[1] Except that here the emphasis is laid on good works and not on faith it is the mediaeval expression of the Lutheran tenet of the priesthood of all true believers, and it is probable that within their own communion the Arnoldists acted on this principle. Whether this be true or no, such an interpretation of sacramental doctrine is merely a particular adaptation of Arnold of Brescia's general teaching on apostolic poverty. This, however, is no proof of the sect's definite descent from the Brescian reformer, for such opinions were current among the Patarini before Arnold's day.

Indeed those who held them could claim a quasi-official sanction for them. Not only were they adopted and diligently propagated by that sturdy champion of the hierarchy, Cardinal Humbert,[2] but in the heat of the campaign against simony and clerical concubinage both Nicholas II in 1059 and Gregory VII in 1074 had appeared to countenance these tenets by issuing decrees forbidding the laity to attend the Masses of priests guilty of such offences.[3] Certainly it might be and was argued that these ordinances were purely administrative in character and by no means intended to prescribe a definite dogma. But though it was possible for the trained theologian to discriminate between the position taken by Nicholas and Gregory and the extreme Donatist principle, it was clearly difficult to carry such a nice distinction to the mind of the

[1] E. Scott Davison, p. 164.
[2] Humbert, *Adv. Simoniacos*, lib. I, M.G.H. *Lib. de lite*, I, pp. 107, 125–6.
[3] Mansi, *Concilia*, XIX, col. 907 seq., XX, col. 408, 433.

average layman or even of the average priest.[1] And in actual practice it proved impossible. Thanks to this hasty decision on the part of the Papacy the Donatist principle gained widespread recognition among orthodox churchmen for a century or more. True, Gregory was no theologian and probably imperfectly understood the doctrinal revolution implicit in his decrees, but it is certainly surprising that so shrewd a judge of men should have failed to discern the political dangers likely to arise out of this innovation or its inconsistence with his own political principles. For by the terms of his decree the laity were given an active part in promoting the papal programme of reform.[2] And this was subversive of that principle of the superiority of ecclesiastical over secular jurisdiction which Gregory was mainly concerned to assert in the contest over lay investiture.[3] It was not so large a step from a refusal to admit the validity of the sacraments of a particular priest to a denial of the efficacy of sacraments *in toto* and of the sacerdotal character of the priesthood.[4] Certainly the Arnoldists and other sects, which held similar opinions, did little more than press to a logical conclusion principles implicit in Gregory's teaching on the subject.

Three further references to the Arnoldists are found in thirteenth-century writers. Under the form of "Arnos-

---

[1] The task was not made easier by Gregory's intemperate language on the subject. See his letter to Robert, Count of Flanders, Jaffé, *Mon. Greg.* pp. 255 seq.: "...quae insania quodve scelus est, uno eodem tempore corpus meretricis et corpus attrectare Christi".

[2] See ante, p. 195. This invocation of lay passions was a particular source of annoyance to the anti-Gregorian writers and a matter of misgiving to some of Gregory's more statesmanlike adherents. Lambert, *Annales*, M.G.H. Script. v, p. 218. Sigebert, *Chronicae*, M.G.H. Script. vi, pp. 362 seq. Cf. Mirbt, *Die Publizistik im Zeitalter Gregors VII*, pp. 447–9, 450–2.

[3] Actually it reversed the position. It exalted the laity as judges over the clergy. Cf. Mirbt, p. 451; Tocco, p. 221; Volpe, p. 7.

[4] Troeltsch, *Die Soziallehren*, loc. cit. ante. Volpe, pp. 7, 22. Tocco, p. 256.

tustae" the Franciscan, David of Augsburg, classes them among various groups of the Waldenses,[1] and the notice is repeated without comment by David's pupil, Berthold of Regensburg.[2] The Dominican Inquisitor, Stephen of Bourbon, likewise mentions the sect in an exhaustive catalogue of heretics purporting to be derived from a captured Waldensian.[3] From these meagre scraps of evidence little can be adduced as to the possibility of the Arnoldists maintaining a separate, independent existence well on into the thirteenth century. Dr Breyer would seem to be right in postulating a close connection between them and the Lombard branch of the Waldenses, but his conclusion that the two bodies coalesced into one is scarcely tenable. Several links are missing in the chain of evidence he submits as proof.[4]

We are now in a position to adjudicate on the main question of the origin of the Arnoldist sect. Did it take its name from Arnold of Brescia or from some other Arnold contemporary with him? A conclusive answer is impossible. The foregoing review of the history and tenets of the body has shown that in general principles it had much in common with the Brescian reformer. The castigation of the worldly and corrupt hierarchy, the perpetual hankering after a life of apostolic poverty, the denial of the Church's claim to Divine authority, all these point to a distinct infiltration of Arnold's teachings. But there is no evidence for a direct continuity; the question can only be resolved

---

[1] "Cum olim una secta fuisse dicantur Povre de Leon et Ortidiebarii et Arnostustae et Runcharii et Waltenses et alii"—Döllinger, *Beiträge*, II, p. 317. Cf. p. 330.

[2] Berthold von Regensburg, *Predigten*, I (ed. Pfeiffer, Vienna, 1862), p. 402.

[3] The full list is "Arnoldiste, Speroniste, Leoniste, Cathari, Patarini, Manichei sive Burgari". Etienne de Bourbon, *Anecdotes historiques*, ed. Lecoy de la Marche (Paris, 1877), p. 281. See whole of section 329, pp. 278 seq.

[4] Breyer, *Arnoldisten*, pp. 403 seq.

on a basis of probability. On the whole the balance is in favour of the identification with Arnold of Brescia, and most authoritative writers on the subject have tentatively accepted the hypothesis.[1] The fact that the tenets of the sect included at a later date elements foreign to Arnold's creed does not disprove that he was its original founder. But the case for acceptance would be infinitely stronger, could it be shown that Arnold held similar doctrines on the sacraments.

Have we any evidence that Arnold was tainted with doctrinal heresy? True, Otto of Freising affirms that Arnold held erroneous opinions on the Eucharist and infant baptism, but his words are avowedly based on hearsay reports[2] and probably refer to calumnies about Arnold spread by the papal and Imperial courts.[3] Also the critic may pertinently ask whether Otto was honest enough an antagonist to give his enemy any charitable benefit of doubt. It is, in fact, questionable whether Otto's statement ought to count for much in the absence of confirmatory evidence from St Bernard and John of Salisbury. More serious is the allegation of the Bergamasque poet that the reformer taught that the laity should not receive the sacraments of priests nor confess their sins to them but to one another.[4]

---

[1] Breyer, *Arnoldisten*, pp. 388–91, 398, 413. Hausrath, *Arnold-isten*, pp. 8 seq. Tocco, op. cit. pp. 187, 258. Those who reject the derivation from Arnold include Guadagnini, *Vita di Arnaldo*, pp. 9 seq. and C. Schmidt, art. "Arnoldisten" in *Herzog's Realencyklopädie*. Giesebrecht (p. 34) occupies a neutral position.

[2] "De sacramento altaris et baptismo parvulorum non sane dicitur sensisse"—Otto of Freising, *Gesta Fred.* p. 133.

[3] De Castro, pp. 197–9. It should also be remembered that the Church's doctrine on these points had not yet been clearly defined.

[4]   "Nec debere illis populum delicta fateri,
          Set magis alterutrum, nec eorum sumere sacra."
                                        Gesta di Fed. lines 784–5.
Cf. Breyer, *Arnoldisten*, pp. 399–400. Arnold appears to have acted on this principle before his execution. *Gesta di Fed.* lines 834 seq. Cf. Ugo Balzani in *Camb. Med. Hist.* v, chap. xi, p. 372.

And this is in perfect accord with the tenets ascribed to the Arnoldists by Durandus and Bonacursus.[1] Also it is worthy of note that John of Salisbury speaks of Arnold's following as the "heresy of the Lombards".[2]

Such evidence is, however, insufficient to convict Arnold himself of dogmatic heresy. Can he be termed a heretic in any sense of the word? Much ink has been used in the discussion of this vexed question. First of all be it noted that only once is the reformer termed *hereticus* in an official document, namely in Eugenius' letter to Wibald concerning the plot of 1152.[3] Both for his exploits in Brescia and his revolutionary activities in Rome he incurred condemnation merely as a schismatic, and even his conviction together with Abailard at Sens was in a sense merely a formal repetition of the decree of exile passed on him in 1139. In face of these facts Giesebrecht concludes that Arnold can in no wise be judged guilty of heresy and the majority of his biographers have concurred in this opinion.[4] Gibbon and Gregorovius have compromised by ascribing to him a "political heresy" on the ground of his rejection of the Temporal Power.[5] For the same cause the Abbé Vacandard has no hesitation in delivering a verdict of "guilty".[6] But the heart of the problem lies deeper. A judgment based merely on the affirmations or negations of contemporary authorities must of necessity be inconclusive and in a case of such gravity may even be misleading. The real question at issue is where schism ends and heresy begins. Can it be maintained that Arnold's repudiation of the claim of the Church of his day to be the

---

[1] See ante, pp. 193–4.   [2] *Hist. pont.* loc. cit. ante.

[3] See p. 143, n. 1.

[4] Giesebrecht, p. 34: "Man kann Arnold den Schismatikern beizählen, aber Häretiker war er mit Nichten." Cf. Odorici, *Arnaldo*, pp. 66–7; Hefele-Leclercq, v, p. 737; Tocco, pp. 248–9.

[5] Gibbon, VII, p. 220; Gregorovius, IV, p. 547.

[6] Vacandard, p. 99.

true Church of Christ was merely an act of schism? Was it not rather tantamount to an act of rebellion against the Divine ordering of the universe as the Middle Ages interpreted it and, as such, heresy of the most heinous kind?

In the light of these considerations Dr Breyer has re-examined the whole problem. His conclusions are decidedly unfavourable to the reformer,[1] though it must be admitted that he does not always seem aware of the complex nature of the investigation; witness his summary and artificial division of Arnold's teaching into three distinct categories: schismatic, heretical and political.[2] Final judgment in a question of such delicacy must of necessity be suspended. Undoubtedly the Church viewed such opinions as Arnold held on the nature of the priesthood as necessarily excluding their holder from the communion of the faithful, and for a modern critic to dissent from this view without any authoritative *locus standi* is sheer presumption.

But this does not imply that Arnold is to be placed in the same category as Wyclif or Luther in respect of his errors. Despite the gulf of time and circumstance dividing them his position is more akin to that of Savonarola. Both were puritan reformers aghast at the paganism and corruption of the Church of their own day, each possessed the instinct and the vision of a prophet, and each came to an untimely end through attacking the Temporal Power and identifying himself with a political party. And like Savonarola after him Arnold could with equal justice have rejoined to his judges that, though he were cut off from the Church militant, the hosts of the Church triumphant were waiting to acclaim him.[3]

---

[1] Breyer, *Arnold von Brescia*, pp. 153 seq.

[2] Breyer, op. cit. pp. 177–8. Cf. *Arnoldisten*, p. 392.

[3] To the Bishop of Vasona's "Separo te ab Ecclesia militante atque triumphante", Savonarola replied "Militante, non triumphante, hoc enim tuum non est". Quoted in Villari, *Life and Times of Savonarola*, 10th ed. 1909, p. 756.

It is the settled conviction of the present writer that Arnold must historically be regarded as primarily a religious reformer. Practical circumstances constrained him to appear as a renegade monk embroiled in a political revolution. Yet at bottom it was not as a constitution-monger or as a demagogue that he appealed to the men of his day. It was rather as a moral teacher, a prophet preaching repentance with the pertinacity and enthusiasm of a man whose zeal had outrun his discretion. For in the last resort it was a way of living that he came to show men, the way of consecration to the ideal of personal sanctity, to be sought not within the cloister pale but in the busy world of men.

A due appreciation of this aspect of Arnold's position will make plainer the threefold significance of his teaching. His chief source of inspiration, it must be repeated, was the example of humility and simplicity set by the early Church, and here was forged a potent link with the past. The immediate channel of transmission was the teaching and practice of the Patarini, which he had assimilated in Lombardy, and which constant study of the Scriptures and the Fathers had served only to strengthen. Yet Arnold's message was not confined to the world of his day, it was also in a measure prophetic of the future. By laying stronger emphasis on the personal side of religion he foreshadowed the individualist development of the Renaissance. Only in this limited sense, however, can De Castro's dictum of Arnold as a son of the Renaissance be accepted.[1] To assert that Arnold represented a reaction from the environment of his age,[2] or to depict him as a harbinger of a brighter and more liberal epoch is to be guilty of a misleading half-truth. Nor is there any evidence for Guerzoni's statement that

---

[1] De Castro, pp. 5–6.
[2] "Arnaldo era tratto a fuggire il suo tempo, a rinnegare il medio evo"—ibid. p. 439.

Arnold preached the virtue of toleration.[1] What we learn of the strictness of his personal life and the vigour of his discourse would lead us rather to expect the contrary. For the fact that Arnold's teaching was so thoroughly ascetic stamps him as a typical child of a century which was the golden age of the Monastic Orders.

If we may indulge in a final comparison, that between Arnold and Gregory VII is likely to be specially illuminating, since the reformer in impotence and the reformer in power are seldom contrasted. Broadly speaking the two men had much in common. Each started with a lofty conception of the Church's moral obligations and a firm resolve to make her life more worthy of her high and holy calling. Both were men of great personal piety, consumed with a white-hot passion for justice which frequently dried up the springs of human charity. Both scrupulously fulfilled in private the canons of their public teaching. Both were endowed with the gift of leadership and the rarer faculty of inspiring confidence in their adherents. Neither possessed much breadth of vision or originality of statecraft, but both proved clever opportunists and knew how to turn a momentary advantage to permanent profit. Each died conscious of the failure of his cherished schemes, leaving problems of a mixed and intricate character for posterity to solve. But here the parallel breaks down. Agreed in the main as to the ultimate objective they were poles asunder in their choice of means. In neither case did the result correspond even remotely with their ambitions. Gregory strove to safeguard the purity of the Church's life from the contaminating influence of the world by securing for her an acknowledged position outside the feudal framework of society. He ended by riveting upon her the chains of a rigid political system. Arnold laboured for a complete reform of the Church both in head

[1] Guerzoni, p. 30.

and members. He merely succeeded in bequeathing his principles to the heretical sectaries beyond the Church's pale. Yet Gregory at least achieved some small measure of success, certain concrete results such as the abolition of lay investiture and the mitigation of simony and clerical concubinage. Arnold, on the other hand, left no constructive work as a memorial of his activities, but merely the shadow of a great name and the example of a pure and disinterested life spent in a vain endeavour to change the working of the ecclesiastical system. The explanation of their diverse fate is not far to seek. Gregory worked throughout in harmony with the enlightened opinion of his age and by virtue of his high office in the Church could always count on a large measure of support for his projects. Arnold was driven to plough a lonely furrow, to engage in a desperate struggle against the prevailing currents of his age, and any encouragement he might have gained from the conservative reformers among the clergy he forfeited by his alliance with the radicals of the city communes.

In one respect Arnold shared the common lot of reformers in the Middle Ages. While he found individuals eager to receive his message, he strove in vain to inspire ecclesiastical institutions with the will to reform. Hence, although his teaching lived on among the various sects in Italy, which waged a desultory warfare with the Church throughout the succeeding century, it left little or no impress on the Church itself. Arnold's failure to remould the Church on democratic lines precipitated the ultimate expulsion of his ideals and accelerated the tightening-up of the reins of government by a process of centralisation in the hands of Pope and Curia. It is one of the unrecognised ironies of history that the men ultimately responsible for this were the conservative reformers within the Church. By thwarting at every step the evolution of Arnold's programme they did much to render the reform of the

Church in head and members impossible of achievement. And when in the days of the Conciliar movement the spirit of reform again revived in men, the psychological moment had long since passed. The constitution of the Church had become too rigid to allow of radical changes, and without these no real progress could be made. From this point of view it might be fairly maintained that the failure of Arnold of Brescia's attempt made the Reformation a historical necessity.

Appendix I

ARNOLD OF BRESCIA: THE
ORIGINAL SOURCES

ALMOST every modern writer on Arnold has re-echoed Giesebrecht's lament on the paucity of original sources (Giesebrecht, *A. von B.* p. 4), and the amount of material extant is indeed singularly small considering the magnitude of Arnold's part in the affairs of his time.

Prior to 1868 the chief authorities were Otto of Freising's *Gesta Frederici primi* and the letters of St Bernard. The facts of Otto's life do not warrant the supposition that he was at any time brought into personal contact with Arnold. Born about the year 1115, in 1126 Otto entered the Cistercian house of Morimond, becoming abbot ten years later. His tenure of office was short, for in 1138 on the accession of his half-brother, Conrad Hohenstaufen, to the German throne, he was appointed to the bishopric of Freising, becoming adviser in ecclesiastical affairs both to Conrad and his successor, Frederick Barbarossa (*Gallia Christiana*, IV, col. 816; cf. Adolf Hofmeister, "Studien über Otto von Freising", *Neues Archiv für ältere deutsche Geschichtskunde*, XXXVII, pp. 747 seq.). From 1145 to 1146 Otto was certainly in Italy but there is no evidence that he accompanied Frederick on the Italian expedition of 1155. During his brief stay at Morimond, therefore, Otto in all probability derived the information he gives concerning Arnold from the circle of his fellow-Cistercian, the Abbot of Clairvaux. Hence it is not surprising to find that his narrative is on the whole a trustworthy guide for the facts of Arnold's life up to the latter's banishment at the Lateran Council of 1139. At the German court the opportunity for gleaning news of Arnold would doubtless be more restricted. In consequence Otto's narrative is sparse for the later part of the reformer's career; he is vague as to the date and circumstance of Arnold's return to Italy (see p. 106 of text) and the account given of his activities in Rome is, as we have noted (p. 141), entirely inaccurate. Fortunately it may be corrected by the more substantial account of the Roman revolution found in

Otto's other work, the *Chronica* (see p. 106). The narrative in the
Gesta Frederici closes with a bare mention of the reformer's
execution and the destruction of his ashes. Much is told us of
Arnold's character, his manner of living, his eloquence and the
radical nature of his opinions. Generally speaking Otto's judgments are prejudiced and hostile, reflecting the ill-informed
opinions of Arnold current in Barbarossa's court. He would see
in the reformer an ecclesiastical renegade tainted with heresy
and an upstart tribune wheedling the fickle and rebellious Roman
populace by the artifices of the demagogue. With the discovery
of other evidence the credibility of Otto's narrative is not now so
assured as was formerly supposed.

The letters of St Bernard (M.P.L. 182) are documents of a
very different order. They are primarily of use for the period
between the Council of Sens (1140) and Arnold's return to
Italy in 1145. But though they add little to our knowledge of
Arnold's life they give a clearer revelation of his teaching. More
especially they serve to illustrate the attitude of enlightened
churchmen towards the more radical wing of the reform movement which Arnold represented. Even so, it remains a little
difficult to account for the hidden springs of the bitterness which
Bernard displays in these letters. It cannot be altogether explained by solicitude for the Church's welfare, though his
appreciation of the dangers attending her through Arnold's
alliance with the "arch-heretic", Abailard, is sensibly apparent
in the letter to Pope Innocent II written in 1140 (see pp. 75–7 of
text). Bernard's impression of Arnold, gained by personal contact at Sens, may have contributed towards increasing his
anxiety.

In the poem *Ligurinus* (M.P.L. 212), ascribed to the Cistercian
monk, Gunther of Paris, some eighty lines are allotted to
Arnold's story. At one time deemed a forgery from the pen of
Conrad Celtes, the fifteenth-century humanist, this work is now
generally accepted as a genuine twelfth-century production.
(See Gaston Paris, *Dissertation critique sur le poème latin attribué
à Gunther* (Paris, 1872); Pannenborg, *Forschungen zur deutschen
Geschichte*, II, pp. 283 seq.) It is not, however, an independent
source but is based on the *Gesta Frederici* of Otto of Freising;
its value is accordingly diminished. No new information is
forthcoming and allowance must also be made for the flowers of
rhetoric associated with verse composition at this period. Too

often the plain statements of Otto receive embellishments which adorn the tale but impair the credibility of the teller.

For the political background of the period the collection of letters published under the name of Wibald, Abbot of Stablo and Corvey, is invaluable (Jaffé, *Mon. Corbeiensia*; given also in Martène and Durand, *Ampliss. Collect.* II). Many of the letters are from Wibald's own pen; those passing between him and the Emperor deal with every ramification of the Imperial politics. In addition the collection includes a large correspondence between Pope Eugenius III, the officials of the Roman Curia and Wibald himself, by means of which the latter was enabled to keep in touch with every change in the situation at Rome. There are also included the several letters addressed to Conrad and Frederick Barbarossa between 1149 and 1152 by the leaders of the Roman commune (see pp. 127–31, 135–8 of text).

For the stormy proceedings of Arnold's latter days the *Vita Adriani IV* of Boso, the English cardinal, is most useful (Watterich, *Pont. Rom.* II). A few scattered notices of Arnold's death in German and Italian chronicles (see Appendix III for texts) complete the scanty information formerly available for the study of the subject. The lack of a clear and circumstantial account from the pen of an accredited and, so far as is humanly possible, impartial witness was sorely felt. In 1868, however, new evidence came unexpectedly to light. This was the work known as the *Historia Pontificalis* and now universally ascribed to John of Salisbury. (For the story of the discovery and publication of the MS. see pp. viii–ix of Dr R. L. Poole's preface to his edition of the work (Oxford, 1927). For a fuller discussion of the document see ibid. chap. viii.)

The work purports to be a history of the Papacy but the fragment that has come down to us only covers the years 1148 to 1152. It is, however, far more than a mere chronicle and deals with every important event between these two dates.

In 1873 Giesebrecht (*A. von B.*) advanced arguments in support of the view that the author was none other than the far-travelled Englishman, John of Salisbury. A few years later Pauli (*Zeitschrift für Kirchenrecht*, XVI (1881)), working on internal evidence, claimed that the writer was both a member of the papal household and an eye-witness of the events he recorded. Finally the last link in the catena of evidence has been forged by Dr R. L. Poole, who has shown that from the Council of Rheims in

1148 till December 1153 John of Salisbury was a clerk in the papal chancery (Poole, Preface, p. lxxiv).

A slight sketch of John's life from his first appearance at the Paris schools to the close of his association with the papal household will make plain the peculiar advantages he enjoyed for recording Arnold's history. From 1136 to 1146 John was studying under various teachers at Paris and at Chartres. He would therefore be in a position to acquaint himself with Arnold's doings from the time of the latter's appearance with Abailard at Sens to his departure for Zürich. In addition he could easily gain first-hand knowledge of Arnold's character and doctrines. By 1146 the period of his studies was concluded, and the same year he crossed the Alps into Italy and journeyed to Viterbo, where Eugenius III was then residing. In all probability he was there an eye-witness of Arnold's reconciliation with the Church, of which he is our sole informant. In 1148 he was again in France and present at the Council of Rheims met for the trial of Gilbert de la Porrée. Henceforward till his return to England *c.* 1153, he was, as we have said, habitually employed in the papal chancery.

The date of the composition of the *Historia Pontificalis* is still a matter of measurable doubt. From internal evidence it was plainly not completed till 1164 at the earliest. Dr R. L. Poole (Preface, p. lxxxii), however, thinks that much of it was written some years earlier. But the possibility of John's first impressions being obscured by a gap of some ten or twelve years between the time of writing and the events recorded has to be considered. Yet, in general, he is so sane and cautious a critic of men and affairs that the *Historia Pontificalis* may safely be judged a first-rate authority for the few years described in its pages.

For the history of Arnold of Brescia its importance can scarcely be over-rated. A lengthy chapter (cap. xxxi, pp. 63 seq.) is devoted to his career. Details of his earlier life are given, and a timely corrective is supplied to Otto of Freising's erroneous statements regarding Arnold's part in the early stages of the Roman revolt. John's witness on this point is unimpeachable and squares well with knowledge gleaned from other sources. It is a matter for deep regret that his well-informed narrative ceases with Arnold's return to Rome; yet in a manner this is counterbalanced by the succinct statement given of the reformer's teachings. In a remarkable degree this corresponds with what we learn from Otto of Freising, the *Ligurinus* and St Bernard.

John's narrative is in all respects the most trustworthy and authentic source for Arnold's history we possess. His attitude towards Arnold's teachings is that of a detached and intelligent critic. There is no trace of the passionate vehemence of St Bernard or the scornful tone of Otto of Freising. On the contrary, the account in the *Historia Pontificalis* may be taken as a fair exposition of Arnold's principles from a critic ably qualified for the function both by tolerance of temper and the fact of his presence in Rome.

The discovery of the *Historia Pontificalis* was followed within twenty years by another find of almost equal interest. In 1887 E. Monaci published under the title of *Gesta di Federico primi in Italia* a remarkable poem found in the Vatican Library, where a hundred lines are devoted to Arnold's life (cf. Giesebrecht's paper in the *Arch. della Soc. Rom.* III (1880); K. Hampe, *Historische Zeitschrift*, CXXX (1924), p. 61; R. Breyer, *Historisches Taschenbuch* (1889), p. 126, n. 2). Written between 1162 and 1166 and of Bergamasque origin it gives a graphic description of the reformer's execution (see Appendix III for text). Poetry is not usually a good medium for exact description, but so precise in detail is this part of the narrative that it is either a remarkable *tour de force* in historical imagination or may fairly be regarded as the work of an eye-witness. In general the author is extremely well-informed and the whole section on Arnold is a much more valuable contribution to our knowledge of the subject than that of the other verse authority, the *Ligurinus*.

There remains one other source of very doubtful value. This is an account, avowedly derived from second-hand information, given by Walter Map, the English satirist, who wrote half a century later and lived far removed from the events he purports to record. The passage occurs in the *De Nugis Curialium* (ed. M. R. James, Oxford, 1914, pp. 39–40). Map explains that he got the story from Robert of Burnham, Archdeacon of Buckingham in 1188 and friend of Gilbert Foliot, who had been often employed in diplomatic missions to the Curia at Rome. The account is, to say the best of it, fantastic, and the picture given of Arnold has undergone a great deal of professional colouring in transit. A ridiculous tale is introduced of Arnold appearing before Pope and cardinals at a lordly banquet and declaiming in fiery tones against the luxury and extravagance of the papal household. Map's well-known love of a good story, his hearty detestation of the Cistercians of his day (an antipathy duly extended to the illustrious apostle of the Order) and the satirical setting of his work; all these factors counsel extreme caution in accepting the information he offers. Dr Poole, however (*Hist. Pont.* p. 66, n. 2), regards it as of substantial value.

This constitutes the sum-total of original authorities; no new material has come to light since the publication of the *Gesta di Federico* and any addition in the future is more likely to be the result of a fortunate accident than the fruit of systematic research.

Besides lack of materials there is another factor of importance. With the exception of that of Walter Map, all contemporary accounts of Arnold come from open antagonists or unsympathetic spectators. Hence a certain readjustment of the balance is needed if an accurate judgment of the issues raised by his career is to be achieved. This is naturally a difficult proposition, and the failure of the earlier biographers to arrive at a satisfactory solution is responsible for not a few of the errors and anachronisms on specific points dealt with in the pages of this work.

Appendix II

ARNOLD OF BRESCIA: SOME MODERN STUDIES

LITTLE more than a rough sketch of the principal secondary works on Arnold can be attempted here. Specific points raised by successive writers are dealt with in the text. At the outset it must be remembered that all the early modern biographers wrote without full knowledge of the facts of Arnold's life, since nothing was then known either of the *Historia Pontificalis* or of the *Gesta di Federico* (see Appendix I). Hence the narratives of Gibbon (*Decline and Fall* (ed. Bury), VII, pp. 219–23) and Milman (*History of Latin Christianity*, 3rd ed. IV, pp. 373–90, 404–13), though generally clear and well-balanced, contain mistakes due to their reliance upon Otto of Freising and the *Ligurinus*. Nor would their general conclusions satisfy modern students of the period. Thus Gibbon focusses attention on the political sphere of Arnold's activities, whilst Milman (p. 380) interprets his teaching on the relationship between the ecclesiastical and the secular power as purely Erastian.

Yet in both cases the authors' final judgments differed widely from those of their contemporaries. When Gibbon wrote, the verdict of historians in general on Arnold was one of unreserved condemnation, and the reformer figured in the page of history as a schismatic and a heretic. Baronius (*Annales Ecclesiastici*, XII (1629 ed.), pp. 275 seq.), Gretser (*Arnaldi Brixiensis redevivi vera descriptio* (1613)), Muratori (*Annali d' Italia* (1823 ed.), XV, pp. 320–1) and other Roman Catholic scholars of the sixteenth and seventeenth centuries had succeeded only too well in perpetuating the ban pronounced against Arnold by the Church in his own life-time. The Lutheran, Mosheim (*Institutes of Ecclesiastical History* (trans. A. MacLaine, III, 2nd ed. 1825), pp. 119–20), upon whom Gibbon drew for information, was indeed a notable exception, and his enthusiastic eulogy of Arnold's life and principles foreshadowed the inevitable reaction.

This was not long delayed. In 1790, three years after Gibbon wrote, appeared *An Apology for Arnold of Brescia* by Giovanni Guadagnini, a pioneer among Arnold's countrymen in the telling of his story. The true import of the book lies not in intrinsic merit—it is decidedly a "livre de circonstance" coloured by the writer's Jansenist principles—but rather in the fact that it cleared the ground for a galaxy of biographers eager to pay their tribute to the memory of the Brescian reformer.

Among these the work of Heinrich Francke, *Arnold von Brescia und seine Zeit* (Zürich, 1825), deserves mention only on account of its remarkable inaccuracy of fact and distortion of environment. The purport of the book is to depict the reformer as a premature incarnation of the spirit and ideals of the Reformation. Many of Francke's errors are repeated uncritically by Clavel (*Arnauld de Brescia et les Romains du XII siècle* (Paris, 1868)). The work of another French writer, Guibal (*Arnaud de Brescia et les Hohenstaufen* (Paris, 1868)), calls for a different criticism. Careful scholarship in execution fails to disguise the fantastic character of the writer's theme. On the ground of Arnold's opposition to the temporal power of the Papacy Guibal acclaims the Emperor Frederick II and the later Hohenstaufen as the true inheritors of Arnold's principles. Despite the author's express disclaimer, the treatment seems to be affected by the contemporary view of the "Roman question".

With the two attempts at sketching Arnold's career made by Odorici (*Storie Bresciane*, IV (Brescia, 1855); *Arnaldo da Brescia, Ricerche istoriche* (Brescia, 1861)) we come to a group of Italian writers with whom the problem of the Temporal Power has become an obsession. In Odorici's works Arnold is presented as before all else a political reformer, imbued with republican sentiments and endeavouring to establish in Rome a commune which should stand as a model of political organisation for the whole of Italy. His activities as a religious reformer are depreciated as mere incidents arising out of his early training and the peculiar situation at Rome, where ecclesiastical and political functions were united in the Papacy.

In the numerous paeans of praise prompted by the celebrations of 1882, when a statue was set up in Brescia to Arnold's memory, the apotheosis is complete. In these the reformer appears as a republican demagogue in the garb of an Italian patriot, a forerunner of the Risorgimento, with a clear-cut programme of separating the activities of "Church" and "State", and working towards the ultimate ideal of *libera chiesa in libero stato*.

The first impulse had been given as early as 1844 by the publication of the tragedy of G. B. Niccolini (*Arnaldo da Brescia* (Florence, 1844)). The vast popularity which it gained was far in excess of its merits. As an attempt to recreate the life and times of Arnold it is of little value. Its success was due solely to the skill with which the author fanned the patriotic aspirations of his own day by ascribing these very sentiments to the hero of his drama.

Among historians of this school the work of Guerzoni (*Arnaldo da Brescia secondo gli ultimi studi* (Milan, 1882)) may be taken as typical. Almost every page of his short sketch is coloured by reminiscences of his own times. Arnold is portrayed as a gallant and premature apostle of the idea of religious toleration, an enemy of sacerdotalism and a champion of civic independence, denying both the papal claim to secular power and the Imperial claim to ecclesiastical privilege. Such a portrait is little less than a travesty of history as narrated in contemporary authorities. (Besides Guerzoni, G. de Castro, *Arnaldo de Brescia e la rivoluzione romana del XII secolo* (Leghorn, 1875); R. Bonghi, *Arnaldo da Brescia* (Città di Castello, 1885) and G. Paolucci, "Arnaldo da Brescia nella riforma di Roma", *Rivista Storica Italiana*, IV (1887) should be included in this group.)

In brief, the indictment to be preferred against this school of biographers is that of constructing an Arnold legend through the creation of an imaginary figure, embodying the ideals, principles and mental processes of the nineteenth-century liberal patriot with Christendom of the twelfth century for the field of action.

Even the monumental work of Gregorovius (*History of the City of Rome in the Middle Ages* (trans. Mrs G. W. Hamilton) IV, pt. 2) is not free from unhistorical reasoning of this kind. That part of it dealing with Arnold was written in 1861 within Rome itself, but the inspiration of local colour so profitable for other sections of the author's subject has in this case produced less fortunate results. A spectator of the stirring struggle going on around him and prompted by his own anti-clerical prejudices, he falls a victim to the trap in which most of the Italian biographers have been ensnared. The monastic garb of the twelfth-century reformer is metamorphosed into the red shirt of Garibaldi's heroes, and the plea for apostolic poverty is translated into the frantic anti-papalism of the nineteenth-century republican. "His .teaching", he writes (p. 548), "was of such enduring vitality, that it is still in harmony with the spirit of our time and Arnold of Brescia would now be the most popular man in Italy." Yet for the substance of the narrative there can be nothing but praise. The historical background is splendidly drawn; all the manifold activities of the century and the measure of influence exerted by each upon the central figure are recorded.

Meanwhile the work stimulated a growing interest in the subject beyond the Alps, and within the last thirty years of the century the careful scholarship of German historians happily succeeded in dispelling the clouds of prejudice and ignorance wreathed round Arnold's figure by his own countrymen. As far back as 1848 Neander (*Der Heilige Bernhard*, re-edited S. M. Deutsch in 2 vols. (Gotha, 1889); *General History of the Christian Church* (trans. J. Torrey), VII, pp. 198–205, 215–19) had paved the way for a more systematic study of Arnold's career. In both works the reformer's ideals are subjected to a clear and impartial analysis and his actions judged solely by their fruits.

The year 1873 is a landmark in the history of our subject. In March of that year Giesebrecht read a paper to the Royal Bavarian Academy ("Arnold von Brescia", *Sitzungsberichte der Königliche Akademie der Wissenschaften* (Munich, 1873), reprinted separately the same year) which, though small in scope, was at the time rich in significance, and still remains the most valuable contribution from a single author that we possess. Both by the scholarly use made of his material and the complete detachment of his outlook Giesebrecht inaugurated a new chapter in Arnoldian historiography. Later writers have for the most part verified the conclusions he provisionally adopted.

At the outset it must be admitted that he found himself placed in a position of peculiar advantage. He was the first modern writer on the subject able to make use of the mine of information available in the *Historia Pontificalis*. Thus he was enabled both to correct errors handed down from writer to writer in the past and to explain certain points which had till then proved difficult to comprehend. The net result is an entire re-orientation of the subject.

Giesebrecht was the first writer to treat Arnold primarily as a religious reformer and to interpret his political activities as a natural outcome of his schemes for ecclesiastical reform. Greater emphasis is laid on the positive elements in the reformer's teaching. Hence the effect of Giesebrecht's treatment is to broaden the foundation of Arnold's activities. He is seen to be less a political partisan and more a practical reformer. For the first time Arnold of Brescia was accorded his true place in history.

A very different estimate of Arnold is given by the Abbé Vacandard in a monograph published in 1884 ("Arnauld de Brescia", *R.Q.H.* xxxv). Unfortunately the tone of this work is palpably affected by the circumstance of its origin. It was written as a protest against the panegyrics occasioned by the Brescian festivities of 1882. As might be expected the swing of the pendulum is much in evidence. An unfavourable environment of composition combined with the natural repugnance of a modern Roman Catholic scholar for a mediaeval "heretic" to produce a judgment unsparing in condemnation. Nowhere is any attempt at a sympathetic understanding apparent; from the beginning of the trial the prisoner's guilt is proven in the mind of the judge. Arnold's proposals for religious reform are ridiculed as the vain illusions of an undoubted heretic and his political activities summarily dismissed as "impolitiques, anti-libérales et anti-patriotiques" (p. 108). Nevertheless the general tenour of M. Vacandard's criticism succeeded in annihilating the Brescian *Epigoni* and in the chapters devoted to Arnold in his later work (*Vie de S. Bernard*, II, chap. xxvi, pp. 243 seq., chap. xxxiii, pp. 477–85) the learned Abbé has both moderated his strictures and given us a more constructive account of the reformer's policy.

There remain to be mentioned the works of two eminent German scholars both of whom, by following the path marked out by Giesebrecht, have achieved impressive results. In 1889 Dr Robert Breyer contributed a valuable monograph ("Arnold von Brescia", Maurenbrecher's *Historisches Taschenbuch* (1889)) in which many of Giesebrecht's tentative suggestions are followed up and the majority of his conclusions verified. It was the first considerable work based on Giesebrecht's foundation and still remains an up-to-date and satisfactory account, though to some degree it has been overshadowed by the larger work of Adolf Hausrath (*Arnold von Brescia* (Leipzig, 1891)). This would be a model biography but for the fact that the author has adopted a curious standard of judgment with regard to the comparative value of original authorities. For the reasons given in Appendix I it would hardly seem defensible to place the narrative of Walter Map on an equal footing with the evidence of accredited contemporary witnesses like St Bernard, Otto of Freising, John of Salisbury and the author of the *Gesta di Federico*. Yet in Hausrath's work this equation of values is persistently made.

With the work of A. de Stefano (*Arnaldo da Brescia e i suoi tempi* (Rome, 1921)) our review of the modern biographies of Arnold closes. This book is, in fact, rather a series of studies of the reformer's environment than a biography proper. The biographical chapter itself is an inferior piece of work and many of the old errors perpetrated by Francke and the earlier Italians are repeated. The succeeding sections are more valuable, particularly that dealing with the increasing interest in religious questions shown by the lay element in society of the twelfth century. The significance of this factor for a right understanding of Arnold's popularity is effectively illustrated (p. 77).

Two great histories by German scholars also touch upon our subject. The arrangement of material in Hefele's *Concilien-geschichte* does not permit the telling of Arnold's story in a consecutive narrative. It is studied mainly in connection with the fortunes of Abailard and in consequence the reformer's personality is overshadowed by that of the Paris master. Dom Leclercq, however, in his French translation (Hefele-Leclercq, *Histoire des Conciles*, v, pt. 1, pp. 733–7, 798, 839; pt. 2, pp. 872–3) has restored the balance by adding a footnote containing a précis of Arnold's teaching and an extensive bibliography. Yet more illuminating are the pages given by Hauck (*Kirchengeschichte Deutschlands*, IV, pp. 215–17), the most successful of the many attempts to sketch the reformer's religious environment.

A few smaller books covering the period make interesting contributions to the subject. Tocco (*L' eresia nel medio evo* (Florence, 1884), pp. 231–5) gives a clear and concise account of Arnold's life, followed by an attempt to assess the influence of his teachings on the political theory of the various heretical sects. Emile Gebhart (*L'Italie mystique* (Paris, 1890), pp. 39–48) interprets Arnold's career as an effort to break down the historic tradition of the Church's government and to substitute for it a Papacy shorn of every political privilege and in consequence deprived of its temporal power. The work is marred by a tendency to make sweeping judgments and to draw conclusions not always warranted by the evidence adduced. Lastly, in the enlarged edition of his epoch-making prize essay Lord Bryce (*Holy Roman Empire* (1904 and later editions), chap. xvi) has indicated the significance of Arnold's political activities for the history of mediaeval Rome.

This concludes our survey of the more important secondary works dealing at all largely with Arnold's career. (This review does not pretend to be exhaustive; for other works dealing in part with Arnold see Bibliography.) If a comparison be drawn for example between the productions of Odorici and Hausrath it is impossible not to be impressed by the progress of the last sixty years. Closer acquaintance with the sources and the discovery of new material have produced greater accuracy in the inferences drawn; whilst deeper study of cognate subjects, particularly of the kind of problem left by the Investiture contest, has shed new light on Arnold's actual plans for ecclesiastical reform and ultimately placed his career in a different setting. It is now possible for the student of the twelfth century to achieve a juster appreciation of Arnold's legacy to the Mediaeval Church.

Appendix III

THE BERGAMASQUE POET'S ACCOUNT
OF ARNOLD'S EXECUTION
Gesta di Federico, lines 832–860
(Ed. Monaci, 1887)

Set cum supplicium sibi cerneret ipse parari
Et laqueo collum fato properante ligari,
Quesitus pravum si dogma relinquere vellet
Atque suas culpas sapientium more fateri;
Intrepidus fidensque sui, mirabile dictu,
Respondit proprium sibi dogma salubre videri
Nec dubitare necem propter sua dicta subire,
In quibus absurdum nil esset nilque nocivum,
Orandique moram petiit pro tempore parvam,
Nam Christo culpas dicit se velle fateri.
Tunc, genibus flexis, oculis manibusque levatis
Ad celum, gemuit, suspirans pectore ab imo,
Et sine voce Deum celestem mente rogavit,
Ipsi commendans animam; paulumque moratus,
Tradit ad interitum corpus, tolerare paratus
Constanter penam; lacrimas fudere videntes,
Lictores etiam moti pietate parumper.
Tandem suspensus laqueo retinente pependit.
Set doluisse datur super hoc rex sero misertus.
Docte quid Arnaldi profecit litteratura
Tanta tibi? Quid tot ieiunia totque labores?
Vita quid arta nimis, que semper segnia sprevit
Otia, nec ullis voluit carnalibus uti?
Heu quid in ecclesiam mordacem vertere dentem
Suasit? Ut ad tristem laqueum, miserande, venires!
Ecce tuum pro quo penam, dampnate, tulisti,
Dogma perit, nec erit tua mox doctrina superstes!
Arsit, et in tenuem tecum est resoluta favillam
Ne cui reliquie superent fortasse colende.

NOTICES OF ARNOLD'S DEATH IN
GERMAN CHRONICLES

Annales Palidenses. M.G.H. Script. XVI, p. 89

Arnoldus quidam seculari callens philosophia, dogmate pere-
grino, divisionem inter summum pontificem et populum Romanum fecerat, propter quod obligatur anathemate, dum insuper
plures urbanorum illi cohererent....Rex Fridericus imperiali
sublimandus honore, militantium sibi non tam numero quam
virtute munitus Romam tetendit, dumque vie moras innectit,
adversantium sibi alias urbes cepit, alias evertit. Tandem fati-
gatus multis laboribus, Sancti Petri sedem adiit....Arnoldus
supradictus et consensu potentum urbis prefecto traditur et
suspendio adiudicatur, qui per mala quae moriens pertulit,
erroris debita solvit.

Annales Isingrimi Majores. M.G.H. XVII, p. 314

Hisdem diebus Arnoldus hereticus, qui plurimas seditiones
Romae concitaverat, in patibulo suspensus est, corpus eius igni
consumptum et in Tiberim missum.

Catalogus Imperatorum. M.G.H. XXII, p. 365

Huius tempore quidam magister Arnoldus nomine predicabat
in urbe Roma reprehendens divicias et superfluitates clericorum,
cuius dicta multi magnates Romanorum sequebantur; captus
tandem ob odium clericorum suspenditur.

Godfrey of Viterbo. *Gesta Frederici*, lines 139–141
M.G.H. XXII, p. 310

Arnaldus capitur, quem Brixia sensit alumnum,
Docmata cuius erant quasi pervertentia mundum.
Strangulat hunc lacqueus, ignis et unda vehunt.

Sigebert. *Auctarium Affligemense.* M.G.H. VI, p. 403

Arnoldus hereticus et scismaticus de Brixia, discipulus magistri Petri Abailart, a quinque apostolicis excommunicatur; tandem sub Adriano papa laqueo suspenditur, corpus eius igne
crematur, et combusti cineres in Tyberim proiciuntur.

Annales Augustini Minores. M.G.H. x, p. 8

Anno 1156. Fridericus rex cum expeditione Romam pergens, ab Adriano papa imperator consecratur. Magister Arnoldus a papa suspendi praecipitur.

Annales Einsiedlenses. M.G.H. iii, p. 147

Anno 1155. Fridericus imperator Rome ab Adriano papa factus est, et Arnoldus hereticus suspensus est.

It will be observed that all the above accounts corroborate Otto of Freising's statement that Arnold was first hanged and not burned alive as Sismondi and Hefele (op. cit.) say.

Compare three interesting accounts by English chroniclers of the fourteenth century:

John of Tinmouth. *Historia Aurea*, iii, p. 128, col. 4

Quidam italicus Arnaldus de Brixia artissimam vitam ducens multos sua doctrina seduxit. Qui dum clericorum divitias et superfluitates redarguit, a quibusdam captus suspenditur et crematur, de quo beatus Bernardus quandam scripsit epistolam. "Iste homo" inquit "erat necque (sic) manducans neque bibens", etc.

(Cf. Bern. Ep. 195. The whole account is patently based on Bernard's view of Arnold, and in this respect is not without interest as indicating that it was this view which survived in popular tradition.)

Henry Knighton, i, cap. x, p. 133. Rolls Series

Circa haec tempora quidam magister Arnaldus praedicavit Romae contra divites et contra superfluitatem hominum. Qua de causa multi sequebantur eum. Tandem captus est et per odium clericorum suspensus est.

Eulogium Historiarum, i, cap. li, p. 386. Rolls Series

Eo tempore quidam magister Arnaudus nomine in urbe Romana praedicans, divitias et temporalia omnino reprehendebat, cujus dicta et monita multi magnates sequebantur, qui postea a concivibus captis in odium clericorum est suspensus.

(The repetition of certain phrases, e.g., "per odium clericorum", "clericorum divitias et superfluitates", suggests a parent source, but whether this can be one of these accounts or some other non-extant, it is impossible to tell.)

The following lines on Arnold of Brescia are inscribed in the margin of a twelfth-century manuscript of two letters of St Bernard to Innocent II found in the library of Valenciennes. See J. Mangeart, *Catalogue des manuscrits de la bibliothèque de Valenciennes*, p. 34 (Paris, 1860). They are interesting as an example of the inimical view of Arnold preserved in France after his death.

> Arnoldus periit, cujus quia perdita vita,
> Mens mala, prava fides, mors quoque fida fuit.
> Papa pater patrum, lux legis, semita juris,
> Scismaticum reprobat, quem revocare nequit.
> Rex damnat, lictor celo terraque perosum
> Inter utrumque levat hunc in utroque reum.
> Ne tamen inficiat corruptio corporis auras
> In subitos cineres igne crematus abit;
> Quos Tiberis magnae reverenter destinat urbi,
> Corpore conciliat sic elementa suo.
> Exitus iste manet, quicumque fidem violarit,
> Quam petra commisit, Petre beate, tibi.

(I owe this reference to Dr Breyer. See p. 176 of his monograph on Arnold in the *Historisches Taschenbuch*, VIII.)

Bibliography

A. PRIMARY SOURCES

ABAILARD, PETER. *Epistolae*. M.P.L. CLXXVIII.

—— *Opera*. 2 vols. Ed. Cousin, Victor. Paris, 1869.

Annales Augustini Minores. M.G.H. Script. X, 1852.

Annales Brixienses. M.G.H. Script. XVIII, 1863.

Annales Casinenses. M.G.H. Script. XIX, 1866.

Annales Einsiedlenses. M.G.H. Script. III, 1839.

Annales Isingrimi Majores. M.G.H. Script. XVII, 1861.

Annales Mediolanenses Minores. M.G.H. Script. XVIII, 1863.

Annales Palidenses. M.G.H. Script. XVI, 1859.

BARONIUS, CARDINAL. *Annales Ecclesiastici*. 1629.

BERNARD OF CLAIRVAUX, SAINT. *Opera*. M.P.L. CLXXXII–CLXXXV *bis*.

—— *De Consideratione*. M.P.L. CLXXXII. English trans. Lewis, G. Oxford, 1908.

BERTHOLD OF REGENSBURG. *Predigten*. Ed. Pfeiffer-Strobl. Vienna, 1862.

BONACURSUS OF MILAN. *Vitae Haereticorum*. M.P.L. CCIV.

BONITHO OF SUTRI. *Liber ad Amicum*. Jaffé, P. *Monumenta Gregoriana*.

BOSO, CARDINAL. *Vitae Pontificum*. Watterich, J. M. *Pontificum Romanorum Vitae* (q.v.).

Catalogus Imperatorum. M.G.H. Script. XXII, 1872.

DURANDUS OF MENDE. *Rationale divinorum officiorum*. Ed. Fust and Schöffer. Mainz, 1459.

ETIENNE DE BOURBON. *Anecdotes historiques*. Ed. Lecoy de la Marche. Paris, 1877.

EUGENIUS III, POPE. *Epistolae*. M.P.L. CLXXX.

GERHOH OF REICHERSBERG. *Opera*. M.G.H. *Libelli de lite*, III, 1897. Also M.P.L. CXCIII and CXCIV.

Gesta di Federico I. in Italia. F.S.I. Ed. Monaci, E. Rome, 1887.

GIOVANNI DE CERMENATE. *Historia*. F.S.I.

GODFREY OF VITERBO. *Gesta Frederici*. M.G.H. Script. XXII, 1872.

—— *Pantheon*. Muratori, *Rerum Italicarum Scriptores*, VII. Milan, 1725.

GREGORY VII, POPE. *Registrum*. Ed. Jaffé, P. *Monumenta Gregoriana* (*Bibliotheca Rerum Germanicarum*, II, Berlin, 1865).

GUNTHER. *Ligurinus. De Rebus gestis Frederici Imp.* M.P.L. CCXII.

HUGH OF ST VICTOR. *Opera.* M.P.L. CLXXV–CLXXVII.

IVO OF CHARTRES. *Epistolae.* M.P.L. CLXII.

JOHN OF SALISBURY. *Opera.* M.P.L. CXCIX.

—— *Historia Pontificalis.* Ed. Poole, R. L. Oxford, 1927.

—— *Metalogicon.* Ed. Webb, C. C. J. Oxford, 1929.

—— *Policraticus.* Ed. Webb, C. C. J. 2 vols. Oxford, 1909.

LANDULPH JUNIOR. *Historia Mediolanensis.* Muratori, V. Milan.

MALVEZZI. *Chronicon Brixiensis.* Muratori, XIV. Milan.

MAP, WALTER. *De Nugis Curialium.* Ed. James, M. R. *Anecdota Oxon. Mediaeval. Script.* XIV. Oxford, 1914.

MATTHEW PARIS. *Gesta Abbatum Monasterii Sancti Albani.* R.S. Ed. Riley, H. T.

OTTO OF FREISINGEN. *Chronica.* M.G.H. S.G.U.S. 1912.

—— *Gesta Frederici I.* M.G.H. S.G.U.S. 1912.

OTTO MORENA. *Annales Laudenses.* M.G.H. Script. XVIII, 1863.

PETER THE VENERABLE. *Opera.* M.P.L. CLIX.

ROMUALD OF SALERNO. *Annales.* M.G.H. Script. XIX, 1866.

SIGEBERT. *Auctarium Affligemense.* M.G.H. Script. VI, 1844.

—— *Continuatio Praemonstratensis.* M.G.H. Script. VI, 1844.

WIBALD OF STABLO AND CORVEY. *Epistolae.* Jaffé, P. *Monumenta Corbeiensia (Bibliotheca Rerum Germanicarum,* I). Berlin, 1864.

WILLIAM OF NEWBURGH. *Historia Rerum Anglicarum.* R.S. Ed. Howlett, R.

YORK ANONYMOUS. Appendix to Dölmnei, II. *Kirche und Staat in England und in der Normandie* (q.v.).

—— M.G.H. *Libelli de lite,* III. 1897.

Collections of Documents, etc.

Codice Diplomatico Bresciano. Ed. Odorici, F. 2 vols. Brescia, 1854–8.

DÖLLINGER, J. J. I. VON. *Beiträge zur Sektengeschichte des Mittelalters.* (Vol. II contains documents.) Munich, 1890.

ESCHER, J. AND SCHWEIZER, P. *Urkundenbuch der Stadt und Landschaft Zürich,* I. Zürich, 1888.

JAFFÉ, P. *Bibliotheca Rerum Germanicarum,* 5 vols. Berlin, 1864–9.

JAFFÉ, P. AND LÖWENFELD, S. *Regesta Pontificum Romanorum.* 2 vols. Leipzig, 1888.

Leges Municipales. M.H.P. Leges, XVI.

MANSI. *Sacrorum Conciliorum Collectio*, XXI and XXII.

MARTÈNE, E. AND DURAND, U. *Veterum scriptorum et monumentorum amplissima collectio*, II. Paris, 1725.

MURATORI. *Rerum Italicarum Scriptores.* Milan, 1723.

WATTERICH, J. M. *Pontificum Romanorum Vitae.* 2 vols. Leipzig, 1862.

B. SECONDARY AUTHORITIES

BALZANI, UGO. *The Popes and the Hohenstaufen.* London, 1889.

BERLIÈRE, URSMER. *L'Ordre Monastique.* Paris, 1923.

BERNHARDI, W. *Konrad III.* Munich, 1883.

BERNHEIM, E. *Lothar III und das Wormser Konkordat.* Strassburg, 1874.

—— *Das Wormser Konkordat und seine Urkunden.* Breslau, 1906.

BIEMMI, G. B. *Istoria di Brescia.* 2 vols. Brescia, 1748. (Untrustworthy.)

BÖHMER, HEINRICH. *Kirche und Staat in England und in der Normandie im XI und XII Jahrhundert.* Leipzig, 1899.

BONET-MAURY, GASTON. *Les précurseurs de la Réforme et de liberté de conscience dans les pays latins.* Paris, 1904.

BONGHI, R. *Arnaldo da Brescia.* Città di Castello, 1885.

BREYER, R. "Arnold von Brescia" in Maurenbrecher's *Historisches Taschenbuch*, VIII. Leipzig, 1889.

—— "Die Arnoldisten" in *Zeitschrift für Kirchengeschichte*, XII. Gotha, 1891.

BRYCE, J. *The Holy Roman Empire.* London, 1920.

Cambridge Mediaeval History, V. Cambridge, 1925.

CARLYLE, A. J. AND R. W. *A History of Mediaeval Political Theory in the West*, IV. London, 1903.

CLAVEL, VICTOR. *Arnauld de Brescia et les Romains du XII siècle.* Paris, 1868.

COMBA, E. *I Nostri Protestanti*, I. Florence, 1895.

COULTON, G. G. *Five Centuries of Religion*, I. Cambridge, 1919.

DAVISON, E. SCOTT. *Forerunners of St Francis.* London, 1928. (Posthumously edited.)

DE CASTRO, G. *Arnaldo da Brescia e la Rivoluzione Romana.* Leghorn, 1875.

DEUTSCH, S. M. *Die Synode von Sens, 1141.* Leipzig, 1880.

—— *Peter Abälard, Ein kritischer Theolog des XII Jahrhunderts.* Leipzig, 1883.

DÖLLINGER, J. J. I. VON. *Beiträge zur Sektengeschichte des Mittelalters,* I. Munich, 1890.

FRANCKE, HEINRICH. *Arnold von Brescia und seine Zeit.* Zürich, 1825. (Full of inaccuracies.)

GEBHART, EMILE. *L'Italie mystique. Histoire de la Renaissance religieuse du Moyen Age.* Paris, 1890. Eng. trans. Hulme, L. M. E. *Mystics and Heretics in Italy.* London, 1922.

GHELLINCK, J. DE. *Le mouvement théologique du XII siècle.* Paris, 1914.

GIBBON, E. *Decline and Fall of the Roman Empire.* Ed. Bury, J. B. VII. London, 1914.

GIERKE, OTTO. *Political Theories of the Middle Age.* Eng. trans. Maitland, F. W. Cambridge, 1900.

GIESEBRECHT, W. VON. *Geschichte der deutschen Kaiserzeit,* III. 5th ed. Leipzig, 1890. IV. 4th ed. Brunswick, 1874.

—— *Arnold von Brescia.* Munich, 1873.

GREGOROVIUS, F. VON. *Geschichte der Stadt Rom im Mittelalter.* Eng. trans. Mrs G. W. Hamilton. IV. 2nd ed. London, 1905.

GUADAGNINI, G. B. *Vita di Arnaldo da Brescia.* Brescia, 1882.

GUERZONI, G. *Arnaldo da Brescia secondo gli ultimi studi.* Milan, 1882.

GUIBAL, G. *Arnaud de Brescia et les Hohenstaufen.* Paris, 1868.

HALPHEN, LOUIS. *Etudes sur l'administration de Rome au Moyen Age.* Paris, 1907.

HAMPE, K. *Deutsche Geschichte im Zeitalter der Salier und Staufer.* Leipzig, 1912.

—— "Zur Geschichte Arnolds von Brescia" in *Historische Zeitschrift,* CXXX. 1924. (Confined to examination of the authorship of Wetzel's letter and of Arnold's execution, criticism exemplary.)

HAUCK, A. *Kirchengeschichte Deutschlands,* IV. Leipzig, 1913.

HAUSRATH, A. *Peter Abailard.* Leipzig, 1893.

—— *Arnold von Brescia.* Leipzig, 1891.

—— *Die Arnoldisten.* Leipzig, 1895.

HEFELE, C. J. VON. *Conciliengeschichte.* French trans. Leclercq, H. *Histoire des Conciles,* V. Paris, 1912–13.

HEYCK, E. *Geschichte der Herzöge von Zähringen.* Freiburg, 1891.

JANSSEN, J. *Wibald von Stablo und Corvey.* Münster, 1854.

LANDON, E. H. *A Manual of the Councils of the Holy Catholic Church.* 2nd ed. 2 vols. Edinburgh, 1909.

LEA, H. C. *A History of Sacerdotal Celibacy,* I. 3rd ed. London, 1907.

—— *A History of the Inquisition of the Middle Ages,* I. New York, 1906.

MCCABE, JOSEPH. *Peter Abélard.* London, 1901. (To be read with caution.)

MANN, H. K. *Lives of the Popes in the Middle Ages,* IX. London, 1914. (Written from the Roman Catholic standpoint.)

MANN, L. *Wibald, Abt von Stablo und Corvei.* Halle, 1875.

MILMAN, H. H. *History of Latin Christianity,* IV. 3rd ed. London, 1883.

MIRBT, CARL. *Die Publizistik im Zeitalter Gregors VII.* Leipzig, 1894.

MORISON, J. COTTER. *Life and Times of St Bernard.* London, 1894.

NEANDER, J. A. *General History of the Christian Church.* Trans. Torrey, J. VII. London, 1857.

—— *Der Heilige Bernhard und sein Zeitalter.* 2 vols. Ed. Deutsch, S. M. Gotha, 1889.

ODORICI, F. *Storie Bresciane,* III and IV. Brescia, 1855–6.

—— *Arnaldo da Brescia. Ricerche Istoriche.* Brescia, 1861.

PALO, M. DE. "Duo Novatori del XII secolo" in *A.S.I.* XIV. Florence.

PAOLUCCI, G. "L'Idea di Arnaldo da Brescia nella Riforma di Roma" in *R.S.I.* IV. 1887.

PAPENCORDT, FELIX. *Geschichte der Stadt Rom im Mittelalter.* Paderborn, 1857.

POOLE, R. L. *Illustrations of Mediaeval Thought and Learning.* 2nd ed. London, 1920.

PREVITÉ-ORTON, C. W. *Outlines of Mediaeval History.* Cambridge, 1916.

RASHDALL, HASTINGS. *The Universities of Europe in the Middle Ages,* I. Oxford, 1895.

RÉMUSAT, CHARLES DE. *Abélard.* 2 vols. Paris, 1845.

REUTER, HERMANN. *Geschichte Alexanders III und seiner Zeit.* 3 vols. Leipzig, 1860.

—— *Geschichte der religiösen Aufklärung.* 2 vols. Berlin, 1875 and 1877.

RIBBECK, W. "Gerhoh von Reichersberg und seine Ideen über das Verhältnis zwischen Staat und Kirche" in *Forschungen zur deutschen Geschichte*, XXIV and XXV. 1884–5.

ROCQUAIN, FÉLIX. *La cour de Rome et l'esprit de réforme avant Luther*, I. Paris, 1893.

SCHAARSCHMIDT, C. *Johannes Saresberiensis nach Leben und Studien, Schriften und Philosophie*. Leipzig, 1862.

SIMONSFELD, H. *Jahrbücher des deutschen Reiches unter Friedrich I*, I. Leipzig, 1908.

SISMONDI, J. C. S. DE. *Histoire des républiques italiennes au Moyen Age*. 2nd ed. 1826.

STEFANO, A. DE. *Arnaldo da Brescia e i suoi tempi*. Rome, 1921.

STURMHOEFEL, K. *Der geschichtliche Inhalt von Gerhoh's von Reichersberg erste Buche über die Erforschung des Antichrists*. Leipzig, 1887.

TARLETON, A. H. *Nicholas Breakspear, Englishman and Pope*. London, 1896.

TAYLOR, H. O. *The Mediaeval Mind*. 2 vols. 3rd ed. New York, 1919.

TOCCO, F. *L' Eresia nel Medio Evo*. Florence, 1884.

TROELTSCH, E. *Die Soziallehren der christlichen Kirchen und Gruppen*. Tübingen, 1912.

VACANDARD, E. "Arnaud de Brescia" in *R.Q.H.* XXXV. 1884.

—— *Vie de S. Bernard*. 2 vols. Paris, 1920.

VILLARI, PASQUALE. *Mediaeval Italy from Charlemagne to Henry VII*. Eng. trans. Villari, Linda. London, 1910.

VOLPE, G. *Movimenti religiosi e sette ereticali nella società medievale italiana*. Florence, 1922.

WATTENBACH, W. *Deutschlands Geschichtsquellen im Mittelalter*, II. Berlin, 1894.

Index